Edinburgh
The story of a city

BY E. F. CATFORD

Hutchinson of London

Hutchinson & Co (Publishers) Ltd
3 Fitzroy Square, London W1

London Melbourne Sydney Auckland
Wellington Johannesburg Cape Town
and agencies throughout the world

First published 1975
© E. F. Catford 1975

Set in Monotype Spectrum

Printed in Great Britain by The Anchor Press Ltd
and bound by Wm Brendon & Son Ltd
both of Tiptree, Essex

ISBN 0 09 123850 1

Contents

Map: The Growth of Edinburgh 4/5

Acknowledgements 8

Illustrations 9

1 Approach to Edinburgh 11

2 Growth of a city 14

3 Tapestry of time 24

4 Tolbooth and luckenbooths 35

5 Lawnmarket residents 47

6 Father of the city 59

7 George Square 67

8 Canongate 81

9 Holyrood sanctuary 96

10 The first new town 109

11 The Edinburgh Burns saw 125

12 The new town grows 143

13 Theatrical events 157

14 Great occasions 179

15 Social problems 184

16 Health pioneer 194

17 Into the twentieth century 204

18 Water of Leith 213

19 Along the city coast 230

20 City of villages 244

21 Western extension 259

Plan: The Former Town Walk 274/5

Reading list 275

Index 279

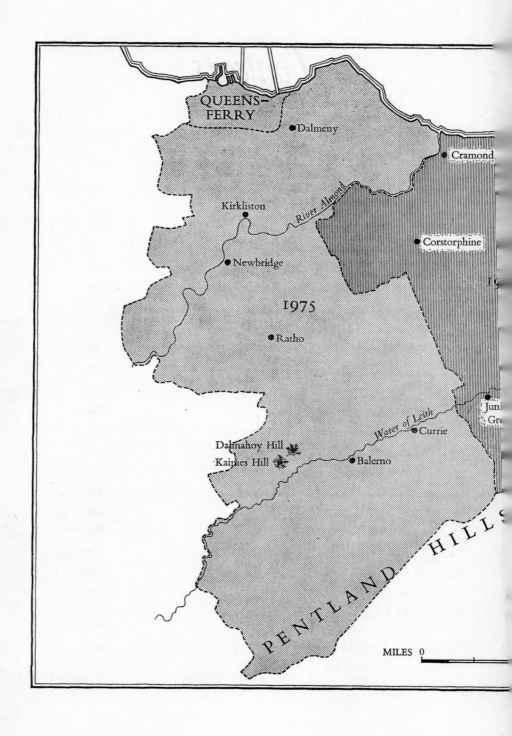

QUEENS-
FERRY

● Dalmeny

● Cramond

Kirkliston

River Almond

● Corstorphine

● Newbridge

1975

● Ratho

Water of Leith

Jun
Gr

Dalmahoy Hill ✳
Kaimes Hill ✳

● Currie

● Balerno

PENTLAND HILLS

MILES 0

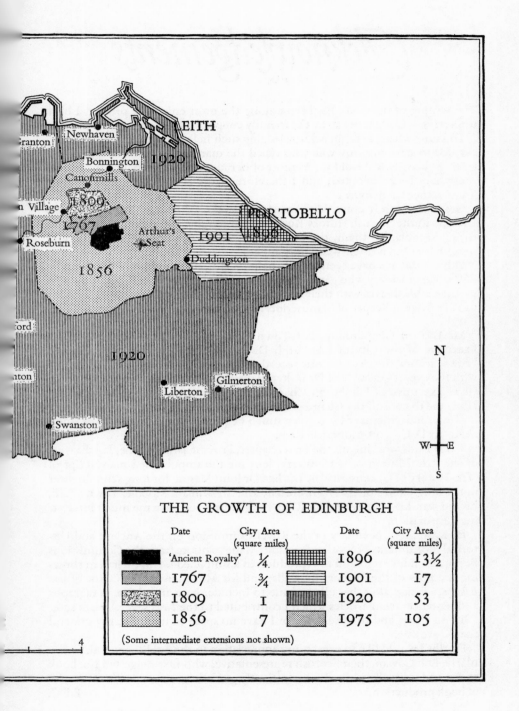

LEITH

Newhaven

Granton

Bonnington

1920

Canonmills

n Village

1809

PORTOBELLO

1767

Roseburn

Arthur's
Seat

1896

1901

Duddingston

1856

ord

1920

nton

Gilmerton

Liberton

Swanston

N

W — E

S

THE GROWTH OF EDINBURGH

Date	City Area (square miles)		Date	City Area (square miles)
'Ancient Royalty'	¼		1896	13½
1767	¾		1901	17
1809	I		1920	53
1856	7		1975	105

(Some intermediate extensions not shown)

4

Acknowledgements

The writing of this book has been among the most enjoyable projects I have undertaken, made more so by the friendly cooperation of so many people.

To know where to begin acknowledging such help is always difficult. I have decided to start with my wife who typed the manuscript, criticizing and suggesting changes as she did so. As most of her ideas were clearly improvements most have beeen adopted; and I therefore gladly acknowledge this book as 'ours' rather than 'mine'.

Next must surely come Mrs Armstrong in the Edinburgh Room and Miss Dickson in the Scottish History Room of Edinburgh Central Public Library and their assistants. To them, the old cliché – 'without whom this book would never have been written' – certainly applies.

Other librarians have been equally helpful – among then Mr G. H. Ballantyne of the Signet Library who gave me access to the volumes of old Court of Session papers on his shelves with their fascinating sidelights on past centuries; and Mr C. P. Finlayson, Keeper of Manuscripts in the Library of the University of Edinburgh.

Mr Edward Glendinning, last Town Clerk of Edinburgh and first Chief Executive of the City of Edinburgh District, kindly gave me permission to browse among the city's historic records which I did pleasurably and profitably with the expert guidance of Dr Walter Makey, City Archivist. Mr David Mowat, Chief Executive of Edinburgh Chamber of Commerce, was good enough to allow me to consult the Chamber's earliest minute-books; and for the chapter on Holyrood Sanctuary I was given much helpful advice by the Bailie of Holyrood, Mr D. C. Scott-Moncrieff, c.v.o.

While I was working on the final chapter, Provost James Milne, last Provost of the Royal Burgh of Queensferry, lent me the unpublished manuscript of 'The History of Queensferry' by the late Dr John Mason, for long schoolmaster in the burgh and noted as its historian; and Mr William Moodie, Town Clerk, his assistant Miss Finlay and Mr Ring, Burgh Surveyor, gave me much interesting information.

Dr K. A. Steer, Secretary of the Royal Commision on the Ancient and Historical Monuments of Scotland, permitted me to quote from the Commissions Report on Edinburgh and to reproduce, in a simplified form, their Plan showing the lines of the former city walls; and Mr Max McAuslane, Editor of the *Edinburgh Evening News*, has allowed me to include, here and there, paragraphs and sentences from articles which I contributed to the *News* several years ago.

To all these, and to others whom I have no space to mention, my grateful thanks are due.

Finally, I would like to express my appreciation to the publishers, and, particularly, Bob Cowan, their Scottish representative, who first suggested the book to me and Julian Watson who has patiently guided me through the intricacies of book production.   E.F.C.

Illustrations

Pages 6/7

Map: The Growth of Edinburgh

Between pages 56 and 57

1 Riddle's Close, Lawnmarket
2 Lord Provost George Drummond (reproduced by permission of the Lothian Health Board)
3 The first Royal Infirmary of Edinburgh (from an engraving lent by Professor David C. Simpson)
4 Vincent Lunardi, balloonist
5 George Square, old and new (copyright photograph by John Dewar Studios, Edinburgh)
6 White Horse Close, Canongate (reproduced by permission of Edinburgh Public Libraries)
7 Holyrood Sanctuary (from an aquatint lent by Professor David C. Simpson)

Between pages 104 and 105

8 Sedan Chair Men
9 The Mound Coach
10 The Lawnmarket in 1822 (reproduced by permission of Edinburgh Public Libraries)
11 Two New Town Architects – Gillespie Graham and Thomas Hamilton
12 Moray Place in 1829
13 The Theatre Royal, Shakespeare Square
14 Mrs Sarah Siddons in Edinburgh in 1784

Between pages 152 and 153

15 Two New Town Residents – Francis Jeffrey and Henry Cockburn
16 'O Felicem Diem' – The arrival of George IV at Leith in 1822 (reproduced by permission of the City of Edinburgh Art Centre)

17 Bailie Fyfe's Close, High Street
18 Sir Henry D. Littlejohn, Edinburgh's first Medical Officer of Health
(reproduced by permission of Edinburgh Public Libraries)
19 St Bernard's Well in 1829
20 A Newhaven Fishwife in 1812

Between pages 200 and 201

21 The Old Town Today – the Canongate (copyright photograph by
Stanley C. G. Lambert, Lasswade, Midlothian)
22 The New Town Today – Charlotte Square, west side (copyright photograph
by Stanley C. G. Lambert)
23 Arthur's Seat, the Castle and the skyline of the Old Town (copyright
photograph by Stanley C. G. Lambert)
24 Duddingston Village and Loch and Holyrood Park (reproduced by
permission of the City Planning Officer)
25 Cramond Village (copyright photograph by John Dewar Studios)
26 Princes Street, old and new (reproduced by permission of the City
Planning Officer)
27 Queensferry – the burgh between the bridges (copyright photograph by
John Dewar Studios)

pages 274/5

Plan: The Former Town Walls

Endpapers

The Old Tolbooth and the luckenbooths – demolished 1817 (from a drawing
reproduced by permission of the Society of Antiquaries of Scotland from the
Proceedings of the Society, Vol. xx – 1885–86).

Where no acknowledgement is made the pictures are from the author's
collection.
Pictures were photographed for this volume by –
John Dewar Studios: nos. 1, 3, 4, 7, 8, 9, 11–17, 19, 20, endpaper
R. R. Inglis Photography: nos. 6, 10, 18, jacket illustration

1 Approach to Edinburgh

To those of us who have lived all our lives in Edinburgh, it is a continuing source of regret that we can never know for ourselves but can only imagine the impressions of a visitor to Edinburgh who sees the city for the first time.

To emerge from Waverley Station as a newcomer to Edinburgh and see, high above one on the left, the spiky skyline of the buildings on the old town ridge dominated by the Castle on its rock, with ahead the classical outlines of the Royal Scottish Academy Gallery and the Scottish National Gallery over the green hollow of East Princes Street Gardens, and on the right the spire of the Walter Scott Monument, gothic and ornate, towering over Princes Street – can there be, anywhere else, so dramatic an introduction to a city and one that comprehends, in a single glance, so much of a city's history?

Nor is the traveller by train, coming up from the railway station, the only visitor to be given so vivid a view of the city. If you come by road from Newcastle, by Coldstream or Jedburgh, your route will bring you over Soutra Hill some sixteen miles south of Edinburgh and 1100 feet above sea level. At several points on that road, if the day is clear – or, better still, the evening just before sunset – you will have before you between the Lothian fields and the Firth of Forth what seems like a cardboard cut-out of the Edinburgh skyline. Though dominated westwards by the high hills of the Pentland range and on the east by Arthur's Seat, the old town ridge, ending in the turreted outline of Edinburgh Castle, will clearly catch your eye.

The traveller from Carlisle, whether he enters the city through Gilmerton or Liberton villages, will be given a different version of the same scene with the details more clearly defined because he will be nearer to them before the buildings come into view. But if his route is by Biggar and the suburb of Fairmilehead he will not see the old town; instead, his first impression will be of a city almost hidden by green and pleasant hills.

Those who approach from the west – from Glasgow, from the Highlands by the Forth Road Bridge, or from the Edinburgh airport at Turnhouse – are given yet another impression. They come in along one or other of the wooded flanks of Corstorphine Hill and have glimpses of Arthur's Seat, but they do not clearly see the sloping ridge of the old town until they are very nearly in the city centre. As they approach, the Castle (from this angle a blunt stone block on its crag) towers above the spires and chimneys of the city's west end.

Visitors who come by the Great North Road, through Berwick, Haddington and Musselburgh, will see nothing at all of the old town or the Castle at its head until they are very near them. For as they come past Portobello (once a town in its own right) it is Arthur's Seat that they will see, its craggy, 823-foot summit straight ahead, flanked by the lesser height of Calton Hill with Grecian columns and the Nelson monument, like a grey telescope upended.

Dr Johnson came that way one August evening in 1773. What he thought of Arthur's Seat is not recorded, but one visitor who came three years after Dr Johnson did not at all like its appearance. He was William Gilpin of Salisbury who, in course of a tour in Scotland in 1776, took one look at the hill and said (as if there was some approved shape that a hill should be): 'Arthur's Seat is odd, mis-shapen and uncouth . . . a view with a staring feature in it can no more be picturesque than a face with a bulbous nose can be beautiful.' Far from finding it mis-shapen, however, generations of visitors and Edinburgh citizens have seen in Arthur's Seat, from this angle, the shape of a sleeping lion – so much so that its two main heights are commonly known as 'the lion's head' and 'the lion's haunch'. Such comparisons, however amusing, add little or nothing to one's appreciation of this striking feature of the Edinburgh scene. Much better is Robert Louis Stevenson's apt description: 'Arthur's Seat – a hill for magnitude, a mountain by reason of its bold design.' It is, indeed a mountain, with crags, whin-covered slopes and lochs all within a short walk from the centre of the city.

I had almost forgotten yet another approach to Edinburgh, that by sea to its port of Leith. Kings and Queens, through the centuries, have landed here and some visitors still come this way, though they are fewer than of old. One who did so was Hugh Miller, stonemason, geologist, writer and editor, who in 1824 arrived by sailing ship from his home in Cromarty in north-east Scotland. As his smack entered the harbour he tells how he gained his first glimpses of the city through a drifting curtain of mist:

At one time a flat reach of the New Town came full into view along which, in the general dimness the many chimneys stood up like stacks of corn in a field newly-reaped; at another, the Castle loomed out dark in the cloud; then, as if suspended over the earth, the rugged summit of Arthur's Seat came strongly out while its base remained invisible; and anon I caught a glimpse of the distant Pentlands, enveloped by a clear blue sky and lighted up by the sun. . . . Leith lay deep in the shade in the foreground.

Despite the many changes of 150 years, that account of the view from the entrance to the port of Leith could have been written yesterday.

From these descriptions it is clear that whenever a traveller comes to Edinburgh – 200 years ago, a century ago, or now – and from whatever direction, the features that chiefly meet his eye are Arthur's Seat and the ancient Castle at the end of the ridge that carries the street known as the Royal Mile gently down from the Castle to the Palace of Holyroodhouse. These are Edinburgh's unique features. Where else will you find a mountain in a city? Or a city with its historic centre raised quite in the same way, as a silhouette against the sky?

2 Growth of a city

The origin of Edinburgh is lost in antiquity. No one knows just when it was that the first inhabitant, seeking a refuge for himself and his family, set up house on the summit of what is now the Castle rock, safely above the forests and lochs that then surrounded it. The fact that such a refuge was there at all was due to two forces which had operated long ages before that first Edinburgh family arrived. Fierce volcanic heat had shaped Arthur's Seat and Calton Hill, as well as forcing up the black mass of the Castle rock; and, much later, the slow relentless movement of the ice from west to east had scooped out hollows both north and south of the rock and left a piled-up ridge of earth, clay and stones tailing away eastwards behind its protective shield.

On that ridge grew the earliest burgh of Edinburgh. The ridge remained the site of the burgh for many centuries and it can still be regarded as the spine of the city despite rival claims of George Street or Princes Street. The ice, by forming that 'crag-and-tail' ridge, had fixed a pattern for the lives of Edinburgh folks for many generations; a pattern which still affects their lives today.

The crest of the Castle rock was an ideal spot for a settlement, for it had springs of water on it and space to graze cattle. That there was an iron age fort upon it seems almost certain, though no traces can now be identified because of the mass of later buildings and it is not until the eleventh century that historians can tell us anything really definite about it. At that time Malcolm Canmore and his Queen, Margaret, made it their home. Only one building of that time remains – St Margaret's Chapel, built for Queen Margaret – and although, of course, it has been almost wholly rebuilt and restored it is now the only building that provides any tangible link with the Edinburgh of that time.

East of the Castle, a little way down the ridge, a cluster of houses grew under its protection and so the nucleus of the town came into being. When its inhabitants organized themselves into a community in any formal sense is another thing at which we can do no more than guess. There must, however, have been a pretty well established form of burgh organization before the twelfth century because in a charter granted by David I in 1128 to the Canons of his abbey of Holyrood he refers to 'my burgh of Edinburgh' implying that he had already declared the little township on the Castle hill to be a Royal Burgh and he would certainly not do that unless there was already a body of worthy citizens there, able to exercise the rights and privileges of such a burgh.

Therefore well before the twelfth century Edinburgh, small and restricted though it was, must have had its merchants and its tradespeople and some kind of burgh organization. There is, however, nothing to justify some of the astonishing statements made by early chroniclers, like John Stow who said in his *Summary of English Chronicles*, written in 1565, that Edinburgh was founded 989 years before the birth of Christ (not, you will notice, 'nearly 1000' or even an approximate 990, but precisely 989!); or even the confident assertion by the magistrates of the city, in the extravagant 'harangue' to which they treated James VI on his visit to Edinburgh in 1618, that 'Edinburgh was founded in 330 B.C.'.

Instead of searching for the first beginnings of the city we are on safer ground if we look at its earliest surviving Royal Charter and take that as our starting-point for its history. That Charter, still preserved in the City Chambers, is written on a quite small sheet of parchment. Leaving out a few words here and there, this is what it says:

Robert, by the Grace of God, King of Scots, unto all good men of his whole land, greeting: Know ye that we have given, granted . . . and confirmed to the burgesses of our burgh of Edinburgh the aforesaid our burgh . . . together with the port of Leith, the Mills and their pertinents. To be held and had to the same burgesses and their successors, in freedom and peace, fully and honourably by all their righteous Meiths and Marches with all the commodious freedoms and easements which were wont of right to belong to the said burgh. . . . Rendering therefrom to us and our heirs, by the year, 52 merks of sterlings. . . . At Cardross, the 28th day of May, of our reign, the 24th year [i.e. 1329].

Two points in that Charter are worth noting. The first is that it confirmed to the people of Edinburgh rights not only in their own little burgh but also over the port of Leith and this was a privilege which the Edinburgh authorities and merchants continued to exercise, sometimes too enthusiastically, for at least 500 years; a circumstance which, lingering even yet in a kind of 'folk memory' may have something to do with the feelings towards Edinburgh still expressed by some of its present-day citizens who live in the part of the city that was formerly the separate burgh of Leith.

The second point of note in the Charter is the reference to the burgh's mills. These were situated on the Water of Leith, in what was formerly known as Water of Leith Village (now Dean Village) and there, only ten minutes' walk from Princes Street, you can still step back in atmosphere to the days when it was a bustling rural community, centre of the millers' and bakers' trades. In a later chapter we will go there.

Students of history will have noted that King Robert the Bruce's Charter was signed at Cardross, in Dunbartonshire, fifteen years after the battle of Bannockburn at which he had so soundly defeated the English. It was, in fact, signed only ten days before his death on 7 June 1329.

Six hundred years later, on 28 May 1929, the anniversary of the granting of the Bruce Charter was celebrated in the city with great pomp and ceremony and, to mark that occasion, the two massive statues of Sir William Wallace by Alexander Carrick RSA, and King Robert the Bruce, by Thos. J. Clapperton, which flank the entrance to Edinburgh Castle were unveiled by HRH the Duke of York (later King George VI) and there the two figures now stand guard, presumably for ever.

At the time of the Bruce Charter the little burgh of Edinburgh must have extended some distance down the streets which we know as Castle Hill and Lawnmarket and into the High Street, at least as far as the Kirk of St Giles where a church had begun to be built in the twelfth century. At the lower end of the ridge, about one mile from the Castle, the abbey of Holyrood had been founded by David I in 1128. In accordance with his charter of 1143 to the Canons of Holyrood, the burgh of Canongate had been formed and it was extending westwards up the ridge. It cannot have been very long before the two burghs met; but they did not merge and become one for several hundred years – not until 1856 in fact.

By the middle of the fifteenth century concern was growing at the danger of invasion from England and a charter granted by James II in 1450 declared that the King had been informed that the people of Edinburgh 'dread the evil and skaith of our enemies of England' and so he gave them full authority 'to bulwark, wall, turret and otherwise strengthen the burgh in what manner of ways or degree that seems most speedful to them'.

Thus the King's Wall, the first Edinburgh city wall of which details are known, was built.* It began about half-way down the south side of the Castle bank which in those days dropped steeply without interruption to the valley which later became the Grassmarket. Then the wall ran eastwards along the side of the steep slope above Grassmarket and Cowgate, protecting the houses above it on the ridge and enclosing St Giles Kirk, until it came nearly to where St Mary's Street crosses the High Street. There it turned at right angles across the High Street ridge and dropped into the valley on the north.

Some vestiges of the King's Wall can still be traced beside the middle section of Castle Wynd (the steps and footpath leading from Johnston Terrace to the Grassmarket) and at the other end of the town that it protected, in Tweeddale Court (at No. 14 High Street).

On the northern side of the ridge the Nor' Loch, which had been formed by damming the stream in the valley where the railway and Princes Street Gardens now are, gave all necessary protection to that side of the town. The loch served other purposes too. With swans as a decorative feature and fish and eels for food, it was also useful for washing clothes, for ducking offenders and for disposing easily of all manner of rubbish and unpleasantness.

*A map of the old walls of Edinburgh can be found on pages 274-5.

B

Edinburgh within the limits of the King's Wall (and excluding the Castle) was no more than half a mile long and a quarter of a mile wide. No wonder, then, that a new wall was soon required for it was not many years before the town had to spill over into the Grassmarket and the Cowgate in the deeply scooped-out valley under the southern slope of the town ridge. When news came to the burgh of the defeat of the Scottish army at Flodden in September 1513 fears arose, once more, that the English might invade the town. So, immediately, arrangements were made to build a new wall that would enclose the larger area which had begun to be built over. To pay for a new wall a tax was imposed on the citizens and fines, collected for various misdemeanours, were allocated to it. Despite the apparent urgency, however, the wall was not completed until 1560, forty-seven years later – a delay which will not greatly surprise those who know their Edinburgh for, even now, it is a city that tends to go slowly and carefully with its major projects.

The Flodden Wall, as this one came to be called, defined the limits of the burgh of Edinburgh for 250 years so it is worth tracing its line and inspecting the few parts that remain. On the east it began at the Nor' Loch, quite close to the King's Wall, about where the main London arrival platform of Waverley Station now begins. The wall came uphill, crossing the High Street where the traffic lights at St Mary's Street are, and at that point, until 1764, stood the Netherbow Port, the main gateway to the burgh from the east. In the roadway at the junction brass plates have been inserted to show the outline of the wall and the gateway which was an imposing turreted affair. A representation of the gateway, cut in stone, can be seen above the door of No. 9 High Street nearby, and this gives a much better idea of its appearance than does the fanciful modern bronze sign a little further up the street marking the Church of Scotland's Netherbow Arts Centre, opened in 1972.

From the Netherbow Port the wall continued downhill, at right angles to the High Street, until it reached the Cowgate in the valley to the south where there was another gate, the Cowgate Port, through which the town's cows were taken to and from their grazing grounds. Uphill then, the wall went, parallel to the street called the Pleasance which is on the line of an ancient roadway leading south from Edinburgh. Here some sections of the Flodden

Wall can still be seen through gaps in the buildings on the right-hand side of the street. At the junction with what is now Drummond Street the wall took a right-angled bend and traces of a tower that must once have been a feature of this corner remain. For some distance along Drummond Street the lower part of the present boundary wall – up to about four or five feet – can clearly be seen to consist of the rough-hewn stones of the original wall.

The route of the wall continued along College Street where the southern side of the University of Edinburgh Old College now marks its line. It then passed through the site of the Royal Scottish Museum in Chambers Street. There, two fragments of it were preserved when an extension to the museum was built around them in the 1930s; but now, unfortunately, they are no longer to be seen.

There were gates, or 'Ports', at Potterrow (between the Old College and the Museum) and at Bristo Place at the southern end of George IV Bridge. The bridge, of course, did not exist when the wall was there and roads leading to Bristo Port came steeply up from the Cowgate as Candlemaker Row still does. Westwards from the Bristo Port the Flodden Wall continued, enclosing the site of Greyfriars Kirk and Kirkyard but excluding the ground on which George Heriot's Hospital (now School) was later built. The only visible evidence of this part of the wall is a gap, filled in with modern stonework, separating the buildings at Nos. 5 and 7 Forrest Road between which it passed. Then, west of George Heriot's School grounds, at the top of the lane and stairway known as the Vennel which led from Lauriston Place down to the Grassmarket, was built the best preserved section of the old wall – the battlemented tower that marked its south-western corner. From here there is a striking view of the Castle and it is easy to visualize the old wall dropping steeply downhill into the Grassmarket, crossing it, and ending against the crags of the Castle rock. In the Grassmarket was the West Port – the gate through which, for centuries, travellers from south-west, west and north-west entered Edinburgh, among them King Charles I in 1633, and Robert Burns in 1786.

To those who take the trouble to follow the line of the wall to the corner-tower at the top of the Vennel a word of warning is due. From the tower an old rugged-looking wall runs south towards Lauriston Place. This should not be mistaken for the Flodden Wall. It is all that remains of a seventeenth-century extension known as Telfer's Wall which was built to enclose George Heriot's Hospital.

For two centuries and a half then, the Flodden Wall, more or less coinciding with the Ancient Royalty (as the burgh's limits were called), defined Edinburgh. The Town Council, it is true, had some rights beyond these limits, but the burgh itself for the whole of that time was enclosed by the Nor' Loch and the Flodden Wall, surrounding an area of just under 140 acres. A man could walk from end to end of Edinburgh in ten minutes and across it from south to north in less. Within that tight-packed area it has been estimated that the population grew from as few as 10000 in 1520 to at least 31000 in 1755, and on that tiny stage much of Scotland's history was enacted. It seems incredible that so small a space could hold so many people and see so much of life. It is no wonder that the early wooden houses on the ridge, with their garden enclosures, soon gave place to stone ones, packed ever closer together and rising steadily higher, some reaching to ten or eleven storeys, with families of all degrees rubbing shoulders daily as they came up and down the narrow stairways to and from their dwellings. In later chapters we will meet some of them but now, having taken the measure of the old burgh within its wall, the time has come to make our way up on to the Castle esplanade – on a clear day, it is hoped – and survey from there the extent of Edinburgh as it has grown over the centuries and as it now is.

First look south from the Castle esplanade. Except for the hills, you must try to imagine away almost everything you see below you – almost but not quite everything. Immediately beneath your feet Johnston Terrace, snaking along the slope of the Castle bank, must be left out for it was not built until the 1830s. Until then the Castle bank plunged 300 feet to the level of the Grassmarket. The Grassmarket is still, in shape, much as it was in medieval times, though its buildings are very different and the bustle of horses, cattle and sheep, carriers' carts and crowds at the fairs that were held there are all a distant memory.

Beyond the line of the Flodden Wall, George Heriot's School, with its many turrets, looks much the same as it did in 1650 when, immediately after its completion, Cromwell commandeered it for his troops though beyond it then there was no Royal Infirmary and in place of the green parkland of the Meadows there was the Burgh Loch, a broad lake from which Edinburgh drew some of its water supply. Beyond the loch was the Burgh Muir, an expanse of common land dotted by occasional towers and mansions and stretching away to the hills of Blackford and Braid, still yellow with gorse in May and June. It was not until the mid-nineteenth century that Edinburgh expanded to the edge of Blackford Hill – easily identified by the round green roof of the Royal Observatory on its crest – and not until 1920 that it encompassed the whole expanse, as far as the Pentland summits which you can see against the sky. These are Caerketton and Allermuir, the latter just over 1600 feet above sea level. Robert Louis Stevenson called them his 'hills of home'. The city boundary now runs along their skyline and below them, within the city, the thatched village of Swanston still retains much of its rural charm that Stevenson knew.

If you walk on now into the Castle and up through its port-cullis gate you will come before long by a steeply curving road to the high rocky outcrop on which St Margaret's Chapel and the ancient cannon 'Mons Meg' stand. Look north from there and once again try to wipe out of sight almost everything except the general lie of the land, the blue waters of the Firth of Forth, the hills of Fife and the Highland hills beyond. Below you, imagine no railway, no gardens, no Mound with picture galleries and no North Bridge, only a marshy hollow with a loch at its foot. Try also to wipe out Princes Street and the buildings beyond it and see only fields and woods rising gently, then falling towards the north. Near the west end of George Street, until the late eighteenth century, there was Wood's Farm and where the modern façade of the St James shopping centre and King James Hotel stand out above St Andrew Square was the hamlet of Multrie's Hill. This was a favourite summer resort of Edinburgh folk until it was swallowed up in the late eighteenth century by St James Square, which itself has now been obliterated by the grey bulk of the new shopping centre.

From the George Street ridge the fields and hedges dropped gently down to the Water of Leith and 200 years ago from your vantage point you would pick out, along its course, the riverside villages of Stockbridge, Silvermills, Canonmills and Bonnington, each a separate small community dependent on the power supplied to its mills by the Water of Leith. Beyond them all and to your right you would see meadows and fields ending in the roofs and masts of the port of Leith. Westwards from Leith would be the isolated fishing village of Newhaven. There, in 1511, James IV built the *Great Michael*, a ship so massive that its construction, it was said, 'wasted all the woods in Fife'. Still further west you would in due time see the nineteenth-century harbour of Granton and beyond it until the 1930s even, little except fields with occasional farms and mansion houses.

It was in 1767 that Edinburgh took its bold decision to escape from the restriction of its ancient ridge and medieval wall. An Act was passed in that year, extending the city's 'royalty' over the rising ground where George Street now runs and, in 1767, the building of the Georgian New Town began. After that, if you could have stood at this Castle vantage point through the years you would have seen almost constant change as the New Town houses were steadily built from east to west and George Street and Princes Street took shape. By 1814 you would have seen the dome of St George's Church (now green and gold in the sun) rising above Charlotte Square. In the next fifty years new roofs would appear as terraces were built further down the slope towards the Water of Leith – Heriot Row, Royal Circus, Great King Street and, to the west, Moray Place; then later, Buckingham Terrace, Belgrave Crescent, Grosvenor Crescent and their neighbours. From 1850 onwards would come less pleasing developments, with Victorian tenements, factories and railways. Indeed there are places where once-elegant Georgian terraces stop abruptly, cut off by railway lines and goods yards. Happily, however, almost all of Edinburgh's Georgian New Town still remains to be explored and relished. Beyond it, towards the north-west, stretch the twentieth-century housing schemes of Granton, Pilton and Muirhouse from which tower-blocks of the 1950s point skywards; and the present century does not come well out of this comparison.

The 'extended royalty' of 1767 carried the City of Edinburgh downhill to the Water of Leith, but not beyond. In 1856, the city's boundaries reached to the borders of Leith – by then a burgh in its own right with full statutory powers of its own, a status which it enjoyed for only eighty-seven years – from 1833 until 1920.

After 1920 everything on this side of the Firth of Forth that you can see from this vantage point became part of the City of Edinburgh, from the wooded crest of Corstorphine Hill on the west along ten miles of coast to the edge of the burgh of Mussel-burgh on the east. Beyond the shoulder of Corstorphine Hill you can just see, from the Castle, a span of the Forth railway bridge, opened in 1890 and the tips of the two towers of the Forth road bridge, completed in 1964. Between these two bridges where they leave the south shore of the Forth is the ancient Royal Burgh of Queensferry. Its name, and that of the ferry that plied there for centuries, commemorates that same Margaret whose eleventh-century chapel is behind you as you look out from your Castle viewpoint. And now, with the coming of local government reform, Queensferry which she knew so well has merged with the City of Edinburgh in which she lived as Queen of Scotland.

So, having had a bird's-eye view of Edinburgh and followed, as it were, a speeded-up film of its growth over many centuries, it is time now to 'zoom in' on some of the landmarks of those centuries and to meet a few of the men and women who have played parts in the city's story.

3 Tapestry of time

The Royal Mile of Edinburgh, stretching down the ridge from Castle to Palace, is really four streets placed end to end – Castlehill, Lawnmarket, High Street and Canongate. Indeed it could be called six streets because the last few yards of the High Street were formerly the Nether Bow (where the Netherbow Port in the Flodden Wall marked the eastern end of Edinburgh) and, between the foot of the Canongate and the Abbey and Palace of Holyrood, there is a short length of street known as the Abbey Strand in which the abbey gateway once stood. Together, these six streets make up the Royal Mile, described (though not by that name) by Daniel Defoe in 1724 as being 'perhaps the largest, longest and finest street for buildings and number of inhabitants, not in Britain only, but in the world'.

Many another traveller was impressed by its length, its width, its tall tenements (known as 'lands'), by its crowded closes and wynds, burrowing under and between the lands; and, it must be owned, by its filth and smells. William Brereton who came here from Cheshire in 1636 wrote: 'This city is placed in a dainty, health-ful and pure air and doubtless were a most healthful place to live in, were not the inhabitants most sluttish, nasty and slothful people.' Joseph Taylor, visiting in 1705, was forced to hold his nose when walking in the street and to tread carefully 'for fear of disobliging his shoes', as he delicately put it. As everyone knows, Dr Johnson, as he was being escorted on the evening of his arrival in Edinburgh from Boyd's Inn off the Canongate to Boswell's house in James Court, Lawnmarket, grumbled in Boswell's ear: 'I can smell you in the dark'; but, Boswell adds, 'he acknowledged that the breadth of the street and the loftiness of the buildings on each side made a noble appearance'.

Despite vigorous though intermittent efforts by the Town Council to remedy matters, how could the town be other than dirty and unpleasant, with so many people living so close together and with only a few wells to supply water which had to be carried in barrels or buckets up six or eight flights of stairs (and in some places even more) to houses with no drains to carry away the waste? Not to mention the cows and horses kept in sheds down many of the closes and the pigs which often occupied spaces under the forestairs that projected from several of the tenements into the street.

Yet noblemen and their families, judges of the high court, college professors, lawyers, merchants, shopkeepers and craftsmen (all with their servants), market stallkeepers, messengers, town guardsmen and many others lived their lives and brought up their families in this higgledy-piggledy community which went far beyond the dreams of present-day town planners seeking to achieve a 'social mix' in the communities they plan.

Not surprisingly, with houses so crowded together and inconvenient, much of life was spent in the streets and closes which must have presented scenes of constant noise and movement. Merchants and lawyers for centuries conducted most of their business at the Market Cross or in one or other of the taverns or coffee houses of the town; and when the day's business was done it was the practice not to go home but to join friends and acquaintances in a favourite oyster-cellar or tavern and pass the evening in convivial talk and enjoyment. After all, the 'cadies' or messengers who were always about in the streets knew not only where everyone lived but also where his favourite haunt was and could quickly take a message to him, failing to find him only if that appeared to be the more tactful thing to do. 'From time immemorial' they had been licensed by the magistrates to ply their useful and responsible trade and, in 1711, these 'cadies' – the same word as the modern golf caddies – were formed into a society with a self-imposed code of conduct. Besides making it their business to find out everything about everyone who came to the city they could be trusted to carry the most private of messages and to hand over safely whatever goods or money might be given to them for delivery.

Within the memory of many today, the Royal Mile and its closes were still dirty and unsavoury places, though the 'social mix' had gone and almost all who lived there were poor and often ill-clad but with still a warmth and friendliness among them. Since then, over the past thirty years or so, a process of renovation has been going on and though much remains to be done several parts of the Royal Mile have become pleasant places in which to live. In this kind of restoration work the problem is to improve and renovate without destroying the character of the street and the aura of the past. This does not mean just replacing derelict and worn out buildings by imitations of what was there before, although here and there in the Canongate that has been well done. It means (or should mean) restoring whatever is worth restoring and is capable of renovation. A seventeenth-century stone wall, strengthened and repaired, has volumes more to tell the passer-by than a modern replica, however skilfully built; and where restoration is impossible, because the old walls have deteriorated too far to be rescued, it is usually better to replace what cannot be restored by something that honestly declares its own period.

This is, indeed, one of the features of the Royal Mile, that five centuries of building – the fifteenth to the nineteenth – all show their own characteristic mark, and now the twentieth century is doing so too. As one recognizes each building's period, one may easily visualize the scenes in which the building must have played its part, even although that part may have been only to provide a back-drop to some historic event or a window as vantage point from which residents cheered a royal procession or hurled abuse or encouragement at a mob in the street below. So, as one walks in the Lawnmarket and the High Street, the buildings one sees fit into place like threads in a tapestry of time, making up a picture of the old town's crowded history.

The only fifteenth-century building still to be seen in the High

Street is the tower and crown of St Giles Church. The tower was built during that century and the crown that surmounts it was completed in 1500. The interior of the church has been altered in many ways and at many times since then, and all the old exterior was either replaced or hidden by the grey stone cladding built around it by the architect, William Burn, in 1829. It is sad that William Burn, who has many fine buildings to his credit, should have given such a dreary aspect to St Giles. Only the tower and crown remain to catch the sunlight on the warm buff-coloured stones laid by workmen who, according to the burgh records, were labouring there in 1491 from 5 a.m. until 7 p.m. each day. Their handiwork, which has looked down on nearly 500 years of history is still the finest of the old town's landmarks.

If there is one building in the Royal Mile more than any other that represents the sixteenth century for us it is the house known as John Knox's at the lower end of the High Street where it narrows to become the Nether Bow. John Knox's House, with red-tiled gable roof and projecting gallery at first-floor level (the only survival of a once common feature) catches the eye from far up the High Street as it projects across the footpath from the other frontages. Though it has been greatly altered since, there are records to show that it was built in the middle of the sixteenth century and thus, so far as its date goes, it could have been occupied by John Knox. Certainly it owes its existence today to the strongly held belief that he lived in it during the last months of his life and died there in 1572. In 1849 when the structure of the house had become dangerous it was condemned and would have been demolished but for the clamour to save it raised by many voices, including the corporate and influential voice of the Society of Antiquaries of Scotland. That clamour was based, not upon the undoubted interest of the house as a surviving example of its period, but wholly upon its traditional association with the great reformer and after a considerable struggle with the authorities the order for demolition was withdrawn and the house was repaired at great expense.

Some forty years later a vigorous controversy was waged within the Society of Antiquaries led, on the one hand, by a member who had painstakingly examined public records and title deeds and had satisfied himself that Knox could not have lived there at any time; and on the other hand, by a learned member who later became a judge of the Court of Session and yet pinned his faith to the 'hearsay evidence' of long-standing tradition, declaring himself satisfied, without any other proof, that John Knox *had* lived in the house. Afterwards it was pointed out that the earliest record of the tradition dated only from 1784, when the Honourable Mrs Murray of Kensington, visiting Edinburgh in course of her tour of Scotland wrote in her diary that she had been shown 'the tottering bow-window to a house whence John Knox thundered his addresses to the people'. That was more than 200 years after Knox's death and, against that story it was stated that there was not any record of Knox preaching from a window and that, at the only possible time of his residence in this house, he was so ill and weak that his sermons from the pulpit could scarcely be heard by his congregation.

The result of the controversy in the Society was inconclusive – but did that really matter? The house is an authentic one of the period and if John Knox did not live in this house in the months before his death the one in which he is known to have lived between 1560 and 1566, on a site marked by a plaque in Warriston Close, opposite St Giles, was probably much like it. There is still, however, a body of informed opinion to support the tradition which in the middle of last century saved the building at the Nether Bow from destruction. Now, as a museum containing many articles connected with the reformer, it is visited by thousands every year whose understanding of Knox and of the Edinburgh of his time is certainly enhanced by what they see around them in its panelled rooms.

Whoever may or may not have lived in that house at the Nether Bow, its balcony would certainly have been a good vantage point from which to see much of the pageantry of sixteenth-century Edinburgh – the century of Mary, Queen of Scots, and of her son James VI. She landed at Leith on 19 August 1561 and rode to Holyrood through one of those damp grey mists or 'haars' blowing in from the Forth that are so familiar and so chilling to Edinburgh folk. It must have been a chilling return for her to her country of Scotland. But a fortnight or so later, on 1 September, she made her formal public progress through Edinburgh in better weather and in great splendour.

Two years later, for the opening of the Scottish parliament in 1563, the Queen came up the Canongate and the High Street on another magnificent occasion, 'her robes upon her back', and a rich crown on her head, with the royal crown, the sceptre and the sword borne in front of her. This time 'she was accompanied with all her nobles and above thirty of her chosen and picked ladies in this realm' – a sight, one would suppose, to delight all but the most churlish as the glittering procession made its way up the crowded and excited street. A churlish one was there, however; he was John Knox, and all that he could find to say on that occasion was: 'Such stinking pryde of women as was seen at that Parliament was never seen before in Scotland.'

These were years of many pageants and processions but the one I would most have liked to see took place in May 1587. James VI, then just twenty-one years old, had been sorely troubled by feuds among the noble families around him. The Earl of Glamis and the Earl of Crawford were 'at daggers drawn'; the Earl of Angus hated the Earl of Montrose; and there were other quarrels, too, among members of the Court. So James decided on one great effort of reconciliation. He invited them all to a banquet at Holyrood Palace where, so the story goes, 'the King drank to them thrice, willed them to maintain concorde and peace' and then ordered them to walk in procession up the Canongate and the High Street to the Market Cross, each hand in hand with his adversary – Glamis with Crawford, Angus with Montrose and so on. The Market Cross was then a little nearer to the centre of the High Street than it is at present; it had not yet been moved to the point a few yards further east, now marked by an octagonal design in the roadway, where it stood from 1617 until 1756. The Cross was draped for the occasion with fine tapestries and beside it, surrounded by all the squalor of the street, the Town Council at the King's command had set a long table 'with bread, wyne and sweetmeats'. The noble lords, who must surely have felt a little foolish, like children told by their teacher to walk nicely together, then feasted and drank each other's health. Debtors, by royal command, were released from prison; 'trumpeters blew, then the people sang for mirth and a great number of musical instruments was employed for the like use'. The feast over, the company again joined hands and, two by two, marched back down the hill to the Palace.

Whether this ceremony achieved its object of reconciling the nobles to one another seems doubtful, though it may perhaps have put them in an agreeable mood to approve, as they soon afterwards did, the marriage of the King to Princess Anne of Denmark. Whatever its results, it was a show I would have been sorry to miss if I had lived in Edinburgh in 1587; and its cost to the town was far from excessive for, according to the burgh records, 'the expenses made upon the banquet after supper to the King's Grace and nobility at the Mercat Cross upon the 15th of this month at which time His Majesty agreed his said nobility, extended to thirty pounds, ten shillings and eight pennies'. As this was Scots money, not sterling, it was a small price, surely, to pay for all that 'concorde and peace'.

Now, to take up the threads of the next century in our tapestry of time in the High Street and Lawnmarket of Edinburgh, two buildings may be picked out: Parliament Hall, in the parliament house complex of buildings behind St Giles, was begun in 1632, completed eight years later and used for sittings of the Scottish parliament until the union of parliaments in 1707; and the Tron Church, further down the High Street, which was opened for worship in 1647.

Parliament Hall, built by the Town Council at the behest of Charles I with the help of subscriptions from individual citizens to house both parliament and the Court of Session, is part of a group of buildings so altered both inside and out as to leave little that is recognizable as original except the Laigh (or low) Hall below street level with the massive stone pillars supporting its roof and the impressive length, breadth and height of Parliament Hall itself with its magnificent oak hammerbeam roof. The Scots parliament first met under that roof in 1639. Their seats were ranged at the south end of the Hall under the great window, the present stained glass of which, however, was not placed there until 1868. Immediately below the window was the throne for the sovereign or, in the absence of the sovereign, for the Lord High Commissioner. Nearby were seats for the nobles and, below these, for the officers of state. Next came a table at which sat the judges of the Court of Session and then places for other members. Commissioners of counties and burghs sat further down the hall and there was also a pulpit, near the present entrance, from which sermons were preached to the assembled parliament.

At other times, and for a century or so after parliament had sat here for the last time in 1707, the hall was used by the Court of Session as the 'Outer House' (in which the judges sat separately) as distinct from the 'Inner House' (with fifteen judges sitting together) for which separate accommodation had been provided when the hall was built. Two judges presiding in the hall each heard a separate cause at the same time amidst the bustle of other business going on around them. As there were, inside the hall, stalls selling books and other articles and even a 'coffee-house', separated only by a low partition, in which the customers moved and chattered among themselves within sight and hearing of the judges, one wonders how justice can ever have been done.

Regularly, the hall was used for a banquet on the King's birthday, 4 June, and Lord Cockburn has described these occasions, as they lingered on into his own day, the late eighteenth and early nineteenth centuries, when sometimes 1500 people were present, 'roaring, drinking, toasting and quarrelling' until a late hour, making the court 'smell for a week with the fumes of that hot and scandalous night'. More sober occasions were the musical festivals held in the hall, the first in 1815, when Handel's *Messiah* and works by Haydn and Beethoven were performed to a crowded audience. Nowadays, Parliament Hall must be just about the only hall in Edinburgh that is not pressed annually into use for a Festival performance of one kind or another.

Now the great hall stands empty except for the gowned and bewigged advocates still pacing up and down its length in twos and threes as they have done for generations discussing learned questions of law (or exchanging gossip and golf stories) while they wait for their next cases to be called; with thirty or more famous judges and advocates of the past looking down on them from the portraits on the walls and from statues round the hall.

Outside, the fine gothic exterior of the hall as shown on Gordon of Rothiemay's drawing of Edinburgh in 1647 has been almost wholly covered and concealed by the nineteenth-century law courts, the Signet Library and the drab façade and unimposing entrance designed in 1808 by Robert Reid. From George IV Bridge, however, a glimpse still remains of the rougher warmer seventeenth-century stonework and window tracery of Parliament Hall.

In Parliament Square King Charles II still sits on horseback, cast in lead, where he was placed by the Town Council in 1685. They were going to put a statue of Cromwell there, but after the Restoration they changed their minds, and then in true Edinburgh fashion took twenty years to have the statue erected. Lord Fountainhall in his historical notices written soon after the event says:

On 16th April 1685, the late King's statue, on horseback, was erected and set up in the Parliament Close. It stood the town of Edinburgh very dear, more than £1000 sterling. Some alleged it was wrong placed, with the tail to the image of Justice above the Parliament House door. He is formed in the Roman manner, like one of the Caesars, almost naked, and so without spurs and without stirrups, because the old Romans used no such help. . . . The vulgar people, who had never seen the like before, were much amazed at it. Some compared it to Nebuchadnezzar's image which all fell doune and worshipped; and others, foolishly, to the pale horse in the Revelation and he that sate thereon was Death.

At intervals, over the centuries, the leaden legs of Charles's horse begin to sag under his weight and repairs become necessary. On the last occasion, in 1972, the statue made the long journey to London for a thorough overhaul and now, perhaps, horse and rider will be able to retain for another 300 years their reputation as the oldest lead equestrian statue in the country.

Like Parliament Hall, the Tron Church (so called from the 'tron' or weighing-machine which was nearby) was built by the Town Council at the command of Charles I and also partly by private subscription. In this case the command had to be given more than once because the Town Council were extremely reluctant to spend the money. Even when they found the King was adamant they dragged their feet and the church was a long time a-building. It was required for the congregation of the south-east parish of Edinburgh, who had hitherto worshipped in a subdivided section of St Giles Church. When Charles I decided to create a Bishopric of Edinburgh he called for the removal of the internal divisions of St Giles so that it could form a worthy cathedral and so the people of the south-east parish were soon to be without a place of worship. Even so, the building of the new church was delayed.

Eventually Charles had to threaten. He had learned that a good many of the merchants of Edinburgh were regularly infringing statutes which forbade the export of money to pay for their overseas trade and he declared that, if the church was not built in accordance with his wishes, proceedings would be taken against offending merchants. Several of the wealthier merchants lived in the south-east parish which included a part of the Cowgate where some of the larger houses were to be found and there must have been some guilty consciences among the parishioners because Charles's warning was followed by quite a spate of contributions to the Tron Church building fund. Nevertheless, progress was slow and, although the Latin inscription on the north front narrates that 'The citizens of Edinburgh consecrated the building to Christ and His Church in the year 1641', it was not in fact ready to receive its congregation until 1647.

The Tron Church has been much mutilated but it is still a distinctive landmark of the Royal Mile. Originally much larger than it is now, its east, west and south arms were all removed between 1785 and 1789 to make way for the building of the South Bridge beside it and the formation of Hunter Square behind it. In 1824 its Dutch-style spire was destroyed in the great fire which swept away almost the whole of the south side of the High Street between the Tron Church and Parliament Square, after which the present spire was built to an entirely different design. So all that remains of the seventeenth-century Tron Church is the rather severe north front, facing across the High Street; and inside, as in Parliament Hall, a fine hammerbeam roof.

The Tron Church ceased to be used for church purposes in 1952. After standing for several years empty and the subject of much controversy about its future it was bought by the government and given to the Town Council on condition that it would be renovated and used for some public purpose. It is now being converted to become an exhibition centre and when that work is completed, everyone will be able to admire the craftsmanship of its roof structure, a privilege reserved in the past for the congregation and, in recent years, only for the man who climbs among the pigeons to adjust the public clock high in the church's spire.

Renovation work inside the building in 1974 gave an opportunity for the city's archaeologist to arrange for excavations beneath

C

floor level and these have uncovered an area, hitherto protected by the floor, which had lain undisturbed since the building of the church was begun nearly 350 years ago. The dig disclosed the cobbled roadway of Marlin's Wynd which led downhill from High Street to Cowgate and was said to have been named after John Marlin, a Frenchman reputed to have been responsible, in 1532, for the first paving of the High Street. He was also said to have been so proud of that work that, by his own request, he was buried at the head of the Wynd.

It would have been good to be able to report that the excavations uncovered his grave, but no such spectacular find was made. Beside the Wynd there appeared the cobbles of a courtyard entered from it. Around the courtyard and on each side of the Wynd are fragments of the thick, strong walls which had carried the weight of the Wynd's tall and congested 'lands'. There are also remains of cellars and drainage channels and traces of the lowest steps of one of the turnpike stairs that once led to the upper floors. At one point, pieces of iron slag were found in a bed of sand suggesting that here may have been a small iron foundry. Broken portions of jugs and other domestic pottery were also discovered.

When reconstruction of the church interior is completed, I hope it may be possible for the remains of the earlier buildings, fragmentary though they are, to be laid permanently open for inspection so that those who view them may conjure up more easily a picture of the busy, bustling activity of those who lived and worked in Marlin's Wynd in the days before the Tron Church was built.

4 Tolbooth and Luckenbooths

Still in the High Street, we must pause to consider some buildings which are no longer to be seen but some of which were already old when Parliament Hall and the Tron Church were new and which, for several centuries, dominated the scene. You cannot picture what life in old Edinburgh was like unless you visualize these buildings as they were, the old Tolbooth immediately west of St Giles and the luckenbooths, which extended down the High Street close to the north wall of St Giles.

You can visualize the site of the old Tolbooth, as originally designated for it in 1385, and the outline of later alterations and additions by looking for the blocks in the roadway, some with dates on them, that mark its outline. At first it provided accommodation for the Town Council, the law courts and the Scottish parliament and, even allowing for its height of five storeys, it must have been pretty cramped accommodation because the ground plan extends to no more than 60 feet by 30 feet. From 1480 it included a prison within it and, latterly, the building came to be used only as a prison except for several small booths, let out as shops and workshops. As a prison it became first notorious and then, through Scott's novel *The Heart of Midlothian*, world famous. Its site is also marked by a heart-shaped design in the roadway and its notoriety acquired such deep roots that, even now, there

are those who, defying the rules of hygiene, still spit upon the
heart as they pass. They are prompted, one can only suppose, by
a folk-memory which they themselves probably could not explain.

The old Tolbooth may well have been the building to which
Queen Mary and her ladies came to open the parliament of 1563
because the new Tolbooth, then being built beside the south-west
corner of St Giles, seems not to have been ready and the records
do not make it clear which building was used on that occasion.
Somehow, the new Tolbooth never gained either fame or notoriety
and it was removed, without any fuss or publicity, in 1811.

The old Tolbooth remained in use as a prison for six more
years, until 1817 when it was demolished and its great wooden
door was removed by Sir Walter Scott to become a curious feature
of his house at Abbotsford, on the bank of the River Tweed, where
it can still be seen.

As a prison, the Tolbooth was not noted for security for there
are many records of escapes from it. Though dark and unsavoury,
far too close to dwelling houses and the bustle of the town, and
hated because of the occasions when it had housed political prisoners and those imprisoned for their religious beliefs it seems, in
part at least, to have been a homely sort of place in which unfor-
tunates, for want of better shelter, sometimes voluntarily took
refuge. In the memoirs of William Chambers (who later was Lord
Provost of the city) there is a vivid description of the prison as
he knew it as a young man shortly before its removal, when he
was frequently in it – not, I hasten to add, as a prisoner but as a
visitor. It then had, it seems, two 'departments' entered through
a large, gloomy hall on the first flat above the street, the east
department being for criminals and that on the west and on the
floors above, for debtors. It was some of these debtors the young
William Chambers had to visit in course of business.

There was, he says, 'a simplicity about the whole system. . . .
So far as the debtors were concerned the prison was little else
than a union of lodging-houses and tavern under lock and key.'
Visitors were admitted by two turnkeys, one below and one above
the stairway, and visitors to the debtors 'might call as often and
stay as long as they pleased' – indeed one was alleged to have stayed,
through the connivance of the keeper, for several years for want
of a better home. 'The inmates and their visitors, if they felt inclined,

could treat themselves to refreshments in a cosy little apartment, half tavern, half kitchen, superintended by a portly female styled "Lucky Laing" from whose premises issued the pleasant sounds of broiling beef-steaks and the drawings of corks from bottles of ale and porter.'

The prisoners in the other department, awaiting trial, serving sentence or awaiting execution, had no such privileges and comforts. They were kept though not always securely in the eastern section. To take one example, there was Robert, the young Master of Burleigh (eldest son of Lord Balfour of Burleigh) who, in January 1710, was due to be executed 'for a most barbarous murder', a crime of passion in which he had shot and killed a school-teacher who had married a girl of humble birth with whom Robert had been in love but whom he had been prevented from marrying because of their unequal rank. A few days before the date fixed for his execution and just after official intimation had come of Queen Anne's refusal to grant him a pardon or reprieve, Robert's mother and two sisters were admitted by the two turnkeys to visit him. The turnkeys, according to the record of the event, 'allowed them to continue in with their plaids on and never took them from them' but whether this was due merely to carelessness or was in recognition of the half-crown gratuity each received from Lady Balfour is not clear. Either way, their lapse enabled one of the sisters to change clothes with her brother and lie down on his bed while he wrapped himself in her plaid and walked out into the High Street with their mother and sister.

Five hours had passed, it was ten o'clock at night, with the prisoner doubtless well out of town, before his escape was discovered and the unhappy keeper of the prison hurriedly sought out one of the city magistrates, Bailie Adam Broun, and reported the sorry business to him. The magistrates immediately raised a hue and cry and (a futile gesture, one might think, in view of the time-lag) ordered the town gates to be instantly shut and kept closed until 8 a.m. next day. However, what chiefly worried Bailie Broun and his fellow magistrates seems to have been the question 'how far the Good Toun [meaning themselves] could be liable to any censure from the Government for this escape' and they hurriedly took the best legal advice on this question. One can almost hear their deep sigh of relief as one reads, later in the record, that learned counsel were satisfied 'that neither by our law nor practices the Good Toun could be anyways censurable for what had happened'. Meanwhile, young Robert Balfour went into hiding and was not recaptured. Five years later, after succeeding to his father's estate, he took an active part in the 1715 rebellion and as a result of this the estate was confiscated. He died in 1757.

A little more than a quarter of a century after that escape the successors in office of Bailie Broun and his colleagues did not get off quite so lightly when they were in trouble over the storming of the Tolbooth and the hanging, by a mob, of John Porteous, ex-Captain of the Town Guard, who was then a prisoner in it. That story has often been told and never better than by Sir Walter Scott who used it as one of the principal episodes in *The Heart of Midlothian*, though he did take minor liberties with some of the facts, as it is a novelist's privilege to do. 'The Porteous Mob' is also the subject of a large oil-painting by James Drummond RSA, painted in 1855, which can be seen in the National Gallery of Scotland on the Mound. It gives a somewhat glamorized impression of the scene at the east end of the Grassmarket, showing members of the mob courteously helping a lady of quality from her sedan chair which has unhappily become caught up in the crowds, just as final preparations are being made for Porteous's execution.

The whole story is fully documented in memoirs of eye-witnesses, in the Town Council minutes and in the voluminous legal and parliamentary papers and press reports that followed the event. Yet its perpetrators were never brought to justice and, despite rumours and legends, no one to this day has discovered who were the ringleaders.

The story began with the hanging, on 14 April 1736, at the place of public execution in the Grassmarket of Andrew Wilson who had been condemned to death, along with his friend George Robertson, for robbing an excise officer in Fife whose activities, the two men thought, interfered too much with their own trade of smuggling. In accordance with custom the two men had been taken from the Tolbooth on the Sunday before the date of execution to attend the service in the part of St Giles Kirk which was then known as the Tolbooth Kirk. During the service, Robertson escaped and got clean away helped, it was said, by Wilson who, at the cost of his own chance of freedom, had created a diversion that gave Robertson the time he needed to make his getaway.

Smuggling in those days was by no means an unpopular activity in the eyes of ordinary folk and that combined with Wilson's self-sacrificing effort on his friend's behalf had made him something of a popular hero. On the other hand John Porteous, Captain of the Town Guard who was in charge of the arrangements for Wilson's execution, was brutal and arrogant and, although (or partly because) he was popular with some of his superiors with whom he curried favour, he was hated by the ordinary people of Edinburgh. As usual in those days a large crowd gathered in the Grassmarket for the grim spectacle of the hanging of Wilson; and, also as usual, when it was over a small group began pelting the hangman with stones and other missiles, injuring him and some of the members of the Guard around him. Though this demonstration was said, afterwards, to have been scarcely more than was customary on such occasions it evidently alarmed and infuriated Porteous and his Guards. On the orders of Porteous, as some said (though he denied giving any such command) shots were fired by members of the Guard into the crowd. Nine people were killed and many wounded, those killed including a young man who had been watching from a window and obviously had taken no part in any riotous activities.

Lengthy inquiries were followed by the trial of Porteous in the High Court of Justiciary and, on 20 July, the jury having 'all in one voice' found him guilty, he was condemned to be executed on 8 September 1736, a verdict and sentence which were warmly welcomed by the public generally. However, while Porteous was a prisoner in the Tolbooth, a group of his well-connected friends applied on his behalf for a reprieve. On 2 September there arrived in Edinburgh official intimation that Queen Caroline (acting in the absence of her husband George II on one of his frequent visits to Hanover) had been graciously pleased to grant a six-week stay of execution, presumably in anticipation of a full reprieve after the King had returned.

When the Queen's message was announced a large section of the public were furiously angry, though, at first, with little outward show. In a day or two it began to be rumoured that a mob intended to take the law into their own hands and hang Porteous. Twice this rumour was reported to the Provost, Alexander Wilson, and twice, unaccountably, he took no action. Then, on 7 September at 9.30 at night, things began to happen. A mob assembled and acted with determination, as if to a well-planned programme. The Town Guard were overwhelmed in their Guard House in the High Street and their weapons seized. The main gates in the town wall were closed by the mob and secured. The Tolbooth was besieged and when its outer door proved too tough for their battering-ram, the mob set fire to it; but they were careful to have buckets of water ready so as to restrict the fire to the door alone. When it collapsed they rushed in, seized Captain Porteous and hustled him, in nightgown, cap and breeches, up the Lawnmarket, to the sound of a drum, and down the steep West Bow to the Grassmarket. On the way, they took a length of rope from a shop, leaving a guinea on the counter in payment, and at precisely a quarter to midnight they hanged the unfortunate captain un-ceremoniously from the pole which marked a dyer's premises at the east end of the Grassmarket. Then, as quickly as they had assembled, the crowd melted away, leaving it to the magistrates next morning to have Porteous's body taken down and buried in Greyfriars churchyard nearby. It has remained there since marked, for 237 years, only by a post inscribed 'P.1736'. Then, in August 1973, the post was replaced by a headstone inscribed 'John Porteous, a captain of the Edinburgh City Guard, murdered 7 September 1736. – "All passion spent" 1973'.

The erection of the stone was suggested and its cost was defrayed by Sir Tresham Lever, author and biographer, of Lessudden House, St Boswells, in the Scottish Borders. His belief (not widely held) is that Porteous was a sadly maligned and misjudged man and so, despite the passage of so many years, he has taken this way of doing some justice to the Captain's memory.

To return, however, to 1736: what were the civic authorities doing during the two and a quarter hours when the mob were going so grimly and efficiently about their unlawful business? It is a question that Queen Caroline, Ministers of the Crown, the Courts and the House of Lords all asked angrily and repeatedly during the months that followed; and the answers they received could be interpreted only as showing, at best, ineptitude and indecision and, at worst, a secret sympathy with the perpetrators of the outrage.

When news of the mob's rising was brought to Provost Wilson (quite unofficially, by his niece) it was 9.45 p.m. and he in company with his Council colleague, Bailie Colquhoun and a former Provost, Patrick Lindsay, was enjoying a convivial evening in a tavern in Parliament Close (now Parliament Square) just east of St Giles and only about 100 yards from the Guard House in one direction and the Tolbooth in the other. Presumably because of the rumours which had been circulating, a troop of soldiers were ready in the Canongate but, of course, outside the walls and beyond the locked gates. Their commander, General Moyle, was in his own house at Abbeyhill, near Holyrood.

After a hasty consultation in the tavern, the Provost asked Patrick Lindsay to go as messenger to General Moyle to seek military assistance; but, as the gates at both the Netherbow and the Cowgate were locked and guarded by the mob, he had to make his way southwards to the next gate, at Potterrow, where he was able to get through and so reach General Moyle's house by a circuitous route. Unaccountably (or, perhaps, as the General later alleged, because he had been drinking too freely with his friends at the tavern) Patrick Lindsay had failed to provide himself with an official request in writing, signed by the Provost. The General, quite legitimately in accordance with the procedures at that time, firmly refused to supply military help in the absence of a written and signed request from a competent authority. So a messenger was sent urgently to the home of the Lord Justice Clerk, which was outside the walls; but by the time his written authorization arrived it was too late to be of any use.

Meanwhile, inside the walls, the Provost and some of his fellow magistrates had sought to call out the Trained Bands, companies of citizens pledged to help in keeping order in times of trouble, but the list of the company captains could not be found quickly enough! They then made their way precariously towards the Tolbooth and, with some show of authority, tried to read the Riot Act to the crowd, only to be sharply repulsed by showers of stones and threats of shooting.

For some extraordinary reason no message, written or otherwise, was sent to the Castle, where, in the absence of any request

for assistance, the major in charge of the garrison was powerless
to take any action though he and his men could hear the shouts
of the mob and the sounds of their battering on the Tolbooth door.

Next day, with Porteous buried and the town quiet, the affair
was far from being finished. Throughout September, October
and November, official inquiries were conducted by such high
officers as the Solicitor-General, the Lord Justice General, the
Lord Advocate and General Wade. The Queen herself, annoyed
and alarmed that her command had been so flagrantly flouted,
offered informers a reward of £200 for information leading to
conviction and a free pardon if they themselves had been impli-
cated; but, though many people were interviewed and several
were arrested on suspicion no one, for lack of evidence, could be
proved to have taken part in the riot. Many who had seen the
crowds in the street declared that they recognized no one and that
the mob must have been strangers to the town – as, indeed, many
of them may have been, for crowds had been seen streaming out
of the gates after the deed was done.

In March 1737, no satisfaction having been obtained, Provost
Wilson and four of the bailies were ordered to appear in London
before the House of Lords to explain their ineptitude in the affair
and, on 2 April, after the Lords' hearing, the Provost was taken into
custody there. A 'Bill of Pains and Penalties' was introduced which,
if passed, would have deprived him of office and caused him to
be imprisoned; and it would also have ordered the permanent
removal of the Netherbow Gate and the abolition of the Town
Guard – though, on the strength of that body's recent record, it
seems unlikely that their discontinuance would have done any
great disservice to the town!

There is, among the Town Council records, a copy of a letter
written at that time by the Provost from London to his colleagues
in Edinburgh which begins:

I am now under the custody of the Usher of the Black Rod. It is attended with
considerable expense, but I must own that, hitherto, my confinement is done
with great civility. My situation cannot be very agreeable. However, had the
community escaped I believe my misfortune would have sat easier upon me.
I have reason to believe that the Bill may be brought in next week and that I
will be served with a copy and allowed to be heard by myself and Counsel
against the Bill.

He then went on to list the documents he required to be sent to him and the action he believed to be necessary to oppose the Bill in the House. He was well served in this by his friends both in and out of parliament for, by 'the Provost's Act' as finally passed in June of that year, though he was deprived of all office for his lifetime, his imprisonment was not required; and, though the burgh of Edinburgh was fined £2000 (to be used for the benefit of Porteous's widow) it was not called upon to suffer the indignities of losing its principal gateway and its picturesque, if ineffectual, Town Guard.

So ended the story of the Porteous riot – but not quite. Even after the passing of the Provost's Act, the government continued to press for action and another Act was passed, which ministers throughout Scotland were required to read from their pulpits on one Sunday each month, calling for all possible steps to be taken to bring to justice those who had taken part in the affair. That Act, however, was more honoured in the breach than the observance for the ministers (some of whom may well have felt some sympathy for the mob) were incensed that they and their pulpits should be used for so secular a purpose as the tracking down of criminals. Besides simply ignoring the Act, various devices were used to avoid making it effective. Of these, my favourite may fittingly conclude this account of the Porteous affair. It is the one adopted by a minister who announced, at the close of his service: 'Though I am required by law to read this Act from my pulpit you are not obliged to listen to me'; and as the congregation withdrew he read it aloud to the emptying pews.

So much for the old Tolbooth and some of its more spectacular incidents. What of the bell-house and the luckenbooths as these are shown alongside it in the drawing on the endpaper? Originally, the bell-house had been an important meeting place for the guild brethren of the city. Under their rules its bell had to be rung three times to call them to meetings, and, after that, those who did not attend were fined. Its bell also announced the time at which selling and buying might begin in the street markets in the High Street; but, long before the drawing was made, the bell-house had become just a part of the eastern section of the Tolbooth.

As can be seen in the drawing which was made not long before their demolition was completed in 1817, the luckenbooths consisted of seven tenements of varying height, mostly timber-fronted and all with shops on the ground flat. It was, in fact, the shops or 'locked booths' (as distinct from open market stalls) that gave these buildings their name. With their projecting forestairs, the luckenbooths must have so restricted the High Street as scarcely to leave room for two carts to pass and for centuries this must have been the busiest and also the most congested part of the city. The crowding and congestion on the north side of the lucken-booths, however, could have been nothing when compared with that on the south side, in the narrow passage between these build-ings and the wall and buttresses of St Giles. Here were the 'krames', otherwise known as 'creams', tiny stalls, some roughly roofed over, others open to the sky, some tucked in between the buttresses and others pressed hard against the wall of the luckenbooths with just enough room for shoppers to squeeze between the two rows.

The shops in the luckenbooths dealt in a wide range of domestic goods and services. Here in the late eighteenth century were grocers, bakers and hardware merchants, shoe-makers, snuff-makers, a hairdresser or two and a 'chymist and druggist'; and there were several woollen-drapers and milliners as well as the very superior-sounding 'Misses Bowie, gold-lace manufacturers'. Many of the shopkeepers lived in the flats above where they had as neighbours a smattering of lawyers, surgeons and teachers. Here also was 'Peter Williamson's Penny Post Office – where Letters and Small Parcels are despatched eight times every day to Leith and as often from thence to Edinburgh and suburbs. Letters circulating within the city or at a moderate distance are delivered every hour and oftener' – which seems a remarkable service for a charge of only one (old) penny.

In the narrow alley of the krames, behind the luckenbooths, the stallholders seem to have specialized in hardware, leather goods (there were several glovers) and children's toys. Lord Cock-burn, looking back through the rose-tinted telescope with which one tends to recall one's childhood, says:

In my boyhood [he was born in 1779] little stands, each enclosed in a tiny room of its own, and during the day all open to the little footpath that ran between the two rows of them and all glittering with attractions, contained everything fascinating to childhood, but chiefly toys. It was like one of the

Arabian Nights bazaars in Bagdad. Throughout the whole year it was an enchantment. Let anyone fancy what it was about New Year when every child got its handsel and every farthing of every handsel was spent there. The krames was the paradise of childhood.

A less rosy picture of the krames appears from the official records of the town. In the first place (Edinburgh not being Bagdad, whatever the young Henry Cockburn may have thought) there was the weather to contend with – and what a biting wind tunnel that narrow passage must have been on a winter day! In 1679, Thomas Glen, a tailor who with his wife kept an open stall there, complained to the Town Council that, when the east wind and rain came on, their wares were altogether spoiled and so he was given permission to build a little covered shop to protect their goods. More serious problems arose from time to time because of the unsavoury practice by the tenants in the flats above the luckenbooths of throwing their household refuse from their windows on to the stalls and stall-keepers and their customers in the narrow lane below. Among many efforts made to curb this practice, an order issued by the Town Council in 1713 required that 'all windows of the dwelling-houses above the luckenbooths be stanchelled or close glass fixed therein so that no nastiness might be thrown out thereat'; an order which had to be renewed from time to time until shortly before the luckenbooths and the krames were removed altogether.

Lord Cockburn also reminds his readers that krames and other little shops not very different from them extended round the end of St Giles Church into Parliament Square, or Parliament Close as it had previously been called and as he preferred to continue to call it. Some of these, right up to the time of their removal, were occupied by watchmakers and jewellers as they had been for centuries. One such little shop, traditionally believed to have been no more than seven feet square, had been the workshop of George Heriot, goldsmith and jeweller to King James VI and his Queen. There, in the presence of the King, George Heriot is said to have laughingly destroyed the bond for £2000 that the King had owed him; and there he laid the foundations of the fortune of more than £23000 sterling from which he endowed his 'hospital for the maintenance, relief, bringing-up and educating poor fatherless boys, freemen's sons of the town of Edinburgh' which was completed in 1650 and the turrets of which we saw, in an earlier chapter, from the Castle esplanade. It became a day school in 1886 and now, with some 1500 boys on its roll, it continues to be governed by George Heriot's Trust, 375 years after its founder's death.

Such is the fortune and enduring fame that George Heriot achieved from his little booth in Parliament Close. But fame of a different kind, though no less enduring, attached to the five-storey building with the flat roof at the eastern end of the luckenbooths, for in it Allan Ramsay opened his circulating library in 1725 and there, to William Creech's bookshop on the ground flat, came Robert Burns in 1786. There we will meet them later, in company with some of their colourful contemporaries.

5 Lawnmarket residents

We have already looked at two seventeenth-century buildings in the High Street: Parliament Hall and the Tron Church. A
third worth pausing at is in the Lawnmarket—No. 438, on the north
side. This is Gladstone's Land. Though it dates in part from the sixteenth century, its main features visible from the street are all of
the seventeenth and are very much as they were left by Thomas
Gledstanes who acquired the house in 1617 and soon afterwards
set about altering and extending it. Seen from across the street,
it is a narrow six-storeyed building with crow-stepped gables and
with two fine dormer windows projecting from the roof. The
two arches of its ground floor and the curved forestair leading to
the first flat set it quite apart from its neighbours.

When Thomas Gledstanes bought the building it had, like so
many houses of those days, a wooden front with a timber gallery
overhanging the ground floor. He substituted a stone front with
the stone-built arcade; and, high up on the west gable, he placed
his initials and those of his wife, Bessie Cunningham. Presumably
he did so out of pride in his achievement but if that was so it is
hard to understand why he placed the initials so far above the
street that they can scarcely be seen.

Over the centuries, as with so many Edinburgh houses, the
building was divided and sub-divided to provide separate dwellings

for many families. The arcade at street level became concealed behind shop-fronts and it was with some surprise in 1935 that the pillars were uncovered. That was during restoration by the National Trust for Scotland to whom the building had been presented by a purchaser who thus saved it from almost certain demolition. In course of the restoration several internal walls were removed and, beneath layers of paper and plaster, some fine seventeenth-century painted ceilings were discovered and renovated. The main rooms of the house are now occupied by the Saltire Society whose aim is to encourage appreciation of Scottish traditions, and the Society are always willing to show the features of these rooms to visitors.

Thomas Gledstanes was a merchant, admitted as a guild brother in Edinburgh in the same year as he bought the house. But it seems that he was not a very successful merchant for there are records of transactions in which he appears to have pawned parts of his property. He and his wife lived in one flat of his tall 'land' and the Saltire Society's booklet on the house contains a list of four of his tenants who occupied other parts of the building at that time, Mr William Strutheris, a minister; Mr John Riddoch, a merchant; Sir James Creichton, Kt, presumably a gentleman of leisure for he is given no 'occupation'; and Mr James Nicolsone, Guild Officer, who, as a fairly lowly official, occupied 'the lowest back dwelling house'.

What sights and events would the Gledstanes and their tenants see as they looked out from their Lawnmarket windows? They would see the street crowded and busy with market stalls, and amongst them well-dressed citizens going about their business. They would see a great deal of squalor and poverty; and also criminals – and later, Covenanters – being led up the Lawnmarket and down the West Bow to the place of execution in the Grass-market. In terrible plague years like 1645 they would see the bodies of victims being carried from houses up and down the street and whole families being removed to the isolation of the Burgh Muir, away to the south of the town, to remain there till the infection had passed. But they would also see happier events, such as the state entry of Charles I to the city on the way to his Scottish coronation at Holyrood Abbey in 1633.

In those days, the principal entry to Edinburgh from south-west,

west and north was by the West Port gateway in the Flodden Wall, along the Grassmarket and thence to the top of the Lawnmarket by the steep zigzag street of West Bow, the uppermost part of which can still be seen where Johnston Terrace joins the Lawnmarket. That way, on 15 June 1633, came Charles I and his richly apparelled train. Sir James Balfour, Lyon King of Arms of that time, recorded that 'for many ages this Kingdom had not seen a more glorious and stately entry, the streets being all railed and sanded; the chief places where the King passed were set out with stately triumphal arches, obelisks, pictures, artificial mountains adorned with choice music and divers other costly shows'. On that occasion even before the King and his company had reached the West Port he was approached by the poet William Drummond of Hawthornden who read a fulsome speech to him. At the gateway a large representation of Edinburgh had been erected and 'by undrawing a veil, the nymph Edina (attended by beautiful damsels) appeared and presented the keys of the city to His Majesty'. These are believed to have been the same keys as are nowadays presented to the Queen on her visits to Edinburgh and on each occasion returned by her for safe-keeping (although, in the intervening years, they had been mislaid for nearly two centuries). Nowadays, the keys are presented by the Lord Provost, accompanied by his Council colleagues who are more dignified but less decorative, perhaps, despite their scarlet robes, than were 'the nymph Edina' and her damsels.

Inside the West Port King Charles was received by the Councillors and Provost who made a speech of welcome, after which the King and his retinue were allowed to proceed – but not for long. At the upper end of the West Bow, perhaps near enough to the top for the residents in Gladstone's Land to catch a glimpse of the proceedings, there was a stately triumphal arch 'on which the lady Caledonia, in rich attire, congratulated his majesty on his safe arrival'. On then, his procession went, beneath the windows of Gladstone's Land to be halted three more times to view scenic effects and listen to music and lengthy poetic effusions before finally passing through the Netherbow Port and riding, with what relief one can imagine, down the Canongate to Holyrood. Yet, to his credit, it is recorded that 'these whole addresses His Majesty, with great pleasure and delight, sitting on horseback as his com-

D

pany did, heard pleasantly', which must have greatly pleased the Provost and Town Council, not to mention the pageant master who had organized it all. He is said to have been Mr John Adamson, Principal of the College (now the University) of Edinburgh who, besides being an elegant scholar was a silver-tongued courtier, much in favour with Charles I.

Such were the colourful ways in which the people of Edinburgh, in those times, greeted their sovereign and entertained themselves and one can readily visualize the excitement in the streets and at the crowded windows of the 'lands' as the cavalcade passed; and the exclamations of wonder, at each halting-place, as a new device of stage-craft was unfolded.

Four years later, on 23 July 1637, there was a different kind of excitement in the streets and inside St Giles. Charles by then had declared the church to be a cathedral and on that day the new episcopal service-book, specially prepared for use in Scotland, was introduced to a crowded congregation. But no sooner had the Dean, James Hanna, ascended the pulpit steps and begun the unfamiliar service than pandemonium broke loose and in the midst of it, to quote an old account, 'one did cast a stool at him, intending to have given him a ticket of remembrance; but jouking [dodging] became his safeguard at that time. . . .' The tumult spread to the street outside and later that day the Bishop of Edinburgh had also to indulge in a great deal of 'jouking' before, having failed to reach the safety of his own home, he was picked up in the Earl of Roxburgh's coach, the unfortunate coachman receiving 'plenty of hard stone coin for his drink silver' as he drove off through the angry crowds.

According to tradition the 'one' who threw the first stool was Jenny Geddes who can scarcely have known to what tragic and far-reaching events the tumult in which she played so prominent a part was prologue. She herself, the story goes, could be seen attending at her cabbage-stall in the High Street for more than twenty years after the occasion that made her famous; and her stool (or one that has, for centuries, done service in its place) can still be seen in the Scottish National Museum of Antiquities in Queen Street.

That picture of Jenny Geddes, her one great gesture made, daily selling cabbages at her market-stance in some way epitomizes how, through the centuries, everyday life went on alongside and around great incidents of Scottish history concerning church and state, inspiring, alarming, joyous and tragic, enacted up and down the narrow, crowded, bustling stage of Edinburgh's main street.

Still more threads and patterns of our tapestry of time begin to appear if we look beyond the street frontages of High Street and Lawnmarket and explore the closes and courtyards that lie out of sight behind them. Riddles Court, off the Lawnmarket, exactly opposite Gladstone's Land, has its own tales of four centuries to tell. Go through the arch at No. 322 Lawnmarket and you will find yourself in Riddle's Close with another archway ahead, leading into the yard of Riddle's Court. Here, with the noise of traffic deadened by tall buildings on all sides, with crow-stepped gables and chimney-stacks at odd angles against the sky, you may well feel you have stepped back through the centuries to the time when the house facing you was the home and also the business premises of a wealthy Edinburgh merchant. The ornamental stone projection above one of the first-floor windows may well have been the fixture for a pulley by which consignments of goods were hauled up to a store-room in his house.

The house was built in the 1590s by Bailie John McMorran who was reputed to have been one of the wealthiest Edinburgh citizens of his day and whose devotion to duty as a Town Council member and a magistrate led only a few years later to his untimely death at the hands of a High School pupil. The building of his house (at that time, hard up against remnants of the King's Wall and of its port or gateway that stood across the West Bow) was sanctioned by the Town Council in January 1591 when they granted his request for permission to rebuild and extend 'ane auld ruinous hoose' which he owned on the site and for that purpose to encroach upon the wall and the old gateway belonging to the town. Being public-spirited and also something of a diplomat he was careful to mention that he desired, 'God willing', to carry out this work not just for his own benefit but also 'in respect that it is needful the house be built for the decoration of that part of the town lying in sight coming up the West Bow'. In this he was as good as his word for the house is even now a handsome one and in his day must have been an impressive mansion, with a long

garden and orchard behind it stretching down to the Cowgate.
Alas, he did not live long to enjoy its amenities.

The High School of those days, which was administered by the
Town Council, stood in High School Yards at the foot of what is
now Infirmary Street opposite the University Old College, less
than a mile away from Riddle's Court. The boys of the school
had given trouble more than once by locking themselves in the
school and defying the teachers in that and other ways – student
sit-ins being not such a modern phenomenon as we are inclined
to think. In September 1595 the pupils were more than usually
recalcitrant. Having been refused a holiday to which they considered themselves entitled a group of boys, several of whom were
from well-to-do families, barricaded themselves into the school and
resisted all efforts of the headmaster and his staff to dislodge
them. In this predicament the headmaster sought help from the
magistrates and Bailie John McMorran was despatched to the
school, with a small posse of town officers in support, to remon-
strate with the boys; but the more earnestly the good Bailie entreated them to come out of the school, the more stubbornly
they refused. For what followed I can do no better than quote
the vivid account of the incident given by Robert Birrell in his diary
of that time (only modernizing some of his spelling):

The said Bailie and officers [says Birrell] then took a great joist and ran at the
back door with the joist. A scholar bade him desist from dinging doon the
door otherwise he vowed to God he would shoot a pair of bullets through
his heid. The Bailie thinking he durst not shoot, he and his assistants ran still
at the door with the joist. Then there came a scholar called William Sinclair,
son to William Sinclair Chancellor of Caithness, and with a pistol shot out
at a window and shot the Bailie through the heid, so that he died presently.

As can be imagined the tragedy caused a sensation, in course
of which the boys concerned (no doubt shocked into submission)
were seized and locked up in the Tolbooth; but because of the
influential position of William Sinclair's father and of the parents
of some of the other boys, they were all set free, says Birrell, 'without any hurt done to them for the same within ane short time
thereafter'.

Although the boys got off scot-free, the unhappy headmaster
and his staff were severely reprimanded by the Town Council
and were ordered in future 'to attend more diligently upon their

school and scholars, teach them sufficiently and keep them in greater awe and discipline than they had done before . . . as the said master and doctors will answer to the guid town upon their offices. . . .' For long afterwards, indeed, until the building was demolished in 1777, generations of schoolboys pointed out to newcomers 'the Bailie's window' from which the fatal shot had been fired.

After the death of the Bailie, the house at Riddle's Court seems to have passed to his brother, Ninian McMorran, and such was its reputation as a mansion of distinction that it was 'borrowed' by the Town Council in the spring of 1598 for the banquet which they gave to King James VI, his Queen, Anne of Denmark, her brother the Duke of Holstein and other Danish nobles who were visiting Edinburgh. On that occasion, to quote Robert Birrell again, 'the King and Queen were present with great solemnitie and merriment'; the 'solemnitie', no doubt, describing the formal opening of the banquet and the 'merriment' its rollicking conclusion. This is not surprising when one learns from the burgh accounts that the cost of the entertainment was £1100 Scots and that, in addition to the food which included venison and hams and 'fowls wild and tame', the Town Council had provided two puncheons and seven quarts of wine, five gallons of claret, a tun of English beer and four barrels of ale. Payments were made to trumpeters and minstrels and to many others who had helped to provide the merriment in more mundane ways, including those whose lowly but necessary function had been to carry water to the kitchen for the cook. There was also a payment of £8 to cover the cost of linen napkins which were lost in course of the evening!

That occasion seems to have been the house's finest hour, or at any rate its most extravagant one, for though in the next two centuries it boasted many noble and distinguished owners and tenants, there is no record of any later celebration on such a scale. Eventually, as did so many other old town mansions, it came wholly into use for such workaday purposes as warehouse, store and brushmaker's workshop. Towards the end of the eighteenth century it was occupied as a hotel known as Shawfield's Lodging. In this complex of buildings, too, Edinburgh's first police court was established in 1805.

From 1850 until about 1890 the old mansion was occupied by

the Edinburgh Mechanics Library and when the need for that institution disappeared with the opening nearby of the Public Library, Bailie McMorran's house and the adjoining property between Riddle's Court and Close were converted into one of the earliest of Edinburgh's student residences. This was done on the inspiration of Professor Patrick Geddes, Edinburgh pioneer of town planning or, rather, of social planning (for his ideas went far beyond paper plans and bricks and mortar to embrace the whole of living). His residence had accommodation for nine or ten students on whom some of the building's atmosphere of ancient conviviality seems to have rubbed off, to judge from a diary kept during its first few years which is preserved in the University Library. The diary records that regular 'smoking-concerts' and other entertainments were held by the students in the old mansion at which the toast list always included 'King James the Sixth' and 'Bailie McMorran' and at which 'the tradition of solemnitie and merriment was maintained'.

By 1946 the properties in Riddle's Court and Riddle's Close had sadly deteriorated. Then, in that year, they were acquired by Edinburgh Corporation and restored for their present use (one which surely would have pleased Patrick Geddes) as an adult education centre. In two rooms there are fine seventeenth-century plaster ceilings, the one in the house that stands between the inner Court and the outer Close having among its decorations the cipher of Charles II and the date, 1684. In another room there are late sixteenth- and early seventeenth-century painted beams; and in the main room of 'Bailie McMorran's house' is a ceiling elaborately painted in the 1890s at the instigation of Patrick Geddes, to record incidents in the story of the University of Edinburgh and also the famous royal banquet of 1598. In the Charles II room were found panels decorated with landscape scenes by James Norrie whose talents as a painter it was fashionable, in the early eighteenth century, to employ in this kind of house decoration. These panels had to be removed for restoration and, if means can be found to protect them against the harmful effects of modern central heating, the intention is to replace them so that once again they can be seen in the setting for which they were created.

In the outer courtyard of Riddle's Close, the outside wooden staircase leading from the first to the second flat above the courtyard has an ancient and romantic appearance but this is deceptive, for it was put there only in the nineteenth century to replace an inside stairway that had become insecure. The words *Vivendo Discimus* (we learn by living) above the inner archway were, as you might guess, suggested by Patrick Geddes as a motto for his students' residence.

As you return to the Lawnmarket through the outer archway you will see a doorway with the date 1726 above it. The block of flats to which the doorway leads has been entirely rebuilt since then, but in one of the flats to which it gave access David Hume first had a home in Edinburgh and here he wrote part of his history of England, published in 1754. From this address he wrote to Adam Smith in 1751:

I have now at last, being turned of forty . . . arrived at the dignity of being a householder. About seven months ago I got a house of my own and completed a regular family, consisting of a head, viz. myself, and two inferior members – a maid and a cat. My sister has since joined me and keeps me company. With frugality, I can reach, I find, cleanliness, warmth, light, plenty and contentment. What would you have more? Independence? I have it in a supreme degree. Honour? That is not altogether wanting. Grace? That will come in time. A wife? That is none of the indispensable requisites of life. Books? That *is* one of them, and I have more than I can use.

A year later that would certainly be true, for it was then that he was appointed Librarian of the Faculty of Advocates.

If, now, we cross the road and go through one of the closes near Gladstone's Land we will meet David Hume again, and other famous people, in James Court where he bought a flat in 1762. In his day, the north side of this courtyard was occupied by a range of tenements built about 1720. Their remarkable feature, upon which almost every visitor commented with astonishment, was that entering from the Court at ground level you found yourself three storeys up on the other side looking out, at first, across the Nor' Loch to the fields of Wood's Farm and, in later years, over the Mound to Princes Street and the roofs of the New Town. The eastern end of these massive buildings still remains. You can see it as you come up the Mound, towering above the stationer's shop: 'Brown of the Mound'. But the western end was destroyed in a great fire in 1857. As originally built, these tenements each contained two well-appointed 'flats' or houses on each floor level and accommodated, in all, perhaps fourteen families. But by the time the fire destroyed the western end, more than forty families lived there and 160 people had to be re-housed and compensated out of a fund raised for the purpose. Appealing at a public meeting for donations for the fund, the Sheriff of the Lothians said: 'This building once canopied affluence, dignity and wealth, these walls once echoed to the accents of wit, learning and eloquence; these firesides once were made brilliant and cheerful by every social luxury but, as years rolled on, the same tenement subsided into the abodes of humbler occupants and, sometimes, the shelter of pinching poverty'.

In David Hume's day, James Court was certainly a fashionable address at which to stay. Its occupants had formed themselves into what they called a 'Parliament' – really just a superior kind of residents' association – to control the courtyard and the common stairs and supervise their amenity. David Hume's flat, later advertised for sale as having 'five rooms and a kitchen with pantries, closets and other conveniences' was on the third floor above the Court and on the east side of the stair. One of the amenities of life in the flat (and, I suppose, of flat life anywhere) seems to have been the benefit of warmth from the adjoining houses. At least, David Hume found it so, for during his absence in France he had let his house to the Rev. Dr Hugh Blair, to whom he wrote: 'I am glad to find you are my tenant. You have got an excellent flat for its size. It was perfectly free of vermin when I left it and I hope you will find it so. Never put a fire in the south room with the red paper. It is so warm of itself that all last winter, which was a severe one, I lay with a single blanket. . . . The fires of your neighbours will save you the expense of a fire in that room', which leads one to wonder whether that informal system of free 'central heating' may have led to the fire that destroyed the building.

Later, Hume had an even more famous tenant here, when James Boswell rented his flat. But it was in another larger flat on the level of the Court in the same building, to which Boswell had moved in 1773, that he entertained Dr Johnson at the start of their tour to the Hebrides in that year. It was there that the long-suffering Mrs Boswell pleased the learned Doctor by serving him as many cups of tea as he could wish to have; and it was there that the Boswells' four-month-old daughter Veronica showed herself

Riddle's Close – *Drawn by James Drummond, RSA, in 1854. The door in the distance belongs to the mansion in Riddle's Court built by Bailie John McMorran in 1591. The doorway in the right foreground led to the flat in which David Hume lived for a time.*

George Drummond (*1687–1766*), *six times Lord Provost. Through the window can be seen the first Royal Infirmary, for the founding of which he was largely responsible. This portrait by John Alexander (1752), hangs in the Board Room of the present Royal Infirmary of Edinburgh.*

The first Royal Infirmary of Edinburgh, *completed in 1747. Drawing by J. Storer, 1818.*

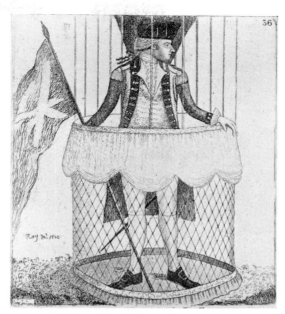

Vincent Lunardi *who made three balloon ascents from Heriot Garden in 1785 and 1786. This portrait, by John Kay, clearly suggests his flamboyant costume and manner. George Heriot's School and its grounds, from which the ascents were made, are seen in the picture below.*

George Square, *built in the 1760s as a quiet enclave for the well-to-do and transformed, 200 years later, into a University precinct. On the west side, in No. 25, Sir Walter Scott lived as boy and young man and No. 27 was the home of the Hon. Henry Erskine. Lord Braxfield lived in No. 13 on the north side.*

White Horse Close *at the foot of Canongate, from a watercolour by James Skene, c. 1818. The building in the centre with the date 1623 above a window, was an inn from behind which stage coaches started for London. The buildings have been restored and adapted as flats.*

Holyrood Sanctuary. *This view of the old town from the slopes of Holyrood Park is from an aquatint by James Gendall, dated 1823. Between Holyrood Palace and the Park are some of the houses, later removed, in which debtors seeking sanctuary were accommodated.*

to be so delighted by Dr Johnson's odd appearance and strange mannerisms that her father then and there decided 'she should have £500 of additional fortune'. Here too, Johnson met (or was exhibited to) several of the leading Edinburgh men of that time; and here he said some harsh and seemingly unprintable words ('something much too rough,' says Boswell, 'which I suppress') about David Hume and his atheism, of which Johnson strongly disapproved. Did Boswell tell him then, I wonder, that if he had come a few months earlier he would have been lodging in a house of which Hume was the owner?

For an entirely different picture of fashionable life in that same James Court tenement about ten years later, we may turn to an unpublished manuscript of James Skene whose delicate water-colour drawings give a pleasing picture of Edinburgh of their day. His manuscript, prepared as an accompaniment to a collection of the drawings which unfortunately was never published, is preserved along with the drawings in Edinburgh Public Library. In it he describes how in 1783 as a boy of eight, he was brought by his mother for the first time to Edinburgh. They lived for a while in 'Shawfields' Lodging' in Riddle's Court and it was while he was there that he first tried his hand at sketching the old buildings nearby.

He also used to attend lessons given by an elderly teacher, 'a most demure and primitive pedagogue, Dominie Austin by name', tutor to the sons of Dr Gregory Grant who lived on the top floor of the same tenement in James Court in which Hume and Boswell had lived. After lessons were over and the Dominie was preparing to leave, 'it was often our practice,' Skene says, 'to slip out and precede him in his more deliberate descent of the long stair, ringing every door-bell as we passed with violence which bringing all the servants to their respective doors just as the Dominie reached them, he had to give exclamations and excuses at every door he passed, to our great amusement as we listened below.'

Dr Gregory Grant, father of James Skene's unruly schoolboy friends, seems himself to have been something of a character, well known in the Edinburgh of his day.

He dressed [according to Skene] like an old beau of Charles II's Court, with a small cocked hat, surmounting a flowing and well-powdered wig which shed its dusty burden over a square-cut coat, generally of a cream-colour and sometimes light blue or crimson, with black breeches, white stockings and with silver-buckled shoes. In this guise, and furnished with a gold-headed cane and a lorgnette he strutted about the streets . . . bowing right and left to those he met. As a practitioner he did little harm, seldom recommending anything beyond the strength of a 'tisanne' [evidently a preparation of barley and water] generally with a little chicken-broth or white wine whey; and into every prescription he added, with most portentous gravity, a drop or two of colourless liquid (suspected to be distilled water) which he carried about in a phial in his long waistcoat pocket.

There is a picture of Dr Gregory Grant in John Kay's *Original Portraits* and in that volume we are told that, despite his eccentricities, his James Court flat was the scene of many fashionable musical suppers attended by the Duchess of Gordon and by other persons of high rank in society. Frequently, also, actors and actresses were there – including the great Mrs Siddons – for the doctor was a devotee of the theatre; and, in return for the pleasure the players gave him, he was always ready to attend them and their families without charging a fee. Perhaps his devotion to the theatre gives a clue to his strange costume and oddity of behaviour; perhaps, in his mind, James Court was a stage on which he was constantly acting a part in some Restoration comedy. Whatever the explanation, such characters seem to have abounded in eighteenth-century Edinburgh, adding humour and sometimes a little pathos to the threads of its history.

6 Father of the city

*A*character of a different kind had appeared on the Edinburgh scene at the beginning of the eighteenth century and for nearly sixty years he played a variety of prominent parts in the city's story. He was George Drummond, who was six times elected to be Lord Provost. No one else has held the position so often and in the last 100 years only two have served more than three years in that office. Clearly, Drummond was no ordinary man and he was a benefactor of the city in many ways. Without his foresight and persistence we might never have had the Georgian New Town which is still our pride and joy, though George Drummond himself did not live to see it take shape.

Born in Perthshire in 1687, Drummond is said to have been 'educated in the schools of Edinburgh' where he acquired such skill in arithmetic that at the early age of eighteen he was asked by a committee of the Scottish parliament to undertake an intricate examination of the Scottish accounts in connection with the negotiations for the union of Scotland and England. He carried out that task so acceptably that after the union in 1707 he was appointed Accountant-General of Excise, with an office at the Nether Bow, an appointment which at that time must have called for a high level of diplomacy and tact. In 1715 he became a Commissioner of Customs with a salary of £1000.

In the same year, as a staunch supporter of the Crown, he rode
out at the head of a company of volunteers to take part in the
battle of Sheriffmuir which, although inconclusive in itself, really
brought an end to the short-lived rebellion of 1715. Thirty years
later, when Bonnie Prince Charlie and his highlanders were
marching on the city and while Provost Archibald Stewart and
his Bailies were anxiously discussing whether or not they should
resist the invaders and, if so, to what extent, George Drummond
again put himself at the head of a volunteer corps and rode down
the West Bow and through the Grassmarket with the intention of
meeting the rebels at Roseburn, to the west of the city; but he had
scarcely reached the West Port when he found that most of his
band, believing discretion to be the better part of valour, had
deserted him and he and his more faithful followers had no option
but to turn back. A day or two later he joined General Sir John
Cope at the battle of Prestonpans and, when that battle was lost,
retreated with him to Berwick where he stayed for some time,
obtaining and passing on to the authorities in London what news
he could about Charles Stuart's brief but colourful stay at Holyrood. Meanwhile Archibald Stewart, the Lord Provost of the day,
because of his indecision at the crucial time (and perhaps also
partly because of his surname) was strongly suspected of compli-
city in the Stuart cause and after Charles's departure he was arrested
and imprisoned, though eventually acquitted. The occupation
had temporarily put an end to the normal Town Council management of the town's affairs and when the Council was reinstated
in 1746, George Drummond (who had had experience as Lord
Provost from 1725 to 1727) was reappointed to that office and had
the task of guiding the Council's activities back on to a normal
basis. He was again elected Lord Provost in 1750, 1754, 1758 and (at
the age of seventy-five) in 1762, serving for two years on each
occasion.

Throughout his long Town Council service, as Councillor,
Bailie and Treasurer as well as Provost, he took a special interest
in the University of Edinburgh, the affairs of which were, in those
days, managed by the Council. Alexander Bower who wrote a
history of the University in 1817 goes so far as to say that Drummond
'was the greatest benefactor the University ever had. From the
year 1715 to the time of his death, nothing was done in the College

without his advice or direction. . . . In the course of the 50 years during which he managed the city he may be said to have appointed all the professors.'

The Royal Infirmary of Edinburgh is another institution that owes a great deal, if not its whole existence, to George Drummond. It was started, as a 'hospital for the destitute sick' in 1729 in a house with six beds in Robertson's Close. The approximate position of the house is marked by a plaque on a wall in what is now Infirmary Street, opposite the University Old College. It was on a site just south of Infirmary Street that the foundation stone of the first new Infirmary building was laid with much ceremony in August 1738. No one among the managers of the new institution worked harder or with more dedication to raise funds for the completion of the building than did George Drummond. Through letters, public appeals and personal visits he sought and obtained money and materials from many different sources. Some came from church door collections, some from proceeds of the 'dancing assemblies' which were so popular at that time, some from commercial firms and some from individuals. Inspired by his appeals, land-owners, quarry-masters and others gave stone, slates and timber; farmers provided carts for carrying the materials to the site; a firm in the north of England gave glass for the windows and many workmen with neither money nor goods to offer gave the only thing they had to give – their labour, without wages, for one day each month. George Drummond frequently visited the building to check progress and to pay the weekly wages of the workmen, sometimes not knowing, at one week's visit, whether any money would come in from which to pay the next week's wages, but it always did.

By the end of 1741, the first half of the building was ready to receive patients and the whole building, to accommodate 228 patients, was complete by 1747. It was a four-storey building, with two side wings, facing northwards across Infirmary Street. In the middle of the centre block was a fifth storey containing a large operating theatre with ample seating, in tiers, from which students could watch the skill of the surgeons – a grim spectacle in those pre-anaesthetic days. Among the features advertised with some pride by the managers was that patients on their way to the operating theatre could be hoisted in a chair, by a pulley arrangement, up the central well of the staircase, thus avoiding the inevitable jolting if they had to be carried up the long stair. Another admirable feature was said to be that every patient was accommodated in a separate bed!

From sensible motives of economy the outside of the building was perfectly plain except for a pillared façade in the centre and a decorative stone scroll at each side of the operating theatre storey. When the building was demolished in 1884 to make way for the two schools and the public baths which are now on the site, the scrolls were acquired by the owner of Redford House, near Colinton Village and there, attached to an out-building beside Redford Road, they are still pointed out to tourists by city coach tour drivers as they pass. The old Infirmary main gate, with its pillars, was rebuilt nearby in Drummond Street, the name of which commemorates George Drummond, where the gate remains as the entrance to a university department. The statue of King George II which stood in the niche on the front of the old Infirmary can be seen outside the main entrance to the present Royal Infirmary in Lauriston Place.

Having seen the Infirmary safely launched in its fine new building, Drummond turned his attention to other city projects and as a member of a 'committee for the improvement of the city', he took a leading part in the planning and building of the Royal Exchange. Now better known as the City Chambers, it is the best example of eighteenth-century building in the High Street. Built on the site of several old closes, the whole building was constructed on steeply sloping ground with the result that although around the quadrangle which faces the High Street it is only four storeys in height, its north wall rises like a great grey cliff to the height of twelve storeys from Cockburn Street. Down among its cellars there can still be found the cobbled way of Mary King's Close, flanked by remnants of ancient houses and shops. Before the Royal Exchange was built above them some of these houses had already stood empty for many years because of the widely held belief that they were haunted by victims of the plague who had died there in the plague years of the seventeenth century.

One of the main purposes of the Royal Exchange and its fine piazza was to provide a proper and dignified place for the merchants and lawyers of the city to conduct their business. However, the Town Council soon found that though you can build a commodious exchange for merchants you cannot make them meet there, and for long afterwards they continued to settle their business deals where they and their fathers before them had always conducted their affairs – in the street beside the market cross, in Parliament Close, or in a coffee house of their choice. Fortunately, the Exchange building had been designed to serve a variety of purposes so the failure of the merchants to appreciate its facilities was less serious than it might have been. Planned by John and Robert Adam and built by a company of wrights and masons described in the contract as 'the Gentlemen of Mary's Chapel' it provided a custom-house (let to the government), thirty-five shops, some with living rooms above them, ten other dwelling houses, two printing houses and three coffee houses. It was not until 1811 that any part of the building came into use for Town Council purposes and from that time, over the years, more and more apartments within it were taken over for the town's use.

In 1904 the west wing was reconstructed to incorporate a handsome new Chamber in which Council meetings are still held. That was intended as the first stage of a complete reconstruction for civic purposes but nothing more was done apart from many minor internal alterations and, in the 1930s, the construction of new east and west extensions facing the High Street. Now, some 220 years after George Drummond, as Grand Master of the Society of Free-masons in Scotland, laid the foundation stone of his new Royal Exchange for Merchants, the building has passed out of the hands of the Town Council to become, under local government reform, the headquarters of the newly-constituted Council of the City of Edinburgh District.

From the Royal Exchange, Drummond turned his attention to his greatest dream: the New Town of Edinburgh. Towards the end of his life he was looking one day from a high window in the old town across the Nor' Loch to the farmlands beyond. Turning to a companion, he said: 'You are a young man and may probably live to see all those fields covered with houses forming a splendid and magnificent city.' Though he worked long and hard to bring that scheme about he did not claim it as his own original idea. In fact, he is on record as saying that he was 'only beginning to execute what the Duke of York [afterwards James VII and II] had suggested so far back as 1681 when residing at Holyrood'. Others too, had spoken of the possibility and, in 1716, some fields beyond the Nor' Loch valley had been bought by the town for possible future use. But there was also great resistance to the idea, partly from vested interests and partly from fear of the windswept site, 'far' from the heart of the old town and difficult of access because of the loch and its marshy surroundings.

George Drummond therefore directed his efforts to persuading his less enthusiastic colleagues to improve the means of communication across the valley and in October 1763 he had the satisfaction of laying the foundation stone of the first North Bridge, a stone bridge with five arches. Even then he had to be careful to describe it, not as the first step towards a new town, but as 'the bridge leading towards Leith, the seaport of Edinburgh'. Three years later the idea of extending the city northwards was at last accepted by the Town Council and entries were invited in a competition to find the best lay-out plan of a new town, 'marking out streets of a proper breadth and by-lanes'. Less than two months after the winning entry had been selected, however, George Drummond died, on 4 December 1766, in his 80th year.

A few days later, the *Edinburgh Evening Courant* reported:

To honour the memory of a gentleman who justly deserves the epithet of 'Father of the City' his funeral, to Canongate churchyard, was attended by the magistrates in their robes, with their sword and mace covered with black crape, the Professors of the University in their gowns, with their mace, the Judges and many hundreds of the principal inhabitants. During the procession the bells, both in the city and in the Canongate, tolled and the crowd of spectators was prodigiously great.

So far, we have looked at George Drummond as a public figure. What of his private life and character? Robert Chambers, in his biographical dictionary, says he was 'of a graceful and dignified deportment', that his manners were 'conciliating and agreeable' and that he was 'highly popular with his fellow citizens'. He was four times married, first at the age of twenty and for the fourth time when he was sixty-eight. By his first and second wives he had fourteen children; his third and fourth wives brought him no children, but each brought with her a considerable fortune, with the result that earlier financial worries, including the sudden reduction of his salary as Customs Commissioner from £1000 to £500, were forgotten and he was able to live for the last twenty-five years of his life in some style.

Before his third marriage, in 1739, he seems to have gone through a period of intense religious introspection in curious contrast to his usual reputation as a man of firm decision and vigorous action. From 1736 until 1738 he kept a diary filling two large folio volumes which are now in Edinburgh University Library; but if one turns to these volumes for new light on George Drummond's part in public affairs one does so almost entirely in vain. There are a very few such items – for example:

8 Sept. 1736. At dinner I got the account that last night the mob had broken open the prison, taken out Captain Porteous and hanged him. It stunned me; ...
16 Sept. 1736. Meeting the Lord Justice-Clerk accidentally, he talked to me about the Porteous murder, in a sort asking my advice. ... All the blood that has been shed and the mischief done is owing to the infatuation or unaccountable stupidity of the present Magistrates. ...

and these entries, about the Infirmary:

15 May 1738. The Infirmary affairs kept me abroad late. ...
3 June 1738. I dined with a number of farmers, soliciting for carts to the building of the Infirmary and they were very frank. I am in constant hurry and bustle about one public thing or another.

Otherwise, the diary consists almost entirely of long accounts of his spiritual doubts and even longer tedious quotations from a similar diary kept by a woman friend, identified only as R.B. On 14 September 1736 he wrote: 'I spent the evening transcribing R.B.'s papers into my own book – my favourite employment.'

In due course, however, another friend advised him to re-marry and even offered to introduce him to a widow who would make a suitable wife. There follow the last two entries in the diary:

23 Nov. 1738 ... In the afternoon I saw the woman at Mrs Fenton's. There is nothing disagreeable either in her manner or person, but I can form no judgment about her yet.
25 Nov. 1738. Though this marriage would probably relieve me out of my distress, yet ... I dare not take one step till I can see the Lord calling me to it.

There the diary ends, and in the following January (the Lord presumably having called him to it) George Drummond and 'the

E

woman' were married and his friend R.B. disappeared from the scene; but this wife died after only three years.

In his earlier days George Drummond lived at Liberton. In 1738 he moved to the estate of Easter Hailes, near Colinton. Finally, in 1757 (two years after his fourth marriage) he bought a fine old mansion in the midst of extensive wooded grounds and named it Drummond Lodge. Its site is now represented by the central garden of Drummond Place, one of the most attractive squares in the New Town, at the eastern end of Great King Street. In his delightful country house, in those days quite in the country and encircled by woodlands though scarcely a mile from the High Street, he and his wife entertained extensively and hospitably. There, round a well-plenished table and over many a bottle of claret, the civic affairs of Edinburgh would often be discussed into the small hours of the morning – and, in all probability, they would frequently be settled there as well, leaving the Town Council on the following day only to go through the formal motions of decision-making.

7 George Square

alf a mile southwards from the High Street is George Square, once a place of elegance, greatly admired as a centre of fashion and gracious living, now strikingly transformed into a modern university precinct and, as I believe, still admirable in a different way.

While George Drummond, towards the end of his life, was striving with public-spirited zeal to have the town extended across the Nor' Loch and to persuade the residents in the old town to bring to reality his vision of the 'splendid and magnificent city' that might one day be sited there, a speculative builder was already cashing in on the old town's desperate need for expansion. He was James Brown, who, early in the 1760s built a small residential square, which he called Brown Square, just within the Flodden Wall where the western end of Chambers Street now meets George IV Bridge. Beyond the wall there had been hitherto little building except in the small ancient burgh known as Portsburgh consisting of two parts, Wester Portsburgh outside the west port where the street of West Port now runs and Easter Portsburgh outside the Potterrow Port, in the district of Potterrow and Bristo. But, some time before James Brown embarked on his schemes, other houses had begun to be built in the neighbourhood of Easter Portsburgh, forming the beginnings of Nicolson Street and Nicolson Square.

These were on the estate of Lady Nicolson whose property lay in an area of fields and crofts with occasional mansion houses spaced here and there among them.

One of these mansions was Ross House, near where the McEwan Hall now is, and its policies stretched away to the south to meet the spacious pleasure-ground of the Meadows which, just at that time, was being formed out of the marsh where the former South or Burgh Loch had recently been drained. A large section of the Ross House policies was bought by James Brown and there, in 1766, he began to build his 'great square' where not the least of the attractions of his 'desirable residences' would be their convenient proximity to the Meadows and the Middle Meadow Walk which an adjoining proprietor was then creating at his own expense as a tree-lined promenade for the enjoyment of the public. Happily, it still remains a pleasant public walk, free from the noise and fumes of motor traffic.

James Brown named his new square George's Square (nowadays, George Square) not, as you might suppose, after the reigning monarch but after his own brother, George Brown. That the project was a profitable one for James is obvious from the fact that a sum equal to the price he had paid for the site (£1200) was very soon being recovered by him annually as feu-duties from the purchasers of the houses in the Square. At an early stage, when the south side was still unbuilt on, proprietors on the other three sides asked that it should be left open to improve the amenity of their houses; but the price of £4000 which James Brown asked in return for this was too great and so all four sides of the Square were eventually completed. This, as it turned out, was a good thing for the residents because only a few years later the buildings of Buccleuch Place immediately south of the Square would have completely blocked the vista which they had sought to preserve.

The mason responsible for many of the earliest houses in the Square was Michael Nasmyth, father of Alexander Nasmyth, the Scottish landscape painter, and grandfather of James Nasmyth, inventor of the steam hammer. Those who know about such things point out on the fronts of several of the remaining houses Michael Nasmyth's characteristic dark-coloured 'sneckings' among the varied hues of the Craigmillar stone from which many of the houses were built. In the centre of the Square, the four and a half

acre garden provided for the private recreation of the early residents still affords a quiet escape from the surrounding bustle of
student life.

The first residents of the Square were expected to preserve its
genteel dignity. Their title-deeds prohibited dealings in trade or
merchandise and 'baking or brewing for sale'. Indeed, to look
through a list of the early residents is to turn the pages of a *Who's
Who* of fashion and rank. Having done so, I was less surprised than
I might otherwise have been by the story of the gentleman who
lingered for an hour or so beside the Market Cross, dressed in his
finest clothes just so that he might mention casually to passing
acquaintances that he was on his way 'to dine with friends in
George's Square'.

Among the galaxy of early residents was Henry Dundas (later
the first Viscount Melville), 'uncrowned king of Scotland', who,
at different times, occupied three different houses in the Square.
In one of these the peace of his evening meal was rudely broken
one June day in 1792 when a mob, angered by his opposition to the
movement for parliamentary reform, attacked the house and could
not be restrained until the military arrived, shots had been fired
and several persons had been injured.

Another early resident was Alexander Fraser Tytler who was
Professor of Civil Law at Edinburgh and later was raised to the
Bench as Lord Woodhouselee. The Navy was represented by Captain
Adam Duncan who became Admiral Duncan and later, taking
his title from his most famous battle, was created Earl of Camperdown: 'one of the biggest and finest men in the Navy – six feet
four in height and of corresponding breadth'. A severe injury to
a finger which remained useless for the rest of his life was sustained,
not in any naval encounter, but in his efforts to repulse some of
the mob outside Henry Dundas' house on that June evening in
1792. For the Army there was General Sir Ralph Abercromby
who, having served in many fields of battle, gained the reputation
of being the most skilful officer in the British service. Scholarship
was well upheld by Dr Alexander Adam, much-loved Rector
of the High School who, as Lord Cockburn succinctly put it, 'was
born to teach Latin, some Greek and all virtue'.

Along with the landed gentry, their families and a formidable
assortment of dowagers and widows of substantial means, lawyers

were perhaps the dominant group taking advantage of this quiet
enclave which was within walking distance of the courts although
in those days, without benefit of either the South Bridge or George
IV Bridge, their walk would involve a steep descent to the Cowgate and a steep climb up again to the Bristo Port. Three houses
among those still remaining in the Square were first occupied
by three very different members of the legal profession. At No. 13,
on the north side, Robert McQueen, Lord Braxfield, prototype
of R. L. Stevenson's Weir of Hermiston lived from 1770 until his
death in 1799. Whatever one may think of this coarse and uncouth
judge whose unfeeling jests and obvious prejudice so disgraced
Scottish justice at the trials of the 'political martyrs' in 1793 and
1794, his courage in walking nightly after these trials, unescorted,
from the court to his George Square home cannot be denied –
unless, that is, you call it foolhardiness. He had blatantly manipu-
lated the juries to ensure that only those opposed to the 'Friends
of the People' served on them; he had, by the power of his personality, played on the fears of his colleagues on the Bench who were
already in a state of near panic lest the evil influence of the French
Revolution was beginning to show itself in Edinburgh; he had
browbeaten witnesses and roughly rebuked those who were on
trial. Then, having expressed his personal view that such people
'would be nane the worse o' a hangin' ', he sentenced them, almost
gleefully, to transportation for fourteen years. And all for what?
For allegedly encouraging the reading of Paine's *Rights of Man*; for
taking prominent part in meetings of the 'Friends of the People'
in a hall in James Court; for urging 'votes for all' in place of the
grossly unrepresentative parliamentary election system of those
days. Unless Lord Braxfield's obsessive prejudice against anyone
who criticized the established order of things had so blinded him
to reality that he did not even notice the sense of outrage his
performance on the Bench had aroused in even quite moderate
fellow-citizens, he must have known that to walk alone to his
house at night was to take a very real risk of attack. Yet he repeatedy
did so; and he came to no harm.

Lord Braxfield's coarse humour and rough manners were not
kept for prisoners at the bar alone. His wife also seems to have been
a target for them. Once, perhaps in their George Square house,
their butler was threatening to give notice because she had

reprimanded him so often. 'Man!' said his lordship, 'ye've little to complain o'. *You're* no' married to her!' And, another time, having ungallantly sworn at a lady who was his partner at whist and who had played a wrong card, he excused himself on the ground that, absent-mindedly, he had thought he was partnered by his wife. From these and many other stories of his behaviour it is clear that his lordship did not aspire to the standards of gentility and good breeding that were supposed to be the hallmark of those first residents in George's Square, but then his ownership of a country estate and his standing as a judge no doubt were sufficient qualifications for acceptance by his neighbours.

Among these neighbours another member of the legal profession certainly qualified. He was the Hon. Henry Erskine, Advocate (and twice, for short periods, Lord Advocate) who lived at No. 27 on the west side, now occupied by the Edinburgh University School of Scottish Studies. Henry Erskine was handsome, urbane and witty, though with a propensity for punning that might seem a trifle tiresome nowadays. He it was who, on his appointment as Lord Advocate, having been offered the gown belonging to Henry Dundas, the outgoing holder of that office, declined it saying that he had 'no wish to put on the abandoned habits of his predecessor'; and, to quote just one more of his atrocious puns, there was the occasion when, for the second time in quick succession he met an acquaintance who was on his way to take the waters at St Bernard's mineral well in the Water of Leith valley and hailed him with the friendly greeting: 'I see you do not weary in well doing.' It was also Henry Erskine who, after being introduced to Dr Johnson in Parliament Hall, pressed a shilling into Boswell's hand explaining that he understood that to be the usual fee to the exhibitor of a performing bear – which, discourteous though it may have been, seems to me to have been an apt comment on James Boswell's well-nigh insufferable habit of showing off his distinguished friend at every opportunity.

Despite the punning, Erskine's pleading in court was both skilful and a pleasure to listen to; so much so that once when he began with the words 'I will be brief, my Lord' the judge is said to have earnestly entreated: 'Na, na, Harry; dinna be brief, dinna be brief.' There was, however, another judge whose wit seems to have been less sharp than Erskine's and who took time to appreciate the point of his jokes. He was Lord Balmuto. The two often walked together in the Meadows after the court had risen and, it was said, the learned judge would sometimes suddenly exclaim: 'I have you now, Harry; I have you now,' and then laugh loudly at some remark that Erskine had made in court an hour or so before.

Henry Erskine was a Whig in politics and that, combined with his natural tendency to support the underdog, may have made him rather less popular than he might otherwise have been with some of the other George Square residents. It certainly would not endear him to Lord Braxfield. However, his readiness to give legal advice and services free, or for a token fee, to those who could ill afford to pay was appreciated by many who could not otherwise have hoped to obtain justice. One grateful client put it in a nutshell when he said: 'There's no poor man in Scotland need want a friend or fear an enemy so long as Henry Erskine lives'; an enviable tribute for anyone to be remembered by after two centuries.

Only two doors away from Henry Erskine, in No. 25, a third member of the legal profession lived when the houses were new. He was Walter Scott, Writer to the Signet, and he and his wife came there in 1772 when their son, the future Sir Walter, was only one year old. Until his marriage in 1797, that house continued to be the young Sir Walter's 'most established place of residence'. It was from there that he went daily to the High School, then in High School Yards, in the building which faces you at the lower end of Infirmary Street, about ten minutes' walking distance from his home; and at the High School he learned from the good Dr Adam (not yet a George Square resident) 'the value of the knowledge which I had hitherto considered only as a burdensome task'.

Here, however, I must digress for a reason which will shortly become clear. George Square was outside the 'ancient royalty' (the extent of the town over which the Town Council had jurisdiction). On the one hand, this meant that its first residents escaped liability for certain civic duties and payments – an advantage which James Brown would not be slow to bring to the notice of prospective purchasers. On the other hand, it also meant that they did not have the benefit of some civic services, such as public lighting and cleansing of the roadway in the Square and the roads leading to it, a disadvantage which he would be less inclined to publicize.

However, in 1771 an Act of Parliament was passed which set a pattern for a whole code of municipal legislation to follow, not in Edinburgh alone but throughout Scotland. By that Act, the area south of the town wall was divided for certain municipal purposes into eight districts known as the Southern Districts, each very small in extent, covering only a few streets, a fact which demonstrates the narrow horizons of those days. For each of these districts five commissioners were elected from among the residents and they met sometimes as district groups and sometimes as a body of forty to deal with general matters. Their functions included arranging for 'cleaning, lighting and watching the several streets and other passages in the south side of Edinburgh and for the removing nuisance' for which purposes they had power to levy rates within their districts.

One of the eight was the District of George Square, including the Square and a few neighbouring streets; and one of the Commissioners was Henry Dundas, the future Viscount Melville. He qualified for election as Commissioner on two counts – first that he was a resident at No. 5 George Square and secondly that nothing of consequence was ever done in Edinburgh in those days without Henry Dundas being in some way involved. At the first meeting of the whole body of Commissioners held in June 1771 he, of course, was in the chair. At that meeting, only one item seems to have been on the agenda and that concerned the age-old and continuing question of the control of exuberant and disorderly youth. The minute of the meeting said: '. . . as it has been and still is the practice in several streets and other passages . . . for boys to meet and play at football, to bicker and cast squibs to the great inconveniency and often danger and damage of the lives of the inhabitants, the meeting consider this a nuisance and recommend to the Commissioners of the proper districts to take proper steps . . . for preventing the above occurrences for the future'.

So, no doubt, the Commissioners of the George Square District would issue 'proper' instructions to their watchmen to take the necessary steps to put an end to the playing of football and the bickering of boys within their bounds; but that would really be an impossible task for the watchmen to perform because 'bickers' between rival groups of youths had been an Edinburgh pastime of very long standing and it was one that continued long after the Commissioners' pronouncement against it. And it is this that brings me back at last to the boyhood of Walter Scott at No. 25 George Square.

In his own notes to the Waverley novels, Sir Walter Scott described the 'bickers' which took place in George Square when he was a schoolboy – that is to say, several years after the Commissioners' meeting had sought to end them. He describes how he and his brothers, with others living in the Square, formed a company which 'as a matter of course was engaged in weekly warfare with the boys inhabiting the Crosscauseway, Bristo Street, the Potterrow – in short, the neighbouring suburbs. These last were chiefly of the lower rank, but hardy loons, who threw stones to a hair's breadth, and were very rugged antagonists at close quarters. The skirmish sometimes lasted for a whole evening until one party or the other was victorious.' He goes on to tell how, on one occasion, one of the opposing 'hardy loons' who was known to him only as 'Green-breeks', was injured so severely that he had to spend a few days in the Infirmary; and how, despite urgent and repeated questioning by those in authority, 'Green-breeks' refused to disclose the identity of the youth who had struck him down although, Scott says, he must have known very well who it was. Could it have been young Walter Scott himself, or one of his brothers? Scott's statement that they afterwards offered 'Green-breeks' a token sum of money as a reward for his refusal to talk suggests the possibility. But 'Green-breeks' declined the offer telling them that 'he would not sell his blood' and that he would never be so 'clam – i.e. base or mean' as to be an informer. 'Afterwards,' says Scott, 'we did not become friends, for the "bickers" were more agreeable to both parties than any more pacific amusement; but we conducted them ever after under mutual assurances of the highest consideration of each other.'

That the rough pastime of bickering could not easily be outlawed from the Edinburgh scene appears also from the pages of George Borrow's Lavengro. There he tells how, as a boy living in Edinburgh when his father was stationed at the Castle, he was in the habit of joining the boys of the old town in their regular battles against their New Town rivals and how pleased he was when one of his companions told him he was 'no' a bad hand at flingin' stanes'. That was in 1813, some thirty years after the 'Green-breeks' incident described by Scott and more than forty years after the Commissioners of the Southern Districts had passed their judgement against such violent activities. Clearly, the problem of unruly youth is not a new one; nor is it one that can easily be solved by the pious resolutions of eighteenth-century commissioners or for that matter twentieth-century committees.

In October 1785 the residents of George Square narrowly missed the opportunity of seeing a novel and exciting spectacle from their own doorsteps. Vincent Lunardi, the dashing and conceited Italian balloonist, had arrived in Edinburgh. He had made several ascents in England but he and his balloon had never before been seen in Scotland. Through the good offices of Henry Erskine he was introduced to the residents in the Square and applied to them for permission to stage his first ascent from their central garden. All were in favour except one determined elderly lady who had no desire to see the peace and quiet of the Square disturbed by the thousands who (even with tickets priced at two-and-sixpence each 'from Mr Creech's bookshop') would doubtless flock there to watch the daring aeronaut. She firmly refused to give her permission; and so the site for the ascent was moved to the garden of Heriot's Hospital and any George Square residents who were anxious to have a close-up view at the moment of take-off would, like anyone else, have to apply for tickets to Mr Creech's bookshop in the luckenbooths. But Heriot's garden was quite near at hand and so, very soon after the balloon was airborne, they would all be able to watch its progress in comfort from the front or rear windows of their houses according to the side of the Square on which they lived.

The excitement over the approaching event was tremendous. The fame of Lunardi's previous ascents had preceded him and everyone in Edinburgh, it seemed, was anxious to witness his first Edinburgh exploit; so much so that, when the great day came, many of the shops in the town were closed. The Heriot Garden was thronged to capacity and everywhere in the neighbourhood crowds watched from streets, windows and roof-tops.

The event was a huge success. Dressed in scarlet and blue, Lunardi stepped into the basket of the balloon which immediately took off. 'He ascended', said a newspaper report, 'in the most grand and magnificent manner . . . and went over the city at a great height, directly across the Firth.' Ninety minutes later he landed, about twenty-five miles away as the crow (or the balloon) flies, in a field near Ceres, a village in Fife. There his descent caused consternation among a group of farm workers who took it as a sign that the end of the world was at hand until they were re-assured by the local minister. Their apprehension becomes less surprising when one reads that Lunardi was in the habit of herald-ing his otherwise unannounced approach from the celestial regions by several loud blasts on a trumpet. After that, Lunardi was fêted in Fife; and in Edinburgh he was given the Freedom of the City, 'an honour certainly due to the first man who ever flew over it'.

His next flight from Edinburgh, three months later, was less successful for he came down in the sea and had to be rescued by the crew of a fishing-boat. Nothing daunted, he was back with his balloon in Heriot Garden again in the following year. This time he offered to take a passenger with him and on 31 July 1786 he was joined in the basket by Mrs Lamash, an actress who was doubtless glad of this opportunity to share in his publicity. But their combined weight proved too great and to the disappointment of the crowd – and, I daresay, the greater disappointment of the lady and Lunardi – she had to step down, whereupon the balloon 'slowly arose in the air, affording by reason of the stillness of the day, a more permanently magnificent spectacle than any of his former ascensions'. This time it remained poised above the city for an hour, before drifting to earth near Musselburgh; and this time George Square did have its share in Lunardi's triumph. On his return, with the balloon, to Edinburgh he was entertained by Henry Erskine at 27 George Square – and here let the next issue of the *Edinburgh Evening Courant* take up the story:

As the balloon had still a pretty strong ascending power Mr Lunardi chose to make his entry into George's Square seated in his triumphal car, the balloon floating in the air a considerable distance above it. The novelty of this sight produced such acclamations as had never before attended any of his perfor-mances. And, after refreshing himself for a few minutes in the Hon. Henry Erskine's house our aerial hero was carried on the shoulders of the populace to his apartments.

The balloon, it seems, was left in George Square for a short time during which many thousands of 'the lower ranks' assembled to see it, but 'not the least damage was done to it'. One can only hope the lady who had been the sole objector to the use of the Square for Lunardi's ascents was not unduly disturbed by this intrusion.

For a short time after this, Vincent Lunardi continued to be enthusiastically entertained and honoured in Edinburgh. Lunardi bonnets, in the shape of his balloon, became popular with the ladies. But before long Lunardi spoiled everything by his vanity. His boastful toast in honour of himself: 'To Lunardi, whom the ladies love' proved too much for his friends in Edinburgh. He left the city and was not seen in it again.

For a century or so, apart from exceptional occasions such as the reform riot and the Lunardi visit, the Square remained a quiet residential quarter, its houses occupied solely as private residences. Then, in 1876 and later years, several houses on the north side were taken over and replaced by the building of George Watson's Ladies' College, the façade of which is still an undistinguished feature of that side of the Square. In the 1920s some houses on the south side were replaced by a residence for students which was also a plain and undistinguished building. Meanwhile, several of the other houses had become boarding establishments, business premises and offices or were occupied by University departments. The time had passed when private families could comfortably occupy these houses with a plentiful supply of servants to fetch and carry up and down the stairs, between basement and attic, for a minimal wage.

These changes had taken place without any outcry being raised. But in 1946 the University of Edinburgh, having already acquired much of the property, began to formulate plans for replacing the houses by modern University buildings to meet the urgent need to provide up-to-date facilities for the rapidly increasing numbers of its students. Then began the 'battle' of George Square – a battle that was fiercer, though not in a physical sense, than any of the old-time bickers could possibly have been. It continued, on and off, for nearly fifteen years between amenity societies on the one hand, nostalgically seeking to preserve the fading aura of an age that had gone and the University on the other, aiming to meet their new needs on this central site where the tradition of the University as 'the Toun's College' and the old link between Town and Gown could be carried on into the future. Here, with a minimum disturbance of households, their new premises along with the Old College, the medical school at Teviot Place and other departments nearby, both existing and planned, could form a compact and comprehensive University precinct. It is one thing for the newly established Heriot Watt University to transfer as they have recently done to their 'grove of academe' among the woodlands of Riccarton on the western outskirts of the city. The place for the ancient Town's College is here, at the city's heart.

Eventually, the University won the day, with the one compromise of leaving the west side of the Square in its original state and using the houses they owned on that side to accommodate some small departments that could be fitted into them. Having organized an architectural competition to find the best possible general scheme for the rest of the Square and having engaged some of the most distinguished architects of the day to carry it out, what has the University achieved? Based on the central garden, still there with its shady trees, the Square is now a college quadrangle which proclaims its own purpose and its own era, with buildings of which the designs, simple and functional, spring from their practical requirements and not from any attempt to pretend to be something different. On the southern side the library building, with reading space for 3000 students, is, nevertheless, low enough not to dwarf the houses of the Square's west side from which its clear, horizontal lines lead the eye easily to the George Square lecture theatre and the Adam Ferguson building, home of Sociology, Social Administration and other studies; then, turning the corner, to the William Robertson building, centre of History and Economics. The horizontal lay-out is punctuated sharply by the Faculty of Arts' fourteen-storey David Hume Tower soaring skywards at the south-east corner and, just beyond the north-east corner, by the Appleton Tower, of nine storeys, designed for science students.

Though rebuilding has only begun on the north side, the whole Square, with its combination of eighteenth-century atmosphere and twentieth-century activity, has a remarkable unity and is a pleasant place in which to be – except, perhaps, when a cold wind is whistling between the blocks. That, however, is something from which George Square has always suffered. In fact, as early as 1779, a lane on the west side was closed in by the single-storey block still to be seen at No. 23a because the early residents found that the narrow lane originally there was 'very inconvenient, especially in the winter season and in high winds and stormy weather'.

Vindication of the University for what they have done in George Square, if vindication is asked for, lies in the fact that, in 1969, the Civic Trust gave formal Commendations to two aspects of the scheme: to the design of the library building which they praised for its strong and effective horizontal lines and to the planning and execution of the whole project, for the 'high degree of order and amenity' which had been achieved.

The names chosen for the new buildings are worth looking at, for they span 200 years of University (and Edinburgh) history. William Robertson, who was Principal of the University for more than thirty years from 1762 was appointed to that post at the instigation of George Drummond, Lord Provost, and it has been said that this appointment 'was one of the last and greatest services rendered by Drummond to the University'. Apart from Dr Robertson's distinction as a preacher, a church leader and a historian, (he was Historiographer-Royal) he is remembered with gratitude for his establishment of the University library fund and also for his promotion of the scheme for the erection of 'the new University building' designed partly by Robert Adam and partly by William Playfair, which is now known as the Old College and, with the added attraction of its patina of age, is still a building of which Edinburgh is justly proud.

Adam Ferguson, Professor of Moral Philosophy from 1764 until 1785, once wrote a book called *Essays on Civil Society* in which he sought to trace man's rise from barbarism to civilization; so, whatever his other claims to fame may have been, that was surely reason enough for giving his name to a building devoted to the study of sociology and kindred subjects. David Hume we have already met, in Riddle's Close and James Court, and we will meet him again in the New Town. Though, in his life-time, he never held any university post of distinction his writings have dominated the world of philosophy and letters to no less a degree than the tower bearing his name dominates George Square.

That leaves only the Appleton Tower; and it is entirely appropriate that this building of the Faculty of Science should commemorate Sir Edward Appleton, a great scientist and, from 1948 until
his death in 1965, a great Principal. Like his eighteenth-century
predecessor William Robertson he too will be remembered for his
promotion of new University buildings, for it was largely through
his vision and his patience and perseverance that the George
Square scheme, despite the persistent 'bickering' of its critics,
was brought to so successful a conclusion.

8 Canongate

The point we have reached in the history of Edinburgh – the building of George Square as a kind of unofficial prelude to the beginning of the New Town – is a convenient one from which to turn back the calendar and take up the story of the burgh of Canongate. Founded by a charter of David I in 1143 in favour of the Canons of Holyrood Abbey, Canongate remained a separate burgh, with its own magistrates and council and its own council chamber until it was merged with Edinburgh in 1856. But, because its principal street was the main road into Edinburgh from the east and formed nearly half the length of the Royal Mile, the townspeople of the Canongate shared closely with those of Edinburgh many events in the history of the two burghs. Several of Edinburgh's prominent people, too, chose to live in the less congested area of the Canongate, commuting daily (by sedan chair) to and from the city.

There was another close link between the neighbouring burghs. By the original charter, the Canons of Holyrood were the superiors of Canongate and could thus influence, or even direct, such affairs of the burgh as the election of its council and its Bailies, though they did not choose to do so to any great extent. After the church's jurisdiction was removed from the burgh in 1587 the superiority passed into the hands of private families until, in 1636, it was ac-

F

quired by the Town Council of Edinburgh, with the approval of
Parliament. So, for 220 years, until the two burghs were combined,
Edinburgh was able to exercise considerable influence over Canongate affairs and, for most of that time, one of the three Bailies of
the Canongate, known as the Baron Bailie, was appointed not by
the people of Canongate but by the Town Council of Edinburgh.

The rights and privileges of Canongate extended northwards
over the barony of Broughton, the little township commemorated
by the names of Broughton Street and Broughton Place on the
edge of the New Town; and also over the Pleasance area, south of
the Cowgate valley. It is, however, sufficient for us to think of
the old burgh of Canongate as represented by the present Canongate street with its cross streets and closes and the two parallel
streets of Holyrood Road (which used to be called South Back
of Canongate) and Calton Road (formerly, North Back of Canongate). In addition, one other adjustment should be kept in mind.
For everyday purposes one thinks of the division between the two
burghs as having been at the Netherbow Port, but this is only
partly true. Edinburgh's territory, in fact, extended further down
the Canongate, but on the south side of the street only, reaching
almost to St John Street. There, in the roadway, is a circular
pattern of stones showing the site of St John's Cross which marked
this extremity of Edinburgh. From the Cross, the boundary ran
up the middle of the street to the Netherbow; and at St John's
Cross, from time to time, the Town Council of Edinburgh would
assemble to greet royal visitors to the city approaching from the
east.

That cross was one of three in the Canongate. There was, as
usual in burghs, the market cross which stood in the middle of
the street almost opposite Canongate Church and around which
markets were held. In 1888 it was moved to the side of the street,
to make way for traffic. In 1953 it was rebuilt inside the churchyard.

At the foot of the Canongate, just before the road branches off
for Abbeyhill, was the Girth Cross, its site, like that of St John's
Cross, now marked by a pattern of stones in the road. Here pro-
clamations were made and executions took place; and, as its
name suggests, this cross marked the extremity of the sanctuary
of Holyrood about which there will be more to say later.

A few yards east of the Girth Cross, on the road to Abbeyhill, stood the Water Gate (taking its name from a nearby horse-pond) for though Canongate, unlike Edinburgh, was never surrounded by a defensive wall it did have a boundary wall of sorts and its own town gate which must have been a fairly substantial one to judge by an instruction given to the Treasurer of Canongate in 1568 'to cause mend sufficiently the Port of the Water-Yett and to cause make ane sufficient lok and kei thereto'. From customs collected at the 'Water-Yett' the Canongate Town Council derived a large part of their revenue.

In the seventeenth century, Canongate was a much less congested place than Edinburgh. So much is clear from Gordon of Rothiemay's drawing of the two burghs prepared on the instructions of Edinburgh Town Council in 1647. It gives a bird's-eye view from a point high in the air somewhere southward from the Royal Mile and shows not just a ground-plan but a view including details of the roofs and façades of many of the buildings. To do this effectively more than a century before Lunardi had demonstrated the means by which such a view could actually be obtained was, in itself, an astonishing flight of imagination. Yet it was imagination combined with realism, for all are agreed that the drawing gives a remarkably accurate impression of the seventeenth-century scene. It shows Edinburgh as a crowded herring-bone pattern of closely packed buildings but Canongate as a main street, flanked, on both sides, largely by detached houses with spacious gardens. Several of these houses remain and still play a useful part in the city's life. Some of the seventeenth- and eighteenth-century tenements built on their former gardens have been reconstructed behind the original frontages while others have been replaced by new buildings reproducing the spirit, though not always the exact design, of the originals.

Having thus set the scene, let us look at some of these buildings which make their contribution to the Canongate's 'tapestry of time'. Walking down the Canongate I would stop first at Morocco Close, No. 273, where a block of flats built in the 1950s occupies the site (and contains many of the stones) of a seventeenth- or early eighteenth-century building that was called Morocco Land. Attached to the wall at about second-floor level, where it was reinstated from the former building, is a stone carving of a Moorish figure wearing a turban, ear-rings, armbands and bracelets. The story of this effigy is a strange one and whether the story was made up to explain the figure or the figure was carved to illustrate the story is anybody's guess; but the intriguing thing is that, however fanciful the events and characters in the narrative may seem to be, some of the events are known to have happened and some of the names are of people who did in fact live in Edinburgh at what lawyers would call 'the relevant dates'.

The bare outline of the story (it has been given many embellishments) is that a young student, Andrew Gray, having been a ringleader in riots in Edinburgh was condemned to death but escaped from the old Tolbooth and fled overseas where, after many adventures, he obtained an important post in the household of the Emperor of Morocco. In the year 1645 he returned on a Moorish ship to Leith and, along with some of the ship's company, came to Edinburgh to demand retribution from the authorities for what he had regarded as their unjust treatment of him. He learned, however, that the daughter of the Provost, Sir John Smith, was a victim of the plague and in imminent danger of death. So, turning aside from thoughts of revenge, he offered to cure her by means of a strange eastern remedy of which he had learned the secret during his travels. The cure was effective, the girl and he fell in love, they were married and they went to live in the Canongate where the tenement named Morocco Land was built and the figure of the Moor set up to commemorate these strange events.

The facts are that there *were* riots in Edinburgh at the 'relevant time'; the year 1645 was, indeed, a terrible plague year in the city; the name of the Provost at that time was Sir John Smith; and the effigy of the Moor carries a shield the arms of which (though now obliterated) used to include an emblem representing the name of Smith. There *was* an Andrew Gray whose life spanned the appropriate years and who could have been a student at the time of the riots (though, for other reasons, he is unlikely to have been involved in such adventures). There are no references in the burgh records to any of the incidents in the story but there are records to show that a building on the site was owned in 1653 by Thomas Gray, merchant, and in 1731 by John Gray, also a merchant; and the building is referred to as 'Morocco Land' in a document of 1710. In the face of all these facts, let anyone who doubts the romantic story of the roving Andrew Gray and the Provost's daughter produce a better explanation of the presence of a Moorish effigy on the wall of a Scottish tenement building; but let it not be just the mundane one that some seventeenth-century Canongate merchant simply chose this way of advertising, or commemorating, his trading connections with faraway lands.

Immediately opposite Morocco Close, in what was the 'extramural' part of Edinburgh, is Chessel's Court, the main building in which is described in the Report of the Royal Commission on the Ancient Monuments of Scotland as 'not only the best preserved but also the finest example of the mansion-flats that were once so common in the old town'. Now effectively restored and with modern blocks beside it carefully designed to be in keeping with it, the main building on the south side of the Court fully lives up to that description. The block was built in 1748 by one Archibald Chessel about whom little is known except that he was a carpenter and worshipped in the Tron Church. His flats were advertised as 'neatly finished and fit to accommodate a genteel family'. Behind them a long garden sloped down to the South Back of Canongate and from their homes his tenants were able to enjoy a magnificent view of Arthur's Seat and Salisbury Crags. Their present-day successors have only a fragment of the garden at their disposal but the view is as striking as ever, especially when the evening sun shines on the russet red of the crags.

Later on, the building became 'Clark's Hotel, for the reception of the nobility and gentry', the situation of which was described as 'airy, cheerful and centrical'; but, by that time, the nobility and gentry were more interested in the new hotels that were being opened in the New Town. So Clark's Hotel was sold and soon afterwards the building came into use as the Scottish Excise Office. In that role it was the scene, one evening in 1788, of events which proved to be the undoing of the hitherto respected Deacon William Brodie. Unlike the story of Morocco Land, the Deacon's story is documented in every detail – in the reports of his trial, conviction and execution five months later.

William Brodie as Deacon of the wrights (or carpenters) had been, for several years, a respected member of the Town Council of Edinburgh. He lived, where his equally respected father had formerly lived, in Brodie's Close in the Lawnmarket. (The Close is still there and still bears the name of Brodie, but the house has long since disappeared.) The Deacon was regularly employed by his fellow citizens to carry out maintenance and repair work on their properties and they knew him as a reliable and efficient tradesman. What they did not know was the extent to which their employment of his legitimate talents helped to advance him in a more lucrative but less public profession by giving him detailed knowledge of the layout of their shops and houses as well as opportunities to take wax impressions of the keys of their premises. These, it seems, several of his customers were so imprudent as to leave on hooks behind their front doors during the day.

For several months a number of unexplained thefts had been taking place, overnight, from lockfast premises in the city. Then, on the evening of 5 March 1788, the Excise Office in Chessel's Court was broken into. The raid had been carefully planned but the plans were badly upset when one of the Excise officials returned unexpectedly to collect papers from his desk. Though he suspected nothing his presence thoroughly demoralized the thieves who fled in confusion taking £16 from a desk drawer as their total proceeds and overlooking £600 lying in another drawer nearby. In their panic they failed to cover their tracks sufficiently and the authorities were soon on their trail.

The excitement caused by news of this latest robbery was intense; but it can have been nothing to the astonishment with which the law-abiding people of Edinburgh and Canongate, opening their newspapers a few days later, read this announcement: '£200 of Reward. Whereas William Brodie, a considerable house-carpenter and burgess of this city has been charged with being concerned in breaking into the General Excise Office for Scotland. . . .' That must certainly have set tongues wagging all up and down the Royal Mile.

After the break-in Brodie, along with the three others who had been involved with him, stayed in Edinburgh for a few days. But as the search became too close for comfort Brodie made for London and, under an assumed name, took boat for Holland. He might have escaped altogether but for his folly in giving a fellow-passenger who was returning on the same boat to Leith, three letters to be delivered to friends in Edinburgh. Through these letters, and by the efforts of the energetic and painstaking King's Messenger who was sent in pursuit of him, he was quickly discovered and brought back to stand trial. The trial took place in August of the same year. Brodie and his principal accomplice were found guilty and suffered the death penalty. In the barbarous manner of those days, they were hanged from a scaffold erected above the platform at the west end of the old Tolbooth, while huge crowds watched from the Lawnmarket. The other two accomplices had turned King's Evidence and were released.

It had long been known that William Brodie, though so respected as tradesman and Town Council member, was fond of keeping low company during his leisure hours and in this he may have differed little from others among his colleagues. It was probably known, to the omniscient cadies if to no one else, that he kept two mistresses who lived within a few minutes' walk of his home and of each other. (To one of these ladies one of the three fateful letters had been addressed.) Matters not known until the whole story was unfolded at his trial were the depth of his involvement with disreputable companions in gambling and in cock-fighting meets held in dark dens off the Grassmarket; and the leading role he had played in the mysterious thefts which had so baffled the authorities. When one thinks of the small area within which all his activities had been conducted and how the robberies must have been a recurring subject of conversation in which, in his guise of city dignitary, he no doubt expressed righteous indignation both at the crime and at the failure to apprehend the criminals, the mind boggles at his effrontery!

The story of Deacon Brodie has taken us away from the Canongate. Back there, if we walk on downhill, we will come, before long, on the north side of the street, to Shoemaker's Land (215 Canongate) and Bible Land (187 Canongate). Both belonged to the Canongate Incorporation of Cordiners or Shoemakers. Both have been reconstructed and are recognizable by the badge of the craft, a shoemaker's rounding-knife, that appears on a carved stone tablet on each. At Bible Land, which belonged to the Shoemakers as far back at 1677, there is also an open bible with the wise words of the 133rd psalm (metrical version): 'Behold how good a thing it is and how becoming well, together such as brethren are, in unity to dwell'. Shoemakers' Land, built for the craft beside their hall (which is no longer there) in 1725, carries the no less laudable message: 'Blessed is he that wisely doth the poor man's case consider'. These craft incorporations, it seems, were always keen on biblical quotations and on keeping salutary words of advice before their members.

For centuries the Cordiners of Canongate held an annual pageant or gala day on 25 October, St Crispin's Day, at which they elected a 'King' who was sumptuously robed and, with his consort and an annually increasing train of attendants, also gaudily dressed, rode through the burgh. As time went on, the cost of this performance steadily increased, eating into the incorporation's funds, until there was little or nothing left from which they could benefit needy members and widows and orphans. So the 'high jinks' of St Crispin's Day were brought to an end about the middle of the nineteenth century. Some of the robes and other regalia of the craft that were used on these occasions can be seen in Huntly House, the city museum, further down the Royal Mile.

Almost opposite Bible Land, there is an archway leading into St John Street, which is now very nearly overwhelmed by the buildings of Moray House College of Education. The historic Moray House, from which all the modern extensions of the College spring, fronts the Canongate just beyond St John Street and is easily recognizable by its stone balcony projecting over the pavement. It has had a colourful history. Built in the time of Charles I, it still has some fine seventeenth-century plaster ceilings. In that century its gardens were described as 'of such elegance and cultivated with such diligence, that they easily challenge comparison with the gardens of warmer countries and perhaps even of England itself. . . . Scarcely anyone would believe it possible to give so much beauty to a garden in this frigid clime'. Cromwell used Moray House as his residence on two occasions. In the days before the union of the parliaments many discussions about the terms of union took place within its walls, and there is a tradition that some who signed the terms of treaty did so in a summer-house in the garden. In 1846 the house was bought by the Free Church of Scotland and altered to become their 'Normal School' for the training of teachers – from which the present College has grown out of all recognition.

St John Street was built about the same time as George's Square and, in its heyday, was almost as fashionable. Originally it was a private street guarded, in the words of one who had lived there, 'by an ancient seneschal in faded uniform who barred the entrance to all carriages except those of residents'.

In St John Street, in the late eighteenth century, lived James Burnett, Lord Monboddo, that eccentric yet learned and kindly Scottish judge who anticipated Darwin's theories by his strange and much ridiculed notion that men were in some way related to the apes; who made all his journeyings on horseback, even as far as London and at an advanced age, because he thought it degrading 'to be dragged in a carriage at the tail of a horse'; and whose custom it was always to walk from the courts to his home though, in wet weather, he would condescend to hire a sedan chair in which to carry his wig and so protect it from the rain.

Of the row of eighteenth-century houses which were formerly ranged down the west side of St John Street only one now remains and it has recently been renovated as the headquarters of the Priory of Scotland of the Most Venerable Order of St John – an order of chivalry which, after a lapse of centuries, was revived in 1947. Lord Monboddo's house, further down the street, was not very different from the one occupied by the Order. In it he loved to give 'literary dinners', and at more than one of these Robert Burns was among the guests. For companion and housekeeper, and as hostess at these dinners, the judge depended on his daughter, Elizabeth, whose beauty was a legend in the city. Sadly, she died at the early age of twenty-five, but not before Burns had immortalized her as 'the fair Burnett' in his poem *Address to Edinburgh*.

In a flat above the arched entrance to the street, Tobias Smollett stayed briefly in 1766 when he visited his sister Mrs Telfer, who lived there. No doubt it was then that he collected some of the material for the Edinburgh scenes in his novel *Humphry Clinker*. Mrs Telfer was an inveterate card player and is remembered chiefly for the occasion when one of the Canongate Bailies, weary after an evening of cards, sought to escape by making the excuse that he had no money left to stake, whereupon she insisted on playing for a pound of candles, a challenge which it would have been difficult for him to refuse, seeing that his trade was that of candlemaker.

When the Bailie was neither playing cards with Mrs Telfer nor making candles he could be found a little further down the Canongate on the opposite side of the road in the Canongate Tolbooth

which served as council meeting room, court house and prison.
Unlike its Edinburgh counterpart it still remains, its preservation
'for the advantage of the inhabitants of the district' having been
one of the requirements of the Act that merged Canongate with
the city in 1856. It now serves as an annexe to the city museum
in Huntly House, across the road.

To browse through the burgh records of Canongate gives a
vivid picture of life in such little burghs through the centuries.
Much of the council's work concerned the control of market
stances and the collection of customs at the Water Gate from which
a large part of the burgh funds came. Consumer protection loomed
large. As far back as 1567, for example, the council (sitting in earlier
premises than the surviving Tolbooth) called upon all hucksters
and stall-holders to produce their weights and balances so that
they could be tested for accuracy and they also bought a complete
set of weights to be kept as standards against which regular checks
could be made. Prices too were controlled, a £40 fine being fixed
as the penalty for selling wine at more than fourteen pence a
pint.

Control of disease and prevention of infection were subjects
that gave much cause for concern. In 1568, victims of the plague
had been isolated in huts 'on the hill', that is to say, Holyrood
Park. Those who were recovering had begun to make their way
back into the town and there was the fear that some might be
returning too soon. So bakers, brewers, butchers and other traders
in food were forbidden to have any direct dealings with such people
for forty days after their return and any money received from them
must be carried 'in a vessel' and 'scalded that it may be purified
from all contagiousness'.

Over the years much good work was paid for by money collected
at the Water Gate customs point. It was used for poor relief and
for the building of a burgh school and for many other civic purposes. But with the opening up of Regent Road along the side of
Calton Hill in the early nineteenth century, much less traffic
into the city came by Canongate and the customs revenue dropped
dramatically. What was left of it tended to be used increasingly
by the council for their own entertainment and, amid criticism
of this, the disappearance of the Canongate as a separate burgh
became inevitable.

For anyone seeking a quick and vivid impression of the growth and history of Edinburgh, Huntly House, opposite the Tolbooth, is the place to go. The house itself was known as the 'Speaking House' because of the Latin mottoes on its walls. It consisted, originally, of three timber houses which were rebuilt in stone in the mid-sixteenth century, but there are no grounds for the story on which its name is based that it was the home of the first Marquess of Huntly who lived from 1576 to 1636, any connection with that family being much later and very brief.

Part at least of the property was owned by the Canongate Incorporation of Hammermen, one of Canongate's eight trade incorporations, by whom it was bought in 1647. The room in which they held their meetings and the 'lockit book' (with two different keys, requiring two office-bearers both to be present before it could be opened) in which their important records were entered can still be seen inside. In the mid-eighteenth century the Dowager Duchess of Gordon rented several rooms from the Hammermen and that accommodation passed, later, to her son. In 1924, when the building like so many others in the Royal Mile was in a badly dilapidated state, it was bought by Edinburgh Corporation and most effectively restored for its present use. In it, you can not only see many relics of old Edinburgh but, given a little sensitivity, you can also acquire as you walk around its rooms, something of the 'feel' of life in a town mansion of two or three centuries ago.

A museum, however, is to be visited not written about, so let us go on, now, to look at its neighbour, Acheson House. Built by Sir Archibald Acheson in 1633 it, too, must once have been a fine mansion. Like so many other houses, it fell on evil days and when it was bought by the Marquess of Bute in 1935 it was occupied by fourteen different families and the haphazard alterations to make this change of use possible had played havoc with the fabric. On his behalf, it was skilfully restored and it is now occupied by the Scottish Craft Centre where the work of Scottish experts in many kinds of craftsmanship can be admired.

Among detailed notes left by the Clerk of Works who was in charge of restoring Acheson House he recalls that, in the years before the reconstruction was begun, 'a visitor walking down the Canongate would be accosted by children, usually girls, who offered their services as guides and told strange tales. "Come and

see the hoose where Lady Jane Grey stayed" and the visitor would
be led to Acheson House; and at the landing of the stone staircase
a curved handrail would be described as John Knox's pulpit. These
legends were repeated so often that, in certain cases, they were
accepted.'

Until I read these notes, I had forgotten the urchins – boys and
girls, usually barefooted and usually asking a penny for their
pains – whom I now remember as a feature of a walk down the
Royal Mile in those days and who had an unerring nose for any
party that included a stranger to the city. While one welcomes the
disappearance of the ragged clothes and bare feet of these self-
appointed conductors their absence from the scene is, on the
whole, to be regretted. What if Lady Jane Grey lived a century
before Acheson House was built and the banister rail never once
shook to the thundering of Knox's sermons or ever saw the inside
of a church? There was a spontaneity about those youngsters
which added interest and amusement to the scene; and I am sure
that the well-briefed corps of voluntary guides who nowadays
take parties down the Royal Mile every summer will forgive me
if I recall, with some nostalgia, the eager inaccuracies of their
juvenile predecessors.

The Clerk of Work's notes also explain a curious feature to be
seen by any passer-by on the outside walls of Acheson House. He
says: 'High up . . . may be seen oyster-shells which have been
placed on the face of the wall probably when pointing was in
progress. . . . In some cases they have been used as pinnings to
steady the stones. . . . There is said to be an old belief that white
shells kept away the witches.' Whatever the reason for their
presence so prominently on these walls there could have been
no difficulty in obtaining supplies of them for in Edinburgh, for
centuries, oysters dredged from the town's own beds in the Firth
of Forth off Newhaven were supplied in their thousands in the
taverns and oyster-cellars that abounded. Now, when the sites
of old buildings in the Royal Mile are being excavated, nothing
turns up with greater regularity than quantities of the oyster-shells
which were discarded from those long-forgotten feasts.

Down Little Lochend Close, on the north side of Canongate,
is Panmure House, a typical Scottish mansion, L-shaped and with
crow-stepped gables, which once stood in its own spacious court-

yard and enjoyed, as it still does, a view of the green slopes of
Calton Hill. Built in the seventeenth century, it had a succession
of noble owner-occupiers from the fourth Earl of Panmure in
1696 until the ninth Earl of Dalhousie, friend of Sir Walter Scott,
in the early nineteenth century. By far its most illustrious occupant
however, was a tenant of the Dalhousies, Adam Smith, who lived
there from 1778 until his death in 1790. When he came to Panmure
House with his aged mother and his cousin Margaret Douglas, as
housekeeper, the author of *The Wealth of Nations* was already famous.
There he was visited, not only by every Scotsman of note but by
statesmen from London as well, Edmund Burke among them.

The Rev. Alexander Carlyle (whose gossipy autobiography
provides all kinds of titbits of information about the people he
knew) says that Adam Smith 'had the most unbounded benevo-
lence'; but although second only to David Hume in learning and
ingenuity he was far inferior to him in conversational talents. It
seems that, in company, Adam Smith was apt to drift off into his
own thoughts, 'moving his lips and talking to himself and smiling
in the midst of large companies'. When brought back from these
reveries to the subject of general conversation, 'he immediately
began a harangue and never stopped till he told you all he knew
about it, with the utmost philosophical ingenuity'.

Like many of Dr Carlyle's stories, that was probably something
of a caricature, for Adam Smith's dinner parties where both food
and conversation were of the highest standard were greatly enjoyed and he was much loved by all his friends. They would have
been unlikely to put up with such absent-minded behaviour and
the subsequent lectures if these had been more than occasional
and rather endearing lapses.

The later history of Panmure House follows what must now be
a familiar pattern. It became part of an iron-founder's premises,
it lay vacant, it fell into decay. Then, in 1957, Mr Roy Thomson
(now Lord Thomson), owner of the *Scotsman* newspaper, generously
restored the building to be the meeting-place of the Canongate
Boys' Club who used it until 1973. Quite recently it has entered
upon a new phase of usefulness in a more official capacity as a
social training-centre for young people.

A little way below Panmure Close at what is now No. 81 Canongate, there was a famous tenement known as Golfer's Land. The

building, unhappily, has disappeared but on its site the legend is there for all to read – how John Patersone, Shoemaker and Canongate Bailie, played golf one day on Leith Links with James VII (then Duke of York) against two English golfers; how his royal partner and he won the match and how, from the proceeds, he built the great five-storey and attic tenement that stood there until recently. The event was commemorated in Latin verse by Dr Archibald Pitcairne, an eminent seventeenth-century physician with a penchant for writing topical rhymes and, in the courtyard behind the modern block of flats on the site, the verse is still there to be read, as is the anagram on the name John Patersone – 'I hate no person' which was also a feature of the old building.

Not far off, on the opposite side of the Canongate, is yet another old mansion which has had many vicissitudes and which once having been the abode of wealth and splendour is now also making a valuable contribution to present-day social needs. Queensberry House was built in the late seventeenth century and even before it was finished ran into trouble when the masons of Canongate objected to masons from outside the burgh being employed on the work. The house took its name from the first Duke of Queensberry who lived there from 1686 until 1695; and it continued until the beginning of the nineteenth century to be the home of noble families except for a short period at the time of the '45 rebellion when it was used as a hospital for wounded Jacobite officers.

An unlikely resident, for a time, in Queensberry House was John Gay, poet and author of *The Beggar's Opera*. When production of *Polly*, his sequel to it, was prohibited in 1729, Gay's patroness, the Duchess of Queensberry (wife of Charles, the third Duke) incurred the displeasure of the establishment of the day by taking him into the household as her private secretary. As such, his duties seem to have left him with plenty of time to linger and gossip in the library and shop of his fellow-poet, Allan Ramsay, in the luckenbooths and for carousing at 'Jenny Ha's', a tavern kept by a hospitable old dame called Janet Hall, nearly opposite Queensberry House whose memory is preserved by the name of a modern public house on almost the same site.

In 1802, Queensberry House was bought by an East Lothian brewer. He sold most of its lavish interior fittings to the Earl of Wemyss who used them in the magnificent new mansion he was building for himself at Gosford, on Aberlady Bay, in East Lothian. The house itself and its grounds were then sold to the Board of Ordnance for use as a barracks. The Board, evidently believing that a barracks should look like a barracks, removed what seem to have been the mansion's most pleasing features: 'a French roof, with storm windows in the style of the palace of Versailles and chimney-stalks sufficiently ornamented to add to the general effect of the building'. Then, having added a fifth storey to the four already there, which upset the proportions and made the whole building look as tall and ungainly as possible, they finished it off with the present plain and unattractive roof. So the building, although used as a barracks for only about 30 years of its long life, was condemned to look like one for the rest of its existence. In 1834 it became the 'House of Refuge for the Homeless' administered under voluntary auspices and, as such, for more than a century it made essential but austere provision for the poor and needy. Now, still under voluntary management but in close co-operation with the official services, it provides hospital accommodation for more than 250 old people in wards that are bright and cheerful in sharp contrast to the building's outward appearance.

At Queensberry House we are nearing the foot of the Canongate and the site of the Girth Cross. Nearby, White Horse Close, with its cluster of houses round a courtyard, has been restored to form one of the most attractive features of the Canongate. The building at the north end of the court, with the date 1623 on it, was once an inn and behind it, in Calton Road, its stables still form useful garage accommodation. The inn had its brief day of fame as head-quarters of the Jacobites during their occupation of the city in 1745; but it is mainly remembered as having been the starting point of the Edinburgh–London coaches, in the days when a journey to London really was a journey. The coaches left from Calton Road, behind the inn, and a handbill advertising their departure may conveniently close this chapter. Beneath a picture of a coach and four galloping horses it says:

February 1754: All that are desirous to pass from Edinburgh to London or any other place on their road, let them repair to the White Horse Cellar in Edinburgh at which place they may be received in a Stage Coach every Monday and Friday which performs the whole journey in eight days (if God permits) and sets forth at five in the morning.

9 Holyrood sanctuary

*I*f you go beyond the site of the Girth Cross at the foot of Canongate you will have arrived within the abbey sanctuary, a fact which will be confirmed when, having taken a few steps further, you reach the beginning of Abbey Strand and find three brass letters – SSS (for sanctuary) – set in the roadway. A century ago, your arrival there might have saved you from being cast into prison, for until the abolition of imprisonment for debt in 1880, many a man came breathless to this point in the Royal Mile, with creditors hard upon his heels, to seek sanctuary in the precincts of the abbey and the palace.

The abbey was founded by David I in 1128. According to legend he founded it in thanksgiving for his escape while hunting one day in what is now Holyrood Park near the site of the abbey. An enraged stag which had unhorsed and wounded the King suddenly fled when he grasped a crucifix which had miraculously appeared between its antlers. The fact that the same story had been told about St Eustache, patron saint of hunters in the second century, and about St Hubert in the forest of the Ardennes in the eighth century did not prevent the abbots of Holyrood giving credence to the story by adopting a stag with a cross on its head as a feature of their seals; nor the burgh and, in due course, the Kirk of the Canongate from using the antlers and cross as their official emblems.

Enough remains of the ruined abbey to suggest that it was once a building of great beauty. Indeed, the Royal Commission on the Ancient Monuments of Scotland go so far as to say of it: 'The façade although mutilated, ruinous and encroached upon by an adjoining wing of the Palace, remains one of the finest early medieval compositions in Britain. Its design is balanced yet rhythmic, while its architectural detail . . . is refined and restrained throughout.'

Only one or two tiny fragments of the early twelfth-century building remain, but the north wall of the roofless nave belongs to the latter part of that century and provides us, almost, with a direct link between ourselves and the abbey's founder who died in 1153. The massive pillars in the nave were built in the early thirteenth century. The great window in the eastern wall, which is such a striking feature as you enter the nave, is seventeenth-century work.

The palace is, of course, later than most of the abbey. The north-west tower, close beside the abbey, was built by James IV around 1500 – about the same time as the crown of St Giles was being built. Much of the rest of the palace including the matching tower at the south-west corner was built for Charles II in the 1670s, by Robert Mylne, King's Master Mason.

The influence of Charles II is seen also in the great picture gallery in which there are portraits of 111 Scottish sovereigns, starting with the more or less mythical Fergus (330 B.C.). They were all painted by a Dutch artist, Jacob de Wet, who had been engaged by Charles to produce portraits of all his royal ancestors. As the palace guides tell the parties they conduct through the long gallery, 'any resemblance of any of these portraits to any of the King's ancestors is purely coincidental'; but, with the passage of time, the portraits long ago acquired a historical interest in their own right.

In the palace, too, can be seen the bedrooms of Mary, Queen of Scots, and Lord Darnley and the room in which Mary's secretary, David Riccio, was murdered before her eyes in 1566. A brass plate marks approximately the place where Riccio's body afterwards lay bleeding from more than fifty stab wounds. When, as a school-boy, I was taken there with others of my class there was no brass plate. Instead, we looked with awe upon the 'actual bloodstains' which, in those days, were annually re-painted to make good the

G

ravages of time and tourism. When one considers that the floor on which the 'bloodstains' appeared was presumably not the floor of 1566 at all, but a replacement of a later date, the brass plate seems to be a more honest, if less emotive, pointer to the spot.

This chapter, however, is not about the palace and its many famous historical associations; it is about a different aspect of Holyrood history not so fully dealt with in the guide-books – the story of the abbey sanctuary.

Historians find much to argue about on the question whether the right of sanctuary at Holyrood belonged primarily to the abbey in the exercise of the church's right to protect criminals or to the palace with its privilege of granting sanctuary in matters of civil law and especially for debtors. These distinctions need not trouble us, since it was as a sanctuary for debtors that Holyrood was famous. In that capacity, for at least 350 years, it sheltered many hundreds of ordinary men and women, as well as a few who were famous and one who was an exiled King of France.

As you walk in the Abbey Strand towards the west gate of the palace, the blank wall on your right, bearing traces of a fine gothic gate house destroyed in 1755, conceals behind it the abbey court house presided over, still, by the Bailie of Holyrood. The holder of that office has now only a few ceremonial duties to perform, but many of his predecessors were busy men. The sanctuary over which they presided sometimes had well over a hundred debtors residing in it, whose rights the Bailie had to safeguard and whose misdemeanours he had to visit with appropriate punishment.

The earliest record of a debtor seeking the protection of the sanctuary of Holyrood was in 1531 but the system developed its formal pattern after Charles I in 1646 appointed James, first Duke of Hamilton, and his heirs to be hereditary Keepers of the Palace, a position still held by the present Duke. Clearly, the dukes themselves could not look after all the details of the sanctuary business and so arose the practice of their appointing a Bailie to carry out that function for them. In a court case in 1799 Henry Erskine, with biting sarcasm and less than his usual good humour, did his best to denigrate the office of Bailie, suggesting that the holder, though dignified with that title 'and vested with something resembling a jurisdiction, can be considered as nothing else than a mere under-keeper or gardener of the Palace'. On that occasion, no one seems to have paid much attention to Henry Erskine and the office continued to be regarded as one of importance and dignity.

In the days when the privilege of sanctuary was sought, the surroundings of the palace and abbey were very different from those of today. Much of the area of the present courtyard and palace garden was occupied by houses, many of which would resemble the seventeenth-century houses still to be seen in Abbey Strand. One of these is now in use as a tea-room and another as a small picture gallery of ancient monuments maintained by the Department of the Environment. The occupiers of the houses around the palace, and of those in the Canongate east of the Girth Cross, made a business of taking as lodgers debtors seeking sanctuary. Small taverns abounded in the area and the 'abbey lairds', as the sanctuary-seekers were jocularly called, spent much of their time in the taverns with their friends for it seems that a good many of them, though unable to meet their just and lawful debts outside the sanctuary, were nevertheless able to live fairly comfortably and congenially within it.

Nor were they 'cabin'd, cribb'd, confin'd' while in sanctuary for its area extended over the whole of what is now Holyrood Park as far as Duddingston Loch and the edge of Duddingston village. Any abbey laird in need of exercise could, if he wished, climb Arthur's Seat before breakfast or enjoy a four-mile stroll round the perimeter of the park without fear of molestation – clearly a pleasanter existence than would await him in a debtor's prison.

The procedure, if you wished to take advantage of this privilege, was to make your way to Holyrood, find lodgings there, and then, within twenty-four hours, have yourself 'booked' in the court book held by the Bailie. This was most important. Anyone failing to have his name entered within the specified time was liable to be forcibly removed from sanctuary by his creditors or officers acting on their behalf. There were also a few other limitations. No one might seek sanctuary with fraudulent intent or while concealing large sums of money. The Bailie could take action against such persons and he could imprison in the abbey court house any of the abbey lairds who incurred serious debts while within the sanctuary. He was also supposed to watch for and frustrate any attempts to fly the country though it is difficult to understand how he could prevent a debtor from walking across the park to Duddingston

and quietly making off from there. Probably the greatest safeguard against that was the relative comfort and friendly social
life combined with security that the sanctuary provided.

A further privilege was available to the abbey lairds. In the period
between midnight on Saturday and midnight on Sunday they
could leave the sanctuary and go where they pleased with impu-
nity. One worthy minister of the gospel, burdened with debt but
determined to continue to serve his parishioners, is said to have
left Holyrood regularly in the early hours of Sunday morning and
to have walked twenty miles to his parish in the country. Then,
having conducted the service in his parish church he would walk
the twenty miles back again before midnight. Such devotion to
their spiritual needs, one hopes, would inspire his parishioners to
subscribe a sufficient sum to pay their minister's debts and set him
free.

For dwellers in the Canongate near the Girth Cross a weekly
source of interest – it would be unkind to call it entertainment –
was provided by the procession of returning lairds late on Sunday
night, sometimes hotly pursued by creditors hoping they would
not reach the boundary line before the clock struck twelve. A
story is told of one gentleman, arriving just too late, who tripped
and fell as he crossed the line. He was dragged back by the heels
and led away to face imprisonment. In the subsequent court case,
however, it was held that as he had lain in the roadway his head and
shoulders had been across the line and, 'the head being the principal part of a man', he was to be regarded as having been within
the sanctuary before he was seized and must therefore be allowed
to return there.

There was also the case in 1709 of one Patrick Haliburton who
was suspected of having enough money to pay his debts but who
chose to live within the sanctuary. One Sunday, a report of his
case states:

he came up to the house of his creditor Mr Stewart and having supped with
him and thereafter stayed till it was past 12 o'clock at night; he is seized upon
by a messenger and put in prison; whereupon he gives in a complaint that
having come to Edinburgh to treat with Mr Stewart . . . he [Stewart] did en-
snare him by pretending much kindness and inviting him to supper and
protracting the time in overtures and terms of accommodation until the
Town Clock struck 12 at night and then had a messenger prepared to take him
to prison by a most illegal and treacherous practice. . . .

The court continued the case to allow proof to be brought as to whether Mr Haliburton had, indeed, been fraudulently detained or whether he had willingly accepted the hospitality lavished upon him; but I have found no report of what finally happened. Perhaps the unfortunate gentleman found the burden of proof too heavy and resigned himself to his fate; or perhaps, as suspected, he had funds available and decided to pay up.

There was undoubtedly a spirit of camaraderie among the residents in sanctuary. In 1724 a Mrs Dilks was enticed by a messenger from her creditor to a meeting in a tavern which although mainly within the sanctuary area could be reached only through a doorway just outside it. As she stepped across the line she was seized triumphantly by the messenger. He, however, had reckoned without Mrs Dilks's fellow-debtors. A bevy of her women friends, having followed close behind her, set upon the messenger, forcibly removed her from his grasp and escorted her back to the safety of the sanctuary.

The court books of the abbey are extant from 1686 until the need for sanctuary disappeared in 1880 with the abolition of imprisonment for debt. They show the names of all who sought refuge there and of those with whom they stayed, none of whom, by the way, was permitted to receive such lodgers without first obtaining the Bailie's 'warrant in write'. In one random four-year period towards the end of the eighteenth century I found nearly 260 abbey lairds recorded as staying, for varying lengths of time, in the houses of about thirty residents. Most of these lodging keepers took only one or two lodgers but James Walker, 'Gardner and Vintner', had ninety such guests during the period, a Mrs Baillie had twenty-five and James Ganty, 'Depute Porter at the Palace', supplemented his wages by taking in about twenty different people.

The abbey lairds were a varied company. James Walker's guests seem mainly to have been country folk. They included several drovers and cattle-dealers, a grazier from Argyllshire, and two or three small farmers. Mrs Baillie had as tenants at least two ministers, the manager of a glassworks in Dundee and a 'Grocer in the New City of Edinburgh'; while James Ganty provided lodging for a surgeon, a 'student of physic', a teacher of English and a merchant and shipmaster, among others.

William Chambers, whose visits to the Tolbooth prison were mentioned in an earlier chapter, gives an interesting account of visits which he made to the sanctuary in the early nineteenth century. Writing of the days when he was apprenticed to a bookseller who also lent books and sold lottery tickets he says: 'Inmates of the Sanctuary of Holyrood were numbered among the steady customers of the lottery' from which, no doubt, they hoped to see a way out of their financial troubles. He goes on:

The Sanctuary, which embraced a cluster of decayed buildings in front and on both sides of Holyrood Palace was, at that time, seldom without distinguished characters from England – some of them gaunt, oldish gentlemen, seemingly broken-down men of fashion, wearing big gold spectacles, who now drew out existence here in defiance of creditors. To this august class of persons, who stood in need of supplies of books from the circulating library, I paid frequent visits; and, conscious perhaps that they gave me some extra trouble, they were so considerate as to present me with an occasional sixpence which I could not politely refuse.

Turning over the pages of the Bailie's book, one comes to the following entries:

> 1833 – Nov. 27   Thomas De Quincey – lodged at Brotherston's.
> 1836 – Nov. 24   Thomas De Quincey – lodged at Mrs Millar's.

In fact, Thomas de Quincey, author of *Confessions of an English Opium Eater*, who lived in and near Edinburgh from 1820 until his death in 1859, was in and out of the sanctuary at Holyrood at different times between 1833 and 1840 and while there he wrote many essays for *Tait's Magazine*, including his recollections of the Lakeland poets. Strangely, it is doubtful whether he ever need have sought the protection of sanctuary at all. He was completely helpless where money was concerned and when creditors were dunning him for payment he seems not to have noticed that others, including publishers, owed him sums from which his debts could have been met. With bills unpaid, he would cheerfully give his last coin to a passing beggar; and, after his death, many bank-notes were found among his papers and tucked away between the pages of his books!

On Sundays, de Quincey would go out to visit friends in Edinburgh, for there were many houses where the conversational brilliance of this quiet little wisp of a man was greatly appreciated. His brilliance, however, tended to flower late in the evening and

so on these excursions out of sanctuary he often missed the midnight curfew. When that happened he usually stayed with his
hosts until the following Sunday – or, sometimes, until several
Sundays later, before returning to his lodgings at Holyrood.

The strangest episodes in the history of the sanctuary, adding
what must have been a lively and colourful interest to life there,
occurred in 1796, when Charles-Philippe, the Comte d'Artois,
brother of the deposed Louis XVIII of France came to Holyrood;
and again, in 1830, when Charles-Philippe after a brief reign as
Charles X of France abdicated and returned once more to Holyrood.
His first arrival there resulted from the massive debts he had
incurred in making supplies available to the émigré army after
the French revolution. When the frigate *Jason* brought him and
his suite to Portsmouth in December 1795 he was unable to land
for fear of his creditors. So orders were given by the Home Secretary
that the palace of Holyroodhouse, where he could have the benefit
of sanctuary, should be made ready to receive him, but 'in a
manner least productive of expense'.

The Count – known as 'Monsieur' during his sojourns at
Holyrood – arrived on the *Jason* at Leith on 6 January 1796, to salutes
of twenty-one guns from Leith battery and from the Castle. He
had declined a military escort but the streets between Leith and
Holyrood were lined by cheering crowds as his small procession
passed, for his arrival, according to the *Scots Magazine* of the time,
'caused a real thrill in the hearts of the Tories of Edinburgh'. Sir
Walter Scott, ever a devotee of the regal and the aristocratic, was
delighted when he 'saw Monsieur come to our old abbey'.

The apartments occupied by Monsieur and the train of dukes,
duchesses, counts and countesses who accompanied him were
mainly in the south wing of the palace, including the present
throne room. Other members of his suite along with footmen and
servants found accommodation nearby. Although the British
government made him an allowance of £6000 a year he had many
expenses to meet and remained deeply in debt. So, like any other
debtor at Holyrood, he could leave the sanctuary only on Sundays
which he did with great regularity, paying many visits in the
neighbourhoood of Edinburgh 'for the good and excellent people
of Scotland looked upon a visit from him as an honour and a
great festival'. He kept one carriage only, for his own use on

Sundays, and lent it during the week to other members of his party who were free to move about at any time.

Among those who came with him to Holyrood, or joined him there soon afterwards, were his son Louis, Duke of Angoulême, then twenty-one years old and Louis's eighteen-year-old Duchess who was a daughter of Louis XVI and Marie Antoinette. Charles's younger son Charles, Duke of Berri, also joined the party and was remembered by the local people as 'an ugly and cheerful young prince . . . a stout country-looking, curly-headed, stirring boy'. Monsieur's wife was not of the company – they had parted long before; but in a cottage at the entrance to Croft-an-Righ (a narrow lane just east of the palace) was installed the Countess of Polastron, Monsieur's 'companion and dear friend' with her eleven-year-old son, of whom the people of Edinburgh firmly believed Monsieur to be the father.

A curious side-light on the temporary influence, locally, of the residence of this French colony at Holyrood is given in the *Anecdotes and Egotisms* of Henry Mackenzie, written about 1825. Mackenzie, famous as author of the sentimental novel *The Man of Feeling*, had at one time lived in St John Street, off the Canongate. Among his *Anecdotes* he has the following paragraph, headed 'Bread for Monsieur':

The bread of Edinburgh was formerly much esteemed. Now, it has miserably fallen off. . . . When 'Monsieur' and his suite were in Edinburgh they employed for their baker a man living close by Holyrood House of the name of Greig, to whom Madame Polastron, the *chère amie* of Monsieur, a very amiable woman, taught the art of baking with leaven a flat-shaped loaf which was called after her a Polastron loaf and was the best I ever ate; but after the French left Edinburgh he lost the art which this lady had taught him and made as bad bread and as sour as all the rest of his trade.

As time went on, Monsieur's creditors seem to have become less pressing and he was able to move about more freely, going occasionally as far as London. In 1802, Napoleon (then First Consul of France) became a trifle worried about Monsieur's popularity and received a report from an agent that 'The comte d'Artois is lodged royally in the Palace, compliments are paid to him by the troops and his sojourn there is the pride of the Scottish Nobility. When he goes to the play, applause breaks out and, in the boxes, everyone rises out of respect.' Not everyone was pleased, however.

Sedan Chair Men. *A drawing by John Kay. Sedan chairs were much used in Edinburgh from the early seventeenth century until the 1850s.*

The Mound Coach. *A cartoon, drawn by John Kay, the humour of which Robert Burns may have enjoyed. For explanation, see Chapter 11.*

The Lawnmarket. *A water-colour by James Skene, dated 1822. On the right is the West Bow, descending steeply towards the Grassmarket. The building on the corner, with projecting upper storeys, was removed in 1877.*

Two New Town Architects – *James Gillespie Graham (1777–1855) on the left, the architect of Moray Place and neighbouring streets, meets Thomas Hamilton (1784–1858), designer of the Royal High School. A drawing from 'Modern Athenians – 1837 to 1847' by Benjamin Crombie.*

Moray Place *when it was new, drawn by Thomas H. Shepherd and published in 1829 in the collection of his drawings entitled 'Modern Athens'.*

The Theatre Royal, *Shakespeare Square. The theatre was opened in 1769. The portico and the three statues – Shakespeare, flanked by Comedy and Tragedy – were added 20 years later. The building was demolished in 1859 to make way for the General Post Office. Drawing by Thomas H. Shepherd, 1829.*

La. RAN. Eternal providence ! What is thy name ?
My name is NORVAL : and my name he bears.

DOUGLAS

Mrs Sarah Siddons *as she appeared in Home's 'Douglas' on her first visit to Edinburgh in 1784. A contemporary drawing by John Kay.*

At a ball which Monsieur attended in the Assembly Rooms in George Street there were some who complained that, from his behaviour, anyone might think he was at home and they were the émigrés! Lord Buchan (elder brother of Henry Erskine) is said to have commented: 'Who is that coming? The King of Shoemakers?' – a reference, no doubt, to the cordiners' annual pageantry.

Monsieur left Holyrood in 1803; but he was back, briefly, in 1810 when it was reported that 'a dark shadow had fallen on his life' through the death of the Countess of Polastron. Then, for twenty years or so, his destiny took him elsewhere; in the 1820s it took him to his country's throne when he became, for a few years, Charles X of France. His ideas, however, seem to have smacked too much of the old pre-Revolution regime and in 1830 he was forced to abdicate. Once more in debt he again sought and was granted asylum at Holyrood.

This time as the exiled King and his party stepped ashore at Leith in October 1830, he must have been delighted with his reception from a Newhaven 'fishwife' who, for many years, had supplied fish to houses in the Holyrood area. Rushing forward as he was about to step into his carriage, she grabbed his hand and exclaimed: 'My name's Kirsty Ramsay, Sir. I'm glad to see you again among decent folk. Mony a guid fish I have gi'en ye, Sir, and mony a guid shillin' I got for it, thirty years sin-syne.'

'Sin-syne', it may be explained, is good old Scots for 'since' or 'ago' or 'long ago', but, more than that, it carries with it a trace of longing for times that have passed and will not come again. Certainly, times had changed and Kirsty's warmth of greeting did not truly reflect the general feeling with which, this time, Monsieur's visit was received. Now, the spirit of liberalism and reform was in the air and there was less open enthusiasm for the arrival of this group of representatives of France's old aristocratic order. Sir Walter Scott, however, came to the rescue with a letter to the press on the day of the ex-King's arrival urging everyone to give him a warm welcome. That seems to have broken the ice to some extent and Charles later expressed his gratitude to Sir Walter.

Charles, this time, had a large suite in attendance, nearly a hundred in all, many of whom lodged in the Canongate. But, by now, he was seventy-three years of age and was doubtless content to live more quietly than during his previous stay. One of his favourite recreations was shooting and it is said that when he went out after snipe in Hunter's Bog, on the slopes of Arthur's Seat, the Canongate urchins would run after him, calling 'Frenchy, Frenchy, dinna shoot the spruggies' – 'spruggies' being 'sparrows' or just any small birds. Other more ambitious shooting expeditions were made to Fordel in Fife, to the Earl of Wemyss's estate at Gosford in East Lothian and to Lord Rosebery's Dalmeny estate, between Cramond and Queensferry where, on one notable day, the ex-King bagged thirty-six pheasants, besides hares and partridges.

Whatever the general feeling, the elderly Monsieur soon endeared himself to the people of the Canongate for he was generous to their poor, as well as to the debtors in Holyrood. He gave donations to the burgh poor-house, and to other charities; and he encouraged his personal medical attendant to practise in the neighbourhood making him an allowance from which to provide medicines for poor patients.

In August 1832, amid massive rejoicings, the Reform Act was passed and a procession of trades representatives 15000 strong marched through the city with banners flying. This overwhelming enthusiasm for what was seen as the dawn of a new era of equality, along with other circumstances, made it advisable for Monsieur to make preparations to leave. He waited for some time in the hope that the government would send a yacht to take him to the continent but none came and he had to make his own arrangements to charter a steam-packet to carry him from Newhaven to Hamburg.

Among those who most regretted the impending departure of the French party from Holyrood were the tradespeople of Canongate who had done well out of supplying their needs. Three days before the company departed, the local tradesmen entertained members of Monsieur's household to a dinner in 'Millar's Tavern' near the abbey. The Lord Provost of Edinburgh, John Learmonth, published a farewell message in glowing language, 'To his most Christian Majesty, Charles the Tenth' but, given the climate of those days, he made a mistake for which he was severely taken to task by the *Scotsman*. In his letter, the Lord Provost expressed the hope that 'brighter days would dawn for the French Royal Family' adding that this was 'the universal feeling of the inhabitants of Edinburgh . . . shared by every individual in this metropolis'. To this the *Scotsman* tartly retorted that, while the Lord Provost was entitled to express any sentiments he chose on his own behalf, he was not entitled to ascribe these sentiments to the people of Edinburgh generally 'who wish to see France free and happy and know that of all Revolutions a Restoration is generally the most pernicious to the freedom and happiness of the people'. The editorial concluded: 'We concur in the compliments paid to the exiles for their unostentatious charity and their quiet unobtrusive manners, but such topics as have been alluded to should not have been introduced into an address purporting to come from the inhabitants of Edinburgh.'

Despite that rather sour note, the *Scotsman* described with enthusiasm the stirring send-off given to the royal party as they embarked on 18 September 1832 from the 'Chain Pier' which, in those days, thrust its 500-foot length seawards at Trinity, a quarter of a mile or so westward of the harbour at Newhaven:

A fine blue sea – a magnificent steam-boat tastefully decorated – splendid banners and flags flying on shore – innumerable well-dressed ladies and gentlemen, with white silk bouquets on their breasts – and the healthy, intrepid sailors of Newhaven, clad in their best true blue and accompanied by their union flags, occupied the entrance to the pier while the French nobles and gentlemen were seen arriving at short intervals in detached parties.

What delighted us most was to see first-rate personages of opposite sentiments in politics, laying aside all political animosity and vying with each other in showing every mark of respect to Charles X and his family. . . . [Soon the ship] clothed in broad canvas, with streamers waving in the wind, rapidly moved towards the east with her distinguished passengers and was very soon out of sight.

Two days later the government steam packet *Lightning* arrived at Leith to take the French party abroad. 'It was too late,' was the wry comment of the author of *The exiled Bourbons in Scotland*, 'and it was probably meant to be so.'

So ended the French connection with the sanctuary of Holyrood. Life for the abbey lairds must have seemed dull and drab for a long time afterwards. Finally, almost fifty years later, came the last entry in the Bailie's court book: '1880 – 9th September – David Gilbert Bain, Solicitor, Edinburgh.' He was the last man to seek sanctuary before the need for doing so disappeared. Thus a long chapter in the history of Holyrood was closed for good.

Yet it was not quite closed. A Bailie of Holyrood is still appointed and, in the present court house beside Abbey Strand, he presides over periodical meetings of his court which are now less judicial occasions, and over meetings of the High Constables of Holyrood, a body of thirty trusty citizens who freely give their services as Guard of Honour at Holyroodhouse. When the Queen is in residence, there, and on other state occasions, they are in attendance resplendent in their uniform – royal-blue trousers, royal-blue tail-coat and cockaded hat – and carrying their ceremonial batons. In June of every second year they assemble with the Bailie and formally perambulate the four-mile boundary of his ancient sanctuary, pausing, in deference to time-honoured custom, to enjoy a ceremonial lunch at the Sheep Heid Inn, in Duddingston village roughly midway on their circuit of the sanctuary.

10 The first new town

'I charge you not to think of settling in London till you have first seen our New Town which exceeds anything you have seen in any part of the world.'

So wrote David Hume to a friend soon after he had moved, in May 1771, from his James Court home to an elegant flat in a newly-completed block at the south-west corner of St Andrew Square, with windows looking into St David Street. The block was demolished in 1955 and an inscription at first-floor level on the building that replaces it is now all that remains to record Hume's residence there – all, that is, except the name St David Street.

That name is said to have originated in a prank played by Nancy Orde, the charming and lively daughter of Chief Baron Orde of the Scottish Exchequer. She and Hume were great friends and it is even said that although she was in her twenties and he a bachelor of sixty, he thought seriously of proposing marriage to her. After one of her visits to him in his new house she chalked 'St David's Street' on the wall outside, as a joke – and one which upset his elderly servant, Peggy Irvine, who threatened to rub out the offending words. Hume, however, told her to leave them, on the grounds that many a better man had been made a saint before. So the inscription was left, the name stuck, and eventually, it was officially adopted.

Earlier, while his New Town house was being built, David Hume
had frequently visited St Andrew Square to see how the work
was progressing. The shortest way from James Court was by a
footpath across the ill-drained eastern end of the former Nor'
Loch. That was the route he generally used and there is a story
that, on one of these journeys, he slipped off the footpath into
the marsh. As he struggled to regain a footing on firm ground he
held out his hand to a passing fisherwoman who was on her way
to the nearby fishmarket and asked her to help him up. His burly
figure and his reputation were well known in Edinburgh, and
recognizing him as Hume the unbeliever, she expressed some doubt
as to whether it would be proper for a Christian woman like herself to help him. When Hume suggested that as a good Christian
she should help even her enemies she agreed to do so but only
if he would first say the Lord's Prayer. To her astonishment he was
able to repeat it perfectly and she duly helped him back on to the
path.

David Hume's enthusiasm for his New Town house would
certainly have delighted George Drummond whose vision of a
great new city covering the fields beyond the Nor' Loch was at
last becoming a reality.

As we saw in an earlier chapter, just two months before Drummond's death in 1766, the Town Council had selected the winning
entry in the competition for a lay-out plan for the great new city.
The winner was James Craig, a young architect of twenty-three
and, until then, almost unknown. There had been several entries
in the competition and it would have been interesting to be able
to compare the other plans with Craig's but, unfortunately, they
were not preserved and we do not even know the names of his
fellow competitors.

The area for which the plans were to provide a scheme was that
now covered by Princes Street, George Street with its two great
terminal squares and Queen Street, the area now known as 'the
first New Town'. Admirable though that first New Town is, its
lay-out plan (and that is all that James Craig was concerned with)
does not show any great originality of thought. Indeed, given the
contours of the ground, it is difficult to see how any very different
plan could have been devised except by some startling and exceptional use of the varying ground levels.

Far from being original, Craig's plan can be seen as being no more than a replica of the old town lay-out. Its principal street, George Street, strides along its ridge of rising ground as the High Street and Canongate stride along the Royal Mile ridge and has Charlotte Square and St Andrew Square at its ends as the Royal Mile has the Castle and Holyrood. To the south, Princes Street reproduces the Grassmarket–Cowgate–South Back of Canongate line while, to the north, Queen Street represents the North Back of Canongate extended westwards. Where James Craig scored was in the majestic breadth of George Street and in his conception of Princes Street and Queen Street as one-sided thoroughfares providing inspiring views for those who lived or walked in them.

Craig's plan envisaged the valley of the Nor' Loch as an open space with an ornamental canal where the loch had been, the water-supply for which would have been provided from the Water of Leith somewhere near Roseburn. So keen was James Craig on this idea that he inscribed on his plan the following lines from a poem by James Thomson, poet of *The Seasons*, who was Craig's uncle:

> *August, around, what public works I see!*
> *Lo, stately streets! lo, squares that court the breeze!*
> *See long canals and deepened rivers join*
> *Each part with each, and with the circling main,*
> *The whole entwined isle.*

Though a tawdry street where Waverley Station is now was named Canal Street, the ornamental canal never materialized. Nor, more fortunately, did the commercial canal which a later generation planned to build through the valley, linking the Union Canal at Fountainbridge by a stairway of locks with the sea at Leith. Instead, we have East and West Princes Street Gardens – and the railway.

The Town Council were so pleased with Craig that, in June 1767, they presented him with a 'gold medal, with the freedom of the City in a silver box as a reward of his merit for having designed the best plan of the new town'. Later, they were less pleased with him when they found that he had sent a copy of his plan to George III with a dedication inscribed on it which made no reference whatever to the Lord Provost, the magistrates or the Town Council

– or indeed to anyone concerned with the project except James
Craig himself. This is what it said:

To His Sacred Majesty George III the Munificent patron of every Polite and
Liberal Art. This plan of the New Streets and Squares intended for His ancient
Capital of North Britain; one of the happy Consequences of the Peace, Security
and Liberty his People enjoy under his mild and auspicious Government, Is
with the utmost Humility Inscribed by His Majesty's Most devoted Servant
and Subject, James Craig.

No wonder the Town Council were displeased. After all they
had done in furtherance of their great development scheme it
was galling, to say the least, to have the whole credit taken by this
young architect who had only devised and drawn the plan!

In the plan as originally drawn and submitted to the King,
Princes Street appeared as 'St Giles Street' but it was reported to
the Town Council that His Majesty disliked that name because it
brought to mind the St Giles district of London which was 'always
infamous for its low and disorderly inhabitants'. He had therefore
been 'graciously pleased to desire that it should be called Princes'
Street'; and so it was.

The first house built in the new town is believed to have been
in Thistle Court, at the eastern end of Thistle Street, the narrow
street lying between George Street and Queen Street, east of
Frederick Street. Thistle Street (with its western extensions, Hill
Street and Young Street) and also Rose Street, lying between
George Street and Princes Street, were described by Craig as being
'for shopkeepers and others'. They were, in fact, to be the service
streets containing shops and modest houses from which the
provisions and also the servants (other than those living in) required by the residents in the more important streets could be
supplied. Off these minor streets there were, and still are, a series
of mews lanes which provided access to stables and coach-houses.
Until well beyond the middle of the nineteenth century several
of these lanes also contained byres for cows kept by some of the
'cowfeeders' and dairymen who provided New Town households
with milk.

The first house in Princes Street was not built until 1769. Partly,
this delay was due to delay in completing the North Bridge for,
until it was built, access from the old town involved either the
muddy walk which David Hume found so hazardous, or a detour

by road round the end of the marshy ground where the loch had been.

At last, in August 1769, the bridge was ready, at least for foot traffic. Then disaster came. The *Edinburgh Evening Courant* of Saturday, 5 August 1769, reported: 'Thursday night, about 8.30, part of the side wall of the south abutment of the new bridge gave way and brought down with it part of the wall but happily all the arches are quite entire. We have reason to be afraid that some few people have suffered and had it not happened at a late hour it might have been attended with more fatal circumstances.' It was later found that five people had been killed and several others injured.

The Lord Provost lost no time in seeking to have the damage repaired. Experts were called in to examine the ruins and report how the bridge could most safely and quickly be restored. It was found that the collapse had been due partly to the insecure foundation of the south abutment which rested upon the accumulated soil and debris along the side of the old town ridge. Mainly, however, it had been caused by the builder, Robert Mylne, having overcome the problem of aligning the road level on the bridge with that of the street from which it led by the simple but hazardous process of heaping large quantities of earth on to the south end of the bridge to bring its road surface to the required height, until the weight had become greater than the masonry could support. The experts all agreed that this was the main cause of the collapse and they reported that 'the most rational step to be immediately taken is the lightening of the Bridge of the earth that is upon it and if it was our own work we would fall about it without loss of time.'

So Robert Mylne and his workmen fell about it and removed the earth as rapidly as possible. The rebuilding, however, was a long process, made longer by a series of disputes between Mylne and the Town Council about responsibility for the accident and other questions relating to his contract with the result that the bridge was not fully opened for traffic until 1772, nine years after the laying of its foundation stone.

The bridge, before its collapse, must have been provided only with some form of temporary railings, for, as the work of repair neared completion, it was decided to substitute for the solid walls that had been specified stone balusters with spaces between them.

H

Whether this was to reduce the weight or improve the appearance of the bridge is not known, but in June 1772 Robert Mylne submitted 'two sample ballisters done in the same proportions as those at Blackfriars Bridge, London' and quoted for 306 of these at £1 each. The design was accepted and the balusters were erected but not long afterwards the spaces between them had, after all, to be filled in because of complaints from pedestrians on the bridge about the unpleasant view, between the balusters, of the slaughter-yards and butchers' stalls which, in those days, occupied part of the valley below.

While the building of the bridge was progressing and while those who had acquired sites at the east end of Princes Street, in St Andrew Square and in George Street and Queen Street were getting on with their building work in accordance with the regulations laid down by the Town Council, something very strange was happening to the site on the eastern side of St Andrew Square. How it happened has never been satisfactorily explained but it resulted in a major departure from the approved scheme.

In Craig's plan, the vista along George Street towards the east was shown as being closed by a church, just as the view to the west was to be effectively terminated by St George's Church. The site for the church on the east side of St Andrew Square, however, adjoined ground belonging to Sir Laurence Dundas who was a wealthy and influential baronet. By some means or other – the records do not make clear exactly how it was done – Sir Laurence managed to acquire the site which had been intended for the church. There he built his house, with the result that when the Town Council came to build St Andrew's Church it had to be placed in a much less effective position on the north side of George Street. Fortunately, Sir Laurence's house (now the head office of the Royal Bank of Scotland) which was designed by Sir William Chambers is a magnificent mansion and its façade, though not what was intended for the site, is a real adornment to St Andrew Square. So Sir Laurence's sharp practice in obtaining the site proved to be less detrimental than it might have been.

About the same time as Sir Laurence Dundas was upsetting the plan for St Andrew Square an encroachment was beginning on the south side of Princes Street which, if it had been allowed to continue, would have changed the whole character of that street and ruined one of the finest and most valued features of the New Town, the valley between it and the old town ridge. Fortunately, the early New Town proprietors – David Hume among them – were quickly alerted to the danger and took action for which they have ever since deserved the gratitude of all who love Edinburgh, residents and visitors alike.

During the year 1771 they were astonished and distressed to find that a coach-builder and a firm of furniture manufacturers had begun to build workshops and houses on ground feued from the Town Council on the south side of Princes Street which it had been understood was to have remained as open space. At once they appealed to the Town Council to put a stop to what they saw as a first step towards the desecration of the valley which, by its width and depth and contours, added so much to the splendour of their brave New Town.

Their petition falling on deaf ears, the proprietors raised two actions in the Court of Session; first, one of interdict, with the object of calling an immediate halt to the building and, second, an action of declarator in which they sought to have it established that such building was in contravention of the terms on which they had been induced to take up their feus. The legal position by no means favoured the aggrieved proprietors. They claimed that the approved plan of development showed open ground south of Princes Street; but it was a fact that the Town Council had said only that it was not intended to build there 'at present' and had given no assurance for the future except that building, if it did come, would not be less than 96 feet from the houses on the opposite side of Princes Street.

In the action for interdict the Court of Session, not surprisingly on the purely legal view, took the Town Council's part. But, when their decision was appealed against to the House of Lords, in April 1772, it was overturned in favour of the complainers. Lord Mansfield's speech on that occasion, on the folly of destroying a beautiful natural asset for purely material ends, has since been singled out as a classic example of bad law making good sense. 'I give my opinion', he concluded, 'not only on the plain and open principles of justice, but from regard to the public and from regard to this misguided Corporation itself.'

The House of Lords decision gave only temporary respite for, in the action of declarator, the Court of Session again upheld the Town Council. This time, instead of an appeal, it was agreed to submit the matter to arbitration and David Rae, Advocate (later, Lord Eskgrove), was selected as arbiter. In his decree dated March 19, 1776 (for much time had been consumed by these proceedings) Rae showed something of the wisdom of a Solomon by declaring:

(1) that the houses which had begun to be built on the site of the present North British Hotel, could be completed, provided they were 'executed in proper taste';

(2) that the furniture workshop alongside them might also be completed provided it did not come above the level of Princes Street; and

(3) that the ground westwards, for half the length of Princes Street, 'shall be kept and preserved in perpetuity as pleasure-grounds to be dressed up at the expense of the town council as soon as may be'.

So the valley and with it the character of Princes Street and its incomparable vista of the old town ridge were saved.

In the years that followed, building continued along Princes Street, George Street and Queen Street, from east to west. Regulations made by the Town Council laid down strict rules. For example, no feus were to be granted for houses above three storeys in height exclusive of the garret and sunk storeys; and plans and elevations of buildings intended to be erected were to be submitted to the inspection of the Council and, if approved, the plans and elevations must be permanently lodged with the Town Council. By these means a reasonable outward uniformity was maintained while leaving scope for internal variations. The idea of the 'palace front', with the façade of a row of houses giving the appearance of one balanced and symmetrical whole as seen to perfection in Charlotte Square had not yet been evolved.

By 1780 houses had been built along Princes Street as far as Hanover Street; and many well-to-do citizens had transferred from their snug but crowded quarters in the High Street to these new and more spacious houses among which shops had not yet begun to intrude.

To No. 30 Princes Street came Bailie John Grieve, soon to be Lord Provost of the city. Among those who had not moved was

George Boyd who had a clothier's shop on the north side of the Lawnmarket and who lived in Gosford's Close, nearby. Between the dwellings of these two still lay the ill-drained site of the Nor' Loch. Whether Bailie Grieve was a customer of Boyd cannot now be known but doubtless there would be some of Boyd's customers among those who had moved from the old town to the new. As George Boyd looked out across the valley, therefore, he must have wished for an easier means of crossing it, for customers who had to make the long circuit from Princes Street by the North Bridge or by St Cuthbert's Kirk, the west side of the Castle rock, the Grassmarket and the steep West Bow would be all too likely to seek a nearer shop. So Boyd, helped by some neighbours, began to make a causeway of stones and rubbish across the muddy remnants of the loch.

From his new home on the fashionable side of the valley, John Grieve was also quick to see the benefit of such a crossing. For one thing, it would shorten appreciably his journeys to the Town Council meetings which were then held in the New Tolbooth beside St Giles. He therefore arranged for earth from nearby foundations to be tipped into the valley opposite his house. Thus began 'Geordie Boyd's Mud Brig' sometimes called 'Bailie Grieve's Brig' which later became 'the earthen mound' and is now universally known as 'the Mound'; that bulky, steep, invaluable link between Princes Street and Lawnmarket.

Soon the scheme for its construction was taken up officially. In February 1781 the Town Council directed that earth from all New Town excavations was to be deposited within lines marked out for the purpose opposite Hanover Street and as almost every New Town house was designed with a deep basement and many with double basements, there was no shortage of spoil from such excavations. For many years the work went on. One account refers to an average of 1800 cartloads being laid upon the Mound daily and in 1793, William Creech estimated that 1305750 cartloads of earth had gone into it 'and it is not yet nearly completed'.

By the end of the eighteenth century the new Mound was in regular use by pedestrians, if not by wheeled traffic. In 1797, an advertisement of a shop for sale in the Lawnmarket declared, by way of inducement to buy, that 'there is now an absolute certainty that this street [the Mound] must soon become the chief communication between the old town and the new'. Yet, even by 1806 (twenty-five years after it had been begun) the *Evening Courant* reported that 'although the earthen mound is a great convenience to the public and in particular to the gentlemen of the law ... at times the access proves extremely dirty and almost impassable'.

Today the Mound is still much used by 'gentlemen of the law'. Judges and advocates, black-coated and bowler-hatted, can regularly be seen striding up it on their daily journeys to the courts from Heriot Row and the neighbouring streets where traditionally the legal profession have their homes and offices. There were, however, two eminent legal gentlemen who did not like the Mound at all. Sir Walter Scott called it 'that huge deformity which now extends its lumpish length betwixt Bank Street and Hanover Street' while, to Lord Cockburn (disapproving, as usual, of anything new under the sun) it was 'that abominable encumbrance by which the valley it bridges was sacrificed for a deposit of rubbish'.

In a way, they were right. Aesthetically the Mound, apart from the two galleries which were later built on it, has little to commend it. Yet, as I walk down it of an evening and see across the shadowy gardens the west end spires sharp against a sunset sky I, for one, am grateful to George Boyd. I also feel rather sorry for him when I recall that, as the Mound which he had begun to build for the benefit of his customers was at last nearing completion his clothing establishment was one of the shops that had to be demolished to provide the connection between the Mound and the Lawnmarket.

By the time the Mound was completed (without the art galleries) houses had been built in Princes Street all the way to the West End. They then formed a long line of plain houses of three storeys and basement, each with a small garden behind and with stables and coach-houses entered from the mews lanes at the rear. There were only a few shops, all at the eastern end of the street. Though most of the original houses have disappeared a few can be glimpsed above modern shop fronts. The best examples are at the two corners of Frederick Street and if you can picture these buildings stripped of their ground-floor plate-glass windows and repeated, with only minor variations, along the whole length of the street, you will have a very fair idea of what Princes Street looked like in its earliest days.

A monotonous line of mediocrity, you may think; but those houses had the merits of uniformity and simple dignity which is more than can be said for the buildings, in a hotch-potch of styles and no style at all, that replaced the houses in the *laissez-faire* years of the late nineteenth and early twentieth centuries. Slowly, very slowly, these in turn are now being replaced by buildings with plain modern frontages conforming, as the original houses had to conform, to strict planning regulations. When these modern buildings are linked eventually (perhaps not until the twenty-first century) in a continuous line along each section of the street, they will bring back a new kind of uniformity to the face of Princes Street which, however different in scale and function, will yet have something in common with the street's first row of unpretentious houses.

While the houses in Princes Street were plain and unadorned, some of those in George Street and Queen Street were very grand. One of the earliest in Queen Street, built in 1770-1 by Chief Baron Orde, father of David Hume's young friend Nancy, is No. 8. Built to a design by Robert Adam it has finely proportioned rooms with enriched plaster ceilings and friezes and some fine fireplaces and mantelpieces. Fortunately, it is now used as an extension of the adjoining Hall of the Royal College of Physicians and so it is likely that all its features will be preserved indefinitely.

It is curious to reflect that, spacious and attractive as those New Town houses were, they fell far short of what we would regard as normal standards in respect of plumbing and hygiene. Here is what Dr Henry Littlejohn, Edinburgh's first Medical Officer of Health had to say about them in his report on the sanitary condition of the city, written in 1863.

At the time of the building of the new town imperfect notions prevailed as to the internal and external drainage of houses. The domestic use of baths was apparently unknown and the conveniences were few in number and awkwardly placed, either so as to deprive a principal room of its amenity, or in such a confined space as to be entirely without ventilation. Besides this . . . where street drains were constructed they were imperfectly built and their communicating branches with the houses, being hastily put together with the chips coming from stones in process of being shaped, were of the most faulty description. . . . The drainage escaped in all directions, infiltrating the neighbouring soil, undermining it everywhere and aiding the operations of those persevering tunnellers, the rats. . . . That such a system is detrimental to the health of the inhabitants need not be insisted on; and there can be no doubt that a town would be healthier without drains, than with such apologies for them.

By the time Dr Littlejohn wrote his report, progress was being made with the substitution of pipe drains for those of the kind of which he complained; but, if a true impression is to be gained of the first New Town and what life in it was like, it is necessary to temper one's vision of gracious living in finely-decorated, high-ceilinged houses with some realization of their unhygienic short-comings which few of those who extol the Georgian splendours of the houses ever mention.

There can be no denying that these Georgian splendours reached the height of achievement in Charlotte Square. By the time building had reached as far west as the Square a new principle had been evolved. Instead of just laying down rules of height, breadth and building line as a framework within which each house could be designed with whatever variations the builder chose, the Town Council required the external appearance of the houses on each side of Charlotte Square to conform to a rigid pattern of design and decoration. The effect of this was to give each group of houses the appearance of being one palatial building; a style of planning which received the seal of royal approval when George IV, on his visit to Edinburgh in 1822, exclaimed to a delighted Sir Walter Scott: 'I always heard the Scotch were a proud people; and they may well be proud, for they are a nation of gentlemen and they live in a city of palaces.'

Having decided on this approach to the planning of Charlotte Square, it is fortunate that the Town Council chose an architect of the brilliance of Robert Adam to design the frontages. Nowhere else in the country, perhaps nowhere in Europe, has anything of the kind been more beautifully achieved. In selecting Robert Adam, they were only just in time, for he died in 1792 very soon after his drawings had been submitted; and his brother James, who was also his partner, died only two years later.

In Adam's drawings the façades of the north and south sides were shown exactly alike, with nine house-fronts making up one balanced design. The east side, broken by the 100-foot width of

George Street was to have two separate 'palace' fronts and the west side was also to have two separate groups of six houses, flanking a central church. Only the north side was completed almost exactly as planned though, even there, roofs and chimney-stalks differed in some details from what had been intended.

Development of Adam's scheme and supervision of the work had to be undertaken by other architects without the benefit of the advice he would have given and the discussions with him that would no doubt have taken place if he had lived. Among these others was Robert Reid who was responsible for one important change. For St George's Church, on the west side of the Square, he produced a bulkier and heavier design than had been intended. While Robert Adam had envisaged the church as taking its place gracefully as part of the Square and in keeping with the Square's domestic character, Reid seems to have seen it as a dominating feature and to have been more concerned with its distant aspect. In this, he was certainly successful. Viewed as one walks towards it along George Street the dome provides an impressive and striking climax to the view; and it is an attractive feature of the Edinburgh sky-line as seen from northern parts of the city.

The church, opened in 1814, had been built by the Town Council to serve those who lived in the western part of their first New Town. Nearly 150 years later, in the 1960s, with ever more New Town houses converted to office and commercial uses, the congregation had dwindled and it was decided that it should merge with that of St Andrew's Church at the other end of George Street. At about the same time, St George's great green and gilt dome was found to be in urgent need of repair at a cost beyond the resources of the church authorities. There was dismay and consternation at what appeared to be the inevitable demolition of the church or, at least, the loss to Edinburgh of a familiar and well-loved landmark by the removal of its dome.

Just in time, the situation was saved by the imaginative vision of a civil servant in what was then the Ministry of Public Building and Works. Faced with a pressing demand for extra accommodation for the historical records of Scotland housed in Robert Adam's Register House at the east end of Princes Street and knowing also of the danger to the west end dome, he contrived a single, happy solution to the two problems. On his suggestion the church building was acquired by the city and leased to the government who undertook full responsibility for its repair and preservation.

A completely new and self-supporting structure was built inside the shell of the church which, with its dome strengthened, took on a new lease of life as the West Register House providing safe and yet easily accessible storage space for important Scottish records. Now, in its spacious entrance hall an exhibition of some of the most interesting of Scotland's historical documents is constantly on public view. There too can be seen a model of the structural solution by means of which it has been possible for the fabric of the church, as a feature of Charlotte Square, to be preserved for future generations.

Over the years, the appearance of the rest of the Square had suffered from time to time by the alteration of windows, the insertion of dormer windows in roofs and other minor changes. On the north side, all such defects were rectified by the public-spirited action of the owners and the whole Square has been protected from further harm by town planning legislation ever since a special Charlotte Square town planning order was made in 1930.

By the end of the eighteenth century, only a part of the north side of the Square had been built and building of the other sides went on intermittently until the last of the houses on the south side was completed about 1820, bringing to completion the development of James Craig's plan. There have been critics of that plan. One called its lay-out 'formal and insipid'; another referred, with a shudder, to its 'draughty parallelograms'. Yet others have decried it because of its awkward approaches from east and west. What they forget is that it was never intended for through traffic. It was designed as a quiet residential quarter for those whose business and professional lives would still be lived mainly in the old town on the ridge above.

When the New Town was new, sedan chairs were in regular use in its streets. They had been introduced in Edinburgh at least as early as the first half of the seventeenth century and there had been a Society of Edinburgh Chair-men since 1740. The chairs were certainly well adapted for use in the narrow closes and the wynds of the old town where carriages either could not enter or were a nuisance if they did. With the migration to the New Town of most of those who could afford to own or hire a chair, there soon came to be as many chairs in the New Town as ever there had been in the old.

A licence to place chairs for hire at a specified stance was first granted by the magistrates in 1687, one of the favourite stances being in the High Street, near the Tron Church, sometimes to the annoyance of shopkeepers who complained that a row of chairs 'foregainst the doors' of their shops hindered their customers and prevented potential customers from seeing the goods on display. By 1814 there were thirty-six registered chair-masters, with 101 chairs, operating from three stances in the old town, two in George Square and at least fifteen in the New Town.

Most of the chair-men were stalwart highlanders – and stalwart they had to be to carry their burdens up some of the steeper streets. Two brothers, Donald and Charles Robertson from Perthshire, had their stance at the crossing of George Street and Castle Street. They were much patronized by Sir Walter and Lady Scott whose servant had only to open the front door at 39 Castle Street and beckon to the brothers when their services were required.

An official booklet issued in 1812 gives the regulations and fares for hackney chairs at that time. From this it appears that the charge for a 'lift' from Castle Street to the Assembly Rooms would be sixpence. The charges were at the rate of threepence a furlong with an extra charge after midnight and double fare if the chair was called after 2 a.m. Not unreasonably, double fare was also chargeable if two adults chose to travel together in the same chair. Every chair had to be numbered on front and back; and if carried or standing on the street 'under cloud of night' it must have a lighted lamp attached to it.

Some of the chairs had their seats fixed on a swivel so that the occupant could remain seated upright even when being carried up or down hill; and travel by chair was said to be very comfortable except, perhaps, when one or both of the chair-men had had a dram too many while awaiting custom. One attraction of this means of travel was that the chair could be brought inside the vestibule of the house for picking up and setting down and places of entertainment like the Assembly Rooms and St Cecilia's Concert Hall at the foot of Niddry Street, had covered areas for their arrival and departure – an advantage for ladies in fine dresses and on a wet or snowy night; and, if the weather was very cold, a warming-pan could be carried in the chair.

If you owned your own sedan, as the best people did, it would not be a drab black box like the hackney-chairs but would be well decorated and upholstered; and it would be kept in the vestibule of your house which may well be one reason why so many New Town houses have such spacious entrance halls. Having your own chair, however, did not necessarily mean that you must also have your own men-servants to carry it. You could call two hackney chair-men who would bring their own carrying-poles from the nearest stance.

The last of the sedan chairs seems to have disappeared from the streets in the late 1850s although a few may have lingered a little longer as a means of carrying patients to the Infirmary, a purpose for which they were much used. The astonishing thing is that the New Town, designed for the days when sedan chairs and carriages were the means of transport, so well serves the entirely different requirements of our own day.

11 The Edinburgh Burns saw

The New Town was less than ten years old when Robert Burns first came to Edinburgh and, during the days he spent there, he would have shared in the excitement of the building developments that were going on. 'There', as he put it in his *Address to Edinburgh*, written within a month of his arrival, 'Architecture's noble pride bids elegance and splendour rise'. But most of the city's life and activity was still concentrated in the old town and it was there, in lodgings off the Lawnmarket, that he spent his first winter in Edinburgh – the months from November 1786 to May 1787. During that visit, as the newly discovered ploughman poet (the Kilmarnock edition of whose poems had recently been published), he was fêted and entertained and fawned upon by the highest society in the city. On his second visit – from October 1787 until March 1788 – he lived in the house of a friend in St James Square, on the edge of the New Town. That was a less public visit for several weeks of which he was confined to the house by an injured knee and spent much of the time in correspondence with his 'Clarinda'. Each of these visits makes a good view-point from which to see the city as he saw it as it was beginning to expand, and to meet some of the people he met as they were becoming accustomed to the new horizons opened up by that expansion.

It was a bleak November evening – Tuesday, 28 November 1786

to be precise – when Robert Burns, then twenty-seven years of age, arrived in the city. On a pony which he had borrowed from a farmer friend, he rode through the West Port along the Grass-market and up the zig-zag of the West Bow into the Lawnmarket at the end of his two-day journey from Mauchline in Ayrshire. On the north side of the Lawnmarket, a little way below James Court, he stopped at Baxter's Close where he had arranged to share with his friend, John Richmond, a room in lodgings kept by Mrs Carfrae, 'a staid sober, piously-disposed, skuldudery-abhorring widow'. Her house has long ago disappeared, but its approximate position is marked by an inscription on the wall of No. 479 Lawn-market.

At the head of the Lawnmarket, then, was the butter-tron or weigh-house, a squat square building; and, at the corner of the West Bow, there still stood the tall timber-fronted house that appears in many old prints, each storey of which projected out-wards further than the one below so that it seemed ready to overbalance at any moment. Yet it had stood there for more than 200 years and remained for nearly another century before it was pulled down. The church at the foot of Castlehill, with its soaring spire, was not yet there – it was not built until 1844; and neither Johnston Terrace nor George IV Bridge had yet been thought of in the 1780s. In their place, steep wynds and closes led down into the Grassmarket and Cowgate and in one of these, Libberton's Wynd, was Johnnie Dowie's hospitable tavern which Burns, you can be sure, would not be slow to find.

Across the valley in Princes Street houses had been built for some distance beyond Hanover Street; and the earthen mound though far from being completed was passable on foot. Another great work on which much faster progress had been made was nearing completion. It was the South Bridge, continuing the road from the North Bridge onwards across the Cowgate valley to provide an easy link with the college (where the present University Old College was built a few years later) and with the southern suburbs of Nicolson Street and Nicolson Square. The South Bridge has twenty-two arches of which only the one spanning the Cowgate Street is open to view. All the rest are obscured by the tall business premises which rise on each side of the roadway, some with as many storeys below bridge level as above it. These were built soon after the bridge, the cost of which was more than recovered from the prices paid for the sites on which the buildings stand, an unusual and highly satisfactory way of financing such an important city improvement.

Three days before Robert Burns arrived in the city, the following notice appeared in the *Edinburgh Evening Courant*: 'This afternoon the last arch of the bridge over the Cowgate was completed. It is one year, three months and 25 days since the foundation stone was laid. It will be passable for people on foot in a few days.' A temporary footbridge of wooden planks was laid above the arches for use by pedestrians and Burns may well have been among the earliest people to cross the valley by means of these planks. Perhaps he asked, as so many have asked since, why the bridge and its roadway descend in a gentle gradient making necessary a sharp climb from its southern end to the level of Nicolson Street. Why was it not built level, or even with a gentle upward gradient from north to south in such a way as to make the link with Nicolson Street easier for the horse traffic of those days? The answer he would have been given was a simple one. In a house in Adam Square where the eastern end of Chambers Street is now, lived Robert Dundas, Lord President of the Court of Session. If the bridge had followed a level course, let alone an upward one, the entrance to his house would have been below the level of the new roadway. So, rather than cause inconvenience to the Lord President, the Commissioners for the building of the bridge (who included among them the Lord President's half-brother, Henry Dundas) agreed to keep the level of the bridge below the level of his doorstep. As it happened, the Lord President died at the age of seventy-five in December 1787 before the bridge had been fully opened to traffic, leaving generations of coach-drivers, carters and 'cabbies' to cope with the short, sharp hill which, but for him, could have been made less steep.

Several circumstances combined to make Robert Burns' first visit to Edinburgh the success it was. The Kilmarnock edition of his poems had been well received. Extracts from it were printed in the October, November and December issues of the *Edinburgh Magazine* and in *The Lounger* Henry Mackenzie reviewed the volume enthusiastically. So everyone in Edinburgh was eager to meet the ploughman poet from Ayrshire.

Then Burns was given an introduction to Lord Glencairn and probably through him he was soon introduced to Henry Erskine who was at that time Dean of the Faculty of Advocates. Erskine had removed from George Square and was living in one of the new houses in Princes Street. He had a wide circle of friends through whom many doors would be opened to the poet. Ten days after his arrival, Burns wrote to Gavin Hamilton in Ayrshire: 'My Lord Glencairn and the Dean of the Faculty, Mr H. Erskine, have taken me under their wing; and by all probability I shall soon be the tenth Worthy, and the eighth Wise Man, of the world' – a prophecy which more or less came true.

Through Lord Glencairn he was introduced to the Duke and Duchess of Gordon and the Duchess, the vivacious and unconventional Jane Maxwell, whisked him off to dancing assemblies, entertainments and social gatherings of all kinds. Of all this, Mrs Alison Cockburn (author of *The Flowers of the Forest*) wrote: 'The town is at present agog with the ploughman poet who receives adulation with native dignity and is the very figure of his profession, strong and coarse, but has a most enthusiastic heart of love. He has seen Duchess Gordon and all the gay world. . . . The man will be spoiled, if he can spoil; but he keeps his simple manners and is quite sober.'

An important event in the city during Burns' first visit was the completion and official opening of the new assembly rooms in George Street. Dancing assemblies had been a feature of Edinburgh's social life for a long time and there had been four earlier assembly rooms in the city. The first, opened about 1710, was in the West Bow. Then, in 1723, a new hall came into use just off the High Street, in what was later called Old Assembly Close. Of this one a visitor wrote: 'They have got an Assembly at Edinburgh where, every Thursday, they meet and dance from four o'clock to eleven at night; it is half-a-crown the ticket and whatever tea, coffee, chocolate, biscuits etc. they call for they must pay for.'

Despite protestations uttered by church dignitaries about the evils of 'promiscuous dancing', the assemblies flourished and after only thirteen years they had to move to larger premises, a little further down the High Street, in New Assembly Close. Here, they were later taken over and managed by a committee of distinguished citizens for charitable purposes, and in a period of about thirty years, more than £7000 was contributed from their proceeds to the Royal Infirmary and other good causes. There was clearly little ground for the concern that had been expressed about 'promiscuous dancing' at these assemblies for one reads that 'none are admitted but such as have a just title to gentility' and the assemblies were conducted under the stern rule of a succession of formidable matrons appointed as 'lady directresses'. Oliver Goldsmith, in 1752, found them a good deal too staid and formal for his liking.

About three years before Robert Burns' arrival in the city new assembly rooms had been built in Buccleuch Place, immediately south of George Square, chiefly for the benefit of the fashionable residents in the Square and the growing southern suburbs nearby. There, the old traditional arrangements were continued. The 'Regulations for George's Square Assemblies – Anno 1785' provided that the assemblies were 'to be held weekly on Wednesday, the one week for Dancing and the other for Cards; beginning with a Dancing Assembly on Wednesday the 5th January 1785 and of course ending with a Card-Assembly on Wednesday the 15th day of June 1785, the hour of meeting to be at half-past Six and of dismissing not later than One in the morning'.

After setting out the rules for subscriptions, the Regulations continued: 'One of the Ladies Subscribers shall be chosen Directress who shall have the sole ordering of the Dancing for the evening she directs; and before breaking up the company she shall name another Lady Subscriber present to succeed her in the direction of the next Card and ensuing Dancing Assembly. The Lady Directress may choose a Gentleman Assistant for the evening.'

The George's Square Assemblies continued until the end of the eighteenth century after which the building in which they were held was converted into dwelling houses and now, as Nos. 14, 15 and 16 Buccleuch Place it is occupied by departments of the University of Edinburgh. It still stands out as a building separate from the other buildings in the street, but internally, there is little or nothing to give a clue to its original use.

Those who attended the assemblies saw to it that they were dressed in the height of fashion and there was always a knot of spectators to watch their comings and goings. But nothing during Burns' visit can have equalled the spectacle which, some fifty years

I

earlier, had become one of the sights of the city. That was the regular procession of eight sedan chairs conveying Susannah, Countess of Eglinton and her seven daughters from their home in Old Stamp Office Close across the High Street to the Assembly Rooms almost opposite; as they were all over six feet tall and each was more handsome than the next, their mother reputedly being the most beautiful of all, that procession must indeed have been a sight worth seeing.

In the 1780s, some of the New Town residents decided to acquire a plot of ground in George Street, between Hanover Street and Frederick Street for the erection of their own New Town assembly rooms and at the time of Robert Burns' arrival, completion of the building was being hurried on so that it could be officially opened for the Caledonian Hunt Ball, fixed for 11 January 1787.

Through the good offices of Lord Glencairn, the Caledonian Hunt, an exclusive body of nobility and gentry had been persuaded to subscribe for 100 copies of the new edition of Burns' poems. For these they sent him, in due course, the sum of £25 and not the 100 guineas he seems at first to have expected. They also graciously authorized the dedication of the volume to 'The Noblemen and Gentlemen of the Caledonian Hunt'.

The Hunt Ball was the social event of the year and as it was, this time, combined with the opening of the new Assembly Rooms, it was undoubtedly the great Edinburgh event of the winter season. Burns does not seem to have been present at the Ball, perhaps because it was too exclusive to admit a ploughman poet, even one with so many aristocratic acquaintances, but he referred to it in a letter he wrote on the day of the Ball to one of his Ayrshire friends which conveys something of the excitement of the occasion. In the letter, after referring to Sir John Whitefoord, one of his patrons, he says: 'His son John, who calls very frequently on me, is in a fuss today like a coronation – This is the great day – the Assembly and Ball of the Caledonian Hunt; and John has had the good luck to pre-engage the hand of the beauty-famed and wealth-celebrated Miss McAdam, our Country woman. . . .'

Two days later, the *Courant* gave a glowing account of the Ball which is worth quoting in full, including its fashion notes.

The Ball given last Thursday evening, at the opening of the New Assembly Rooms, by the Noblemen and Gentlemen of the Caledonian Hunt, was, in the highest degree, magnificent and brilliant. The company, which consisted of about three hundred and forty, included all the people of fashion in town. The dresses of the Ladies were in the highest stile of taste and elegance. The gowns were chiefly of different coloured sattins, covered with crape, and ornamented with flowers; the prevailing cap was the turban, decorated with feathers, and some few with pearls and diamonds. Several ladies wore pink-coloured Spanish hats, which had a very pretty appearance. The dress of the gentlemen was neat and elegant, but no way remarkable. Owing to the supper room not being finished, and the tables being laid in the great room, the company danced in the tea room, which being too small for their accommodation, there was dancing also in the card rooms, and this circumstance no doubt prevented that regularity and propriety which otherwise would have taken place. There were no minuets danced. Lord Elibank and Lady Haddo (who was elegantly dressed suitable to the uniform of the Hunt) began the ball.

The company sat down to supper between two and three o'clock, which, as well as the dessert, consisted of every variety the season afforded, and was served up in a stile that gave general satisfaction. – The Ladies retired about four o'clock, but the morning was pretty far advanced before the Gentlemen left the rooms.

It is but justice to remark, that the above entertainment exhibited a degree of taste and magnificence that reflected honour on the very respectable body by whom it was given: and the community at large must be benefited by the great sums expended in dress, etc.

Of the new premises, the *Courant* said:

The Assembly Room is the largest in Britain, except the Great Room at Bath, and is said to exceed it in elegance and just proportion; it is ninety-two feet long, forty-two broad, and thirty feet high. The building of the rooms etc. has cost about eight thousand pounds.

Rules were drawn up for the conduct of regular assemblies in the new rooms, but despite the magnificent setting the assemblies never seem quite to have regained their former importance in the life of the city. After all, the grand apartments of the New Town houses, unlike those of the old town, provided ample room for private entertainment. So regular assemblies were less necessary and the Assembly Rooms came to be used more for important public functions than for regular social gatherings. Now, along with the Music Hall which was added in the 1840s, the great room, with its glittering chandeliers, makes an impressive setting for such occasions as civic receptions at which conference delegates from all over the world are entertained; and every year, at the time of the Edinburgh International Festival, it becomes a cosmopolitan centre as the Festival Club.

Robert Burns had not come to Edinburgh just to be fêted and to enjoy a round of social activities, however enjoyable these might be. He had come on business, his main object being the publication of a new edition of his poems. For this, he was directed to William Creech, Edinburgh's leading publisher of the day, whose bookshop was at the east end of the luckenbooths, in the building in which Allan Ramsay had opened his circulating library some sixty years before. The shop faced down the High Street and was noted for the view it gave down the long canyon of the Royal Mile to the distant Lothian coast. If, braving the traffic of today, you stand in the middle of the High Street at a point level with the east end of St Giles you will look, as Creech and his customers did, away across Aberlady Bay to the fields near North Berwick, the view sharpened and its colours heightened by contrast with the grey tenements that frame it.

Both in his shop and in his house in Craig's Close nearby William Creech was wont to entertain all the literary figures and Edinburgh worthies of his day. These meetings – known familiarly as Creech's levées – were usually held in his house in the mornings and in his shop in the afternoons and Creech seems to have spent much of his time presiding over them, leaving the day-to-day business of the shop to his clerk, Peter Hill. Lord Cockburn described Creech's shop as 'the natural resort of lawyers, authors and all sorts of literary idlers who were always buzzing about the convenient hive. All who wished to see a poet or a stranger or to hear the public news, the last joke by Erskine, or yesterday's occurrence in the Parliament House, or to get the publications of the day, congregated there.'

By mid-December, Burns had arranged with William Creech for the printing of his new edition. That business concluded, he would be able to enjoy to the full the social, conversational side of Creech's levées where, you may be sure, every current topic would be thoroughly thrashed out. Creech himself was a much-respected though reputedly tight-fisted bachelor of forty-one when Robert Burns first met him. A member of the Town Council, he became a Bailie two years later and, in the same year, served on the jury who found his Council colleague, Deacon Brodie, guilty of theft. In 1811 he was elected Lord Provost. He was the first Secretary of the Edinburgh Chamber of Commerce, founded in 1785, and he served in that capacity for many years, 'politely declining', as the Chamber's minute-book puts it 'to accept of any pecuniary remuneration for his services'. That goes some way towards refuting his reputation for meanness; but, on the other hand, Burns had to ask many times and wait many months for the money due to him by Creech under their agreement.

From Creech's own writings, mostly newspaper articles which were afterwards collected into a volume of *Fugitive Pieces*, he emerges as a serious-minded man with a strict sense of decorum and little sense of humour. Yet he was sociable and popular and when business took him to London for a spell in the spring of 1787, Burns wrote a poem 'To William Creech' which recorded for posterity Edinburgh's distress at the temporary loss of 'her darling bird that she lo'es best – Willie's awa'!'

A later verse in the same poem commiserated with the Chamber of Commerce in having to manage for a while as best they could without their Secretary to keep them right.

> *The brethren o' the Commerce-Chaumer*
> *May mourn their loss wi' doolfu' clamour;*
> *He was a dictionar' and grammar*
> *   Amang them a';*
> *I fear they'll now mak' mony a stammer –*
> *   Willie's awa'!*

Among those whom Burns met at William Creech's shop was Henry Mackenzie, nicknamed 'the Man of Feeling' after his sentimental novel of that name which had been published fifteen years before and which Burns had once described as 'a book I prize next to the Bible'. Mackenzie, the same age as Creech, was an official of the Exchequer. He lived in Brown Square about ten minutes' walk away from Creech's shop. Apart from his official duties he was one of Edinburgh's leading literary figures and editor of *The Lounger* in No. 9 of which, issued on 9 December 1786, he began his review of Burns' poems: 'I know not if I shall be accused of enthusiasm and partiality when I introduce to the notice of my readers a poet of our own country with whose writings I have lately become acquainted; but if I am not greatly deceived I think I may safely pronounce him a genius of no ordinary rank.' That tribute and the laudatory review that followed it did much to hasten the poet's acceptance by Edinburgh society and to boost the sale of his poems.

Any company in which Henry Mackenzie was included could be assured of enjoyment, for he was a great raconteur and conversationalist. A visitor to Edinburgh who met him a few years later described his conversation as 'easy, eloquent and elegant' and added, 'he treats the subject before you as it demands, either with the solidity of reasoning or the graceful levity of humour'. Did he, I wonder, regale the company at Creech's levées with some of the stories which, much later, were collected as his *Anecdotes and Egotisms* – many of them stories about phases of Edinburgh life that were disappearing as the population were moving from the old town to the new?

One, which he called 'Stealing a Room', illustrates the congested and complicated internal planning of the tenements from which they were removing. It happened, he said, in the Lawnmarket where a tenant 'contrived to remove a partition from the adjacent house on the same floor during the proprietor's absence in the country', thereby adding the room to his own house. 'I have no doubt of the fact,' he added, when someone seemed to be taking his story with a pinch of salt, 'improbable as it is.'

When subjects for conversation failed – which, amid all the bustle and gossip in and around the luckenbooths cannot have been often – Creech and his friends would not have far to go for new ideas because only a few steps away in Parliament Close was the print shop of John Kay. Kay had been a surgeon-barber but, having discovered that he had an aptitude for drawing, he devoted himself to that and, from 1784 until his death in 1826, he produced a series of caricature-portraits almost all of which were of topical interest and spiced with a humour which was sometimes none too kind in its thrusts. He displayed his drawings daily in the window of his shop and it became quite the regular thing for Edinburgh folk in all walks of life to gather round his window eager to see whose was the latest portrait on view and what was the latest local incident to be lampooned. There must often have been hilarious groups outside the shop enjoying the wit of his most recent production and it can, surely, be taken for granted that during the winter of 1786–7, Robert Burns would often be among the crowd. Though some of John Kay's caustic comments on persons in authority are unlikely to have appealed much to William Creech, these are just the drawings that Burns would most appreciate.

After Kay's death 360 of his drawings were published as *Kay's Original Portraits*. Almost all of them are dated, so it is possible to identify those that Burns may have seen and chuckled over with his friends. Altogether, fifty-nine were drawn during Kay's first three years as printseller, 1784 to 1786. Two of those dated 1784 are of Lord Monboddo, Burns' host in St John Street on more than one occasion and one is of Dr Alexander Wood ('Lang Sandy Wood') the much-loved surgeon who attended on Burns during his second visit to Edinburgh, after he had fallen and injured his knee. One of the drawings dated 1785 shows Lunardi, in magnificent uniform, standing proudly in the basket of his balloon awaiting 'take-off' for one of his flights over Edinburgh in that year. That Burns would be given full accounts of these flights and of Lunardi's behaviour in the city is certain, the last ascent from Edinburgh having taken place only four months before Burns' arrival.

Seventeen of the drawings are dated 1786 and would, therefore, be really topical. One of the best of these is 'A Whim – or a Visit to the Mud Bridge' and it is one Burns would certainly enjoy. Some time before, a self-appointed group mainly consisting of Lawnmarket shopkeepers who styled themselves the 'Committee of Burgh Reformers' had collected money with the object of speeding up the building of the Mound but their efforts were not welcomed by the authorities. So the Committee decided to spend the money, instead, on entertaining themselves and some friends to dinner in Dunn's Hotel, in St Andrew Square, and in hiring a coach-and-six which they intended should be the first vehicle to ascend the Mound. Their wives and lady friends were to ride in it, while the Committee would walk alongside, from the hotel to the Lawnmarket.

Alas for their plans. Shortly before the day fixed for the event, their honorary treasurer inconsiderately absconded with the Committee's funds and the ceremonial dinner and procession had to be abandoned – a denouement that was received with unkind mirth by many people in Edinburgh and gave John Kay an opportunity, far too good to be missed, to exercise his talents.

His drawing is reproduced between pages 104 and 105. It shows the coach and horses about to climb up the Mound, signposted as 'B's Bridge' and, fittingly, the coachman is George Boyd, originator of the mud brig, in person. He is being urged on by his friend and neighbour, Willie Yetts, a hairdresser and hosier in the Lawnmarket, in the character of footman. Bailie Grieve, Boyd's early collaborator in the mud brig project from the Princes Street end, is not included in the party but the Bailie's wife is in the coach, almost certainly the lady who is so imperiously directing the coachman. The six 'horses' and the postilion are merchants and shopkeepers, most of them with premises in the Lawnmarket. They and their lady passengers were all well-known characters who would be easily identified by their fellow citizens; while the gentleman in front is Jamie Duff – nicknamed Bailie Duff – a simple-minded fellow well known in the city at that time. He is carrying a flag said to be one that George Boyd was in the habit of displaying outside his shop.

Although John Kay drew portraits of many visitors to the city he did not produce one of Robert Burns or, if he did, it has not survived. During that first winter in Edinburgh, however, Burns sat for his portrait to Alexander Nasmyth who was then a successful portrait painter, though he later became more widely known as 'the father of Scottish landscape-painting'. During the sittings poet and artist, who were about the same age, became firm friends and after each day's work was done they would walk together, sometimes only as far as a nearby tavern and sometimes over Calton Hill or Arthur's Seat.

Once they walked, overnight, across the Pentland Hills and came down to the village of Roslin about eight miles from Edinburgh. At the old inn close beside Roslin Chapel in the steep valley of the North Esk they breakfasted and there Burns composed his impromptu verse in honour of the landlady: 'My blessings on you, sonsie wife. . . .' Meanwhile Nasmyth made a rough sketch from which, after the poet's death, he painted a full-length portrait of Burns. Both portraits are now in the Scottish National Portrait Gallery in Queen Street, Edinburgh. The one of head and shoulders only, painted in the Lawnmarket lodgings, is accepted as the most authentic likeness of the poet and has been reproduced very many times.

Burns, the Ayrshire poet, depicted in vivid lines and in their own language the people of the countryside in which he lived; but Edinburgh, too, had had her own poet who described, sometimes humorously, sometimes harshly, but always in life-like terms his fellow townsfolk and their foibles. He was Robert Fergusson for whom Burns had the deepest admiration but he had died, in tragic circumstances, when he was only twenty-four years old, twelve years before Burns came to Edinburgh. Naturally, Robert Burns visited Fergusson's grave in Canongate churchyard and he was shocked to find that no memorial stone had been placed upon it. So he wrote at once to the Bailies of the Canongate asking permission 'to lay a simple stone over his revered ashes to remain an unalienable property to his deathless fame'.

The Bailies re-directed his letter to the correct authorities who were the Managers of the Kirk and Kirkyard Funds of Canongate and thereupon, in the formal language of their minute-book, 'the said Managers in consideration of the laudable and disinterested motion of Mr Burns and the propriety of his request did, and hereby do, unanimously grant power and liberty to the said Robert Burns to erect a headstone at the grave of the said Robert Fergusson and to keep up and preserve the same to his memory in all time coming'.

The stone commissioned by Burns was designed and erected by Robert Burn, later the architect of the Nelson monument on Calton Hill, who was father of the more famous William Burn. The architect took his time over the commission and Burns took his time over paying him. In 1792 he wrote from Dumfries to his friend Peter Hill, Creech's former assistant and by then a bookseller in his own right, sending £5 10s. to be passed on 'to Mr Robert Burn, Architect, for erecting the stone over poor Fergusson. . . . He was two years erecting it, after I commissioned him for it; and I have been two years paying him, after he sent me his account; so he and I are quits. – He had the hardiesse [sic] to ask me interest on the sum; but considering that the money was due by one Poet, for putting a tomb-stone over another, he may, with grateful surprise, thank Heaven that ever he saw a farthing of it.'

The stone (with Fergusson's year of birth given wrongly as 1751 instead of 1750) is still there, on the west side of Canongate

Kirkyard. There, you can read the inscription written for it by
Robert Burns, his testimony from one poet to another.

No sculptured marble here, nor pompous lay,
No storied urn, nor animated Bust;
This simple stone directs Pale Scotia's way
To pour her Sorrows o'er the Poet's Dust.

Having read that tribute to Robert Fergusson you can look up and
see, on the slope of Calton Hill beside Regent Road, the circular
Greek temple designed by Thomas Hamilton and erected in 1830
as Edinburgh's monument to Robert Burns. Across the kirkyard,
against its eastern wall, is a bronze head of Mrs McLehose, 'Clarinda',
who was buried there in 1841, having survived Burns by forty-five
years, reaching the age of eighty-two.

Not far from Fergusson's grave there is an unusual tombstone
which Burns would see when he visited the kirkyard and which
always fascinates me. It was erected in 1765 by the Society of Coach-
Drivers in Canongate to mark the ground designated for burial
of the society's members; and its chief interest for us is the representation upon it of a stage-coach with four horses crossing a
bridge at a spanking pace. Despite its worn condition, which is
not surprising after more than 200 years, it gives a lively impression
of coach travel. Whether, as has been suggested, it also symbolized
the coach-drivers' alternative to Charon's boat as a mode of
crossing the river Styx is another matter.

At some time or other during Burns' first winter in Edinburgh
occurred his one and only meeting with Sir Walter Scott who was
then a boy of about fifteen. It happened at the house of Dr Adam
Ferguson, at Sciennes, only about a mile south of the High Street
but then thought to be quite a long way out of town. Ferguson
was then aged sixty-three and had recently given up his appointment as Professor of Moral Philosophy; in the fashion of the day,
he liked to have frequent academic and literary gatherings at his
home and to include among those invited any interesting visitors
to the city.

On one such occasion which Burns attended young Walter
Scott was among a group of juvenile guests. 'Of course,' said Scott,
'we youngsters sat silent, looked and listened.' Nevertheless, he
had his chance. Burns seemed deeply affected by a print on a

wall of the room which depicted a soldier lying dead in the snow with his widow and dog beside him, and by some rather mawkish lines of poetry inscribed below it. He asked if anyone knew who had written the lines and only the young Sir Walter remembered that they came from a poem by John Langhorne, an eighteenth-century English poet. 'Burns,' he said, 'rewarded me with a look and a word which, though of mere civility, I then received, and still recollect, with very great pleasure.'

The house where their meeting took place can still be seen. It is at No. 7 Sciennes House Place (until recently, Braid Place) off Causewayside, a short distance south of the Meadows. For very many years the house has been sub-divided to form separate flats and from the street it appears to be just an ordinary tenement but if you go through the passage-way at No. 7 into the drying-green at the rear and turn round you will see what used to be the front of Adam Ferguson's house with a plaque on it recording the meeting. You will then be standing in what was part of the garden of the house which had an entrance-drive leading from a gate that stood roughly at the end of Melville Terrace. What is now the back of the building has ornamental stonework and other signs of having been the front wall of a handsome mansion, including the built-up front door, at first-flat level. The door would originally be approached from the garden by a graceful flight of steps up which Burns, the young Walter Scott and the other guests would go on that memorable evening.

In May Burns and his friend Bob Ainslie set off on a tour of the Borders, and during that summer he made a series of tours in different parts of the country with occasional short stops in Edinburgh. Then, on 20 October 1787 he returned to the city partly with the object of persuading William Creech to pay him the money he owed, partly to discuss with James Johnson, whom he had met during his first visit, the production of further volumes of the Scots Musical Museum, containing many of his songs, partly to further his candidature for the excise appointment which he eventually obtained in July 1788 and partly to meet old friends and acquaintances. Many, like James Johnson and Peter Hill, still a clerk in the luckenbooths shop, were pleased to see him; but this time he was not lionized. Fashionable Edinburgh society seems not to have taken long to lose interest in the ploughman poet.

During this visit Burns did not stay in the old town but in a top flat in St James Square, the home of his friend William Cruickshank, a classical master in the High School, whose twelve-year-old daughter Janet used to pick out for Burns on the harpsichord some of the tunes to which his songs were written. In return, he gave her lasting fame as 'young Jenny fair' in his poem beginning: 'A rose-bud by my early walk'.

St James Square was immediately east of the New Town. The Square had been laid out in accordance with a plan prepared by James Craig and had begun to be built in 1779. Its four sides of grey stone blocks, mostly of four storeys and attics, had a certain dignified appearance but the houses fell far short of the standards of those in the New Town proper. In nearly 200 years they were divided and sub-divided and they deteriorated so badly that, by the 1960s, demolition – whatever single-minded conservationists might say – was the only practical solution. Now replaced by the St James shopping centre and a massive office block, the Square is commemorated by a stone in the forecourt of the centre, taken from one of the old buildings, with the inscription 'St James Square, 1779'. In celebration of the bicentenary of the new town in 1967, the name 'James Craig Walk' has been given to a pedestrian way which now leads across the site of the square in which Robert Burns was the guest of his schoolteacher friend.

There is little in Burns' correspondence during this visit that relates to the building work going on all around, though he did refer to it tersely among some other aspects of life in the city in a letter to John Richmond who, by this time, had left Edinburgh and was practising law in Mauchline, in his native Ayrshire. 'I shall not trouble you with a long letter of Edinr. news,' he wrote. 'Indeed there is nothing worth mentioning to you; everything going on as usual – houses building, bucks strutting, ladies flaring, blackguards sculking, whores leering, etc. in the old way.'

Besides the 'houses building', one of the more spectacular feats of construction which he would see this time was the completion of St Andrew's Church, in George Street, with its slender steeple designed by William Sibbald. The press, on 23 November, reported that 'Mr Stevens, contractor for building the steeple of St Andrew's Church, has finished that elegant piece of architecture and fixed the spire and weathercock upon the top of it. Though the whole

is about 186 feet high yet not the smallest accident has happened to
any of the workmen during the building' – which the paper was
happy to attribute to the great care taken in erecting the scaffolding, 'which was very beautiful'. In those days the intricate wooden
scaffolding required for major building projects was often admired
in its own right.

Early in December, at a tea party, Burns was introduced to Mrs
Agnes McLehose, whose husband had left her three years before
and who was living on a small annuity in a house in Potterrow, in
the 'southern suburbs' in an area now demolished to make way for
University development. Having contrived the introduction, the
lady lost no time in inviting Robert Burns to call on her. She
was an attractive woman and he readily accepted her invitation.
Here, however, fate stepped in. Late on the evening before the
day fixed for his visit he injured his knee so severely 'by an unlucky
fall from a coach' that he was unable to leave the house. So six
weeks passed before he could pay her a visit and then he had to
hire a sedan chair for the journey – but he left it in Nicolson
Square and managed to walk the last few yards to her flat in case
the arrival of a gentleman in a chair should provide too much
gossip for neighbours' tongues. In those six weeks he had written
at least fifteen letters to her, progressing from the first – 'I am,
Madam, with the highest respect, Your very humble servant,
Robert Burns' – to the fifteenth, 'I am not proof against the applauses of one whom I love dearer and whose judgement I esteem
more, than I do all the world beside – God bless you. Remember –
Sylvander.'

After Burns was out and about again, their correspondence
continued. In all, he wrote forty letters to her (that, anyway is
the number preserved and published) and she, no doubt, as many
to him, before he left Edinburgh. The two were served well by the
penny post operated by Peter Williamson from his luckenbooths
shop, a service which, it will be recalled, undertook to deliver
letters within the city or at a moderate distance 'every hour or
oftener'. There was a collection point for letters at a grocer's
shop in St Andrew Street, only a few minutes' walk from St James
Square and, no doubt, young Janet Cruickshank or an obliging
neighbour would hand in his letters there while he was unable to
go himself. Only once did Burns have cause to complain of the

service. In a letter headed 'Two o'clock, 14 Feb. 1788' he said: 'I just now received your first letter of yesterday, by the careless negligence of the penny post.' It must, indeed, have been a good service if delivery in the early afternoon of the day after posting counted as 'careless negligence'.

One cannot help wondering whether the affair with 'Clarinda' would have developed as it did if 'Sylvander's' injury had not made it necessary for 'Lang Sandy Wood', the surgeon who attended him, to confine him to his room for so long. In the first place his intention, but for that, had been to stay in Edinburgh for only ten days or a fortnight – and he stayed for twenty-two weeks. In the second place, the exchange of affectionate letters with a charming and intelligent woman who was also something of a poet, made a pleasant occupation for dreary hours when, otherwise, he would have longed to be out meeting old friends and making new ones. Having once started the correspondence, it would not have been easy to bring it to a close sooner than he did, on leaving Edinburgh on 24 March 1788 to take up his tenancy of Ellisland Farm and, soon afterwards, to marry his Jean Armour and provide a home for her and their children.

12 The new town grows

The first New Town, as has been said, was planned as a self-contained residential unit. It is probable that those who created it never dreamed that they were setting a precedent for a whole series of New Town extensions to follow, each with its characteristic features, and all combining to form a satisfying whole. That, however, is what happened. The fashion for living in a self-contained house with airy apartments and servants conveniently consigned to basement or attic instead of in a cramped, ill-ventilated flat where family and servants constantly rubbed shoulders, grew and gathered momentum; boosted, as fashions are in every age, by that strange human urge for keeping up with the Joneses. As a result, the city's present-day New Town conservation boundary, within which special efforts are made to preserve its Georgian heritage, covers an area larger than those of York, Chester, Bath and Chichester added together.

Before Charlotte Square was even half finished, plans had been prepared for the second new town, reaching downhill from below Queen Street towards the Water of Leith. These plans were drawn by Robert Reid who later designed St George's Church and who was the last holder of the office of King's Architect for Scotland and by William Sibbald, Superintendent of Works to the Town Council. Building began in 1802, at No. 13 Heriot Row, about half-way between Dundas Street and Howe Street. In *Walks in Edinburgh*, published in 1825, Robert Chambers says that the building of Heriot Row was thought by many to be a mad speculation and that residents in Queen Street regarded the family who first lived in No. 13 Heriot Row as being 'out of the world'. Comfortably settled themselves, they evidently did not see why others should come and spoil their rural outlook.

Sir John Carr, an English traveller who visited Edinburgh in 1809, was also none too pleased with the new extension. He said that the fine prospect from Queen Street was 'beginning to be interrupted by the recent elevation of new streets and particularly by the houses on a piece of ground called Heriot's Row'. He waxed lyrical over the view from Queen Street. 'The eye,' he said, 'enchanted, wanders over parks, plantations and villages . . . to the Firth of Forth which exhibits a noble expanse of water; its shores decorated with every variety of rural beauty and its bosom embellished with gliding vessels and rocky islets whilst the elevated hills of Fifeshire and the mountains of Perthshire form a beautiful background to this magnificent scene.' Then – surely an anticlimax – he added, 'In my opinion it greatly surpasses the view from Richmond Hill.'

However, there was another aspect of his enjoyment of the prospect from Queen Street that was not affected by building further down the hill: 'It is truly delightful,' he said, 'to join an evening promenade in this street when the sun is shedding his last light upon this exquisite prospect, and also shining upon a number of well-dressed and beautiful females who add not a little to the witchery of the whole.'

Almost all the lands covered by the Reid and Sibbald plan belonged to George Heriot's Trust and the whole scheme was strictly controlled by a contract to which the Trustees and the Town Council were the principal signatories. As a result of that control the streets have dignity, symmetry and a sense of proportion combined with an interesting variety which give pleasure and delight no matter how often one walks along them.

Once again the layout was based on three parallel streets, though this is less obvious than in the earlier plan. The principal street is Great King Street, with the trees of Drummond Place garden, where George Drummond's house once stood, closing the vista to the east and those of Royal Circus at its western end. As with the earlier plan, Heriot Row to the south and its extension, Abercromby Place, are one-sided, facing on to gardens, but in this case the gentle curve of Abercromby Place, the first crescent in the new town, introduces an attractive variation – the first attempt to get away from those 'draughty parallelograms'. To the north, Fettes Row and Royal Crescent were also to be one-sided but these streets were never quite completed, and as for their north-ward view, the less said the better. Later development, and lack of development, have ruined it completely. Royal Circus, with its axis on the road leading downhill to the village of Stockbridge, was built about 1821. Designed by William Playfair its frontages successfully overcome the problem of the sloping ground and it is ingeniously linked by India Street to the west end of Heriot Row and by Gloucester Place and Doune Terrace to the slightly later Moray Place.

As before, lesser streets run parallel to the main ones. Two of these, Northumberland and Cumberland Streets, have good Georgian features and Cumberland Street, after years of neglect has recently benefited from renovation. A third, Jamaica Street, was always inferior and it deteriorated so badly that, not long ago, it had to be demolished. It had, nevertheless, one claim to literary fame for, in a top flat there the young Thomas Carlyle was, briefly, a lodger. He had come to this address in November 1821, in course of his ceaseless search for a quiet place in which to work, as he could never write amidst noise of any kind. Here on the extreme edge of the New Town he thought he had found the quiet he desired. But he had chosen the wrong place, or rather, the wrong time. His window overlooked Royal Circus, the houses of which were then being built and he wrote to his mother: 'There are about 50 masons chipping away at a new Circus on my right hand and on my left by day; and when their rattling has ceased various other noises take up their nightly tale. . . .' So, in a few weeks, in his continuing search for peace he had to move, this time to Spey Street (then called Moray Street) near Pilrig, on the road to Leith where, strange though it may seem to us, he found quietness amid rural surroundings which were more to his liking.

The masons who disturbed Thomas Carlyle must have chipped away to some purpose, because the *Edinburgh Magazine* for December

K

1821 reported, as 'the most extraordinary instance of rapid building', that in just over twelve months the whole circus except for one house had been begun and completed and almost all were occupied. So, if only Carlyle had had a little patience, the constant chipping of the masons would soon have ended and he could have remained in Jamaica Street unless, of course, those 'various other noises' were too disturbing.

While the Reid and Sibbald scheme was progressing another massive project was under way, east of Princes Street. Here, Regent Road was being cut in a great sweep round the shoulder of Calton Hill; and Waterloo Place, with the Regent Arch spanning the valley below, was being built. This was a public scheme undertaken by a statutory body of commissioners and financed, more or less heedless of expense, by the Town Council and the District Road Trustees. The roadway and bridge were engineered by Robert Stevenson, grandfather of Robert Louis Stevenson, and the buildings and screen walls were designed by Archibald Elliot who also designed the Calton Gaol in the likeness of a gigantic toy fort on the edge of Calton Crag. In the 1930s the gaol was taken down to make way for the more austere shape of St Andrew's House, seat of Scottish government departments. As a reminder of the past, however, the gaol governor's house was left and, turreted and battlemented, it still stands absurdly but effectively, on the lip of the cliff that overhangs Calton Road and the end of Waverley Station. The foundation stones of the gaol and of the Regent Bridge were laid on the same day in 1815. Inevitably, in that year, this great approach road to Princes Street was given the name Waterloo Place.

In those days, before the Burgh Reform Act of 1833, the city was governed by the old-style Town Council, self-electing and totally undemocratic. Their civic affairs were heading for bankruptcy of which they had been warned by one of their members years before, a warning on which they had taken no action except to see that he was not re-elected to their ranks. Recklessly, they went on with this costly scheme which added greatly to the city's debt. In response to public demand, they even paid for the reduction in height of some newly erected buildings on the site of the present North British Hotel at the east end of Princes Street so that the view of the Castle from Waterloo Place would not be impeded. Commonsense and present-day civic accountants would have said that such extravagance as was lavished on this Regent Road scheme could not be contemplated in the city's circumstances but, if commonsense and financial prudence had prevailed in 1815, what then? The city might forever have been deprived of the finest approach to the city centre, with its vistas of Arthur's Seat, the old town and the Castle. Assuredly, there are occasions when imprudence can be amply justified by its results, and this is one of them.

The next development to be planned was also on the slopes of Calton Hill and on the lower ground north of it. For that area William Playfair, in 1819, submitted a plan based largely on a report which had been prepared for the Town Council some years before by another Edinburgh architect, William Stark, who was less well known than Playfair although in fact Playfair had been his pupil. In contrast to Craig's squares and parallelograms, Stark urged that streets should follow the contours of the ground, thus achieving 'variety and unexpected change of form both in the streets and buildings'. So, clinging to the hillside and curving round it, three terraces were planned. For the first of these (on the northern slope of the hill) the authorities adopted, once more, their favourite name, 'Royal'. Having already named Royal Crescent and Royal Circus on the edges of the Reid and Sibbald plan, they named this Playfair project Royal Terrace and extended it round the hill as Carlton and Regent Terraces. The three terraces enclose a charming garden for the use of their residents which was laid out by Sir Joseph Paxton on the eastern crest of the hill.

The houses of Royal Terrace make up the longest continuous pattern in the whole of the New Town, extending for nearly a quarter of a mile in a series of seventeen sections, seven adorned by impressive colonnades. These houses, now mostly hotels and offices, look down over a wooded slope to Hillside Crescent, facing the hill, with three wide streets radiating from it. This idea was compared by Stark to the streets radiating from the great Piazza del Popolo in Rome – but any such similarity began and ended with the paper plan. Long before building had reached that far, a new era had dawned and the three radiating Georgian streets end abruptly among Victorian tenements.

In contrast to the rapid completion of Royal Circus, some interesting contemporary comments on the slow progress of the Calton Hill developments can be found in a diary covering the years 1823 to 1833 which is in the Edinburgh public library. The author is unknown but he was clearly much interested in the building projects that were going on.

1823: October 10. The Royal Terrace, notwithstanding its elevated and commanding position, is feuing out but slowly and as yet only three of its houses are inhabited.

1825: June 30. The Royal Terrace which for a long time consisted of 7 houses not the half inhabited, from the digging going on, is about to receive some additions. On the south-east side of Calton Hill there will soon be a long range of houses if we may judge by the extent of the foundations digging.

1826: June 30. The Royal Terrace, after standing long at 7 houses is now increased to 12. . . . The Regent Terrace, where 12 months ago there were only foundations digging, now presents us with 17 houses nearly complete, besides 6 lately begun.

Obviously, Regent Terrace with its southern aspect and its view over Holyrood Palace to the green slopes and crags of Arthur's Seat was more popular with house-hunters than its north-facing counterpart.

Meanwhile, at the opposite end of the New Town another scheme was going ahead on Lord Moray's estate, north of Charlotte Square. From 1812 Henry Cockburn (later Lord Cockburn) had lived in the Square and he recalls in his *Memorials* the appearance of the estate in 1822, just before building began.

It was then an open field of as green turf as Scotland could boast of, with a few respectable trees on the flat, and thickly wooded on the bank along the Water of Leith. . . . That well-kept and almost evergreen field was the most beautiful piece of ground in immediate connection with the town, and led the eye agreeably over to our distant northern scenery. . . . But how can I forget the glory of that scene on the still nights on which, with Rutherford and Richardson and Jeffrey, I have stood in Queen Street, or the opening of the north-west corner of Charlotte Square, and listened to the ceaseless rural corn-craiks nestling happily in the dewy grass.

The plans for the Moray Estate were provided for the Earl of Moray by James Gillespie Graham. (Originally James Gillespie, he married an heiress and added her surname to his own.) His plans certainly departed from squares and parallelograms and ventured into a variety of shapes – the segment of Randolph Crescent, the oval of Ainslie Place and, most mjaestic of all, the circular or, rather many-sided of Moray Place, linked by short connecting streets with Craig's lay-out and that of Reid and Sibbald.

Our anonymous diarist dealt with these developments in his usual matter-of-fact manner allowing himself just a brief expression of astonishment at the amount of building going on.

1823: March 1. The feuing of Lord Moray's grounds which commenced last year, is likely to lead to the formation of a third grand division of our new town. The addition of from 700 to 800 new dwelling-houses in Edinburgh every year for some years past, one would think, must through time over-stock the market and lower the rents, but this state of matters has not yet taken place.

1823: October 10. The most remarkable increase as to buildings of expensive architecture are those on Lord Moray's ground. . . . Now a great part of three or four sides of the Octagon are visible.

1826: June 30. Moray Place wants just five stances of being completed, all on the south side. A great part of it is now inhabited; . . . the north side of Ainslie Place is wholly roof'd in but only one or two houses are inhabited.

The architect had expressed the view that the Earl had done 'everything in his power, consistent with his own interest, to render the plan ornamental to the City and convenient for the inhabitants'. By the detailed requirements of his feuing conditions he had ensured a high standard of amenity while at the same time seeing to it that none of the expense of streets, sewers, boundary walls or pleasure-grounds would fall on him, but would be borne in appropriate proportions by the purchasers of the building lots.

The steep wooded bank between the houses and the Water of Leith, known as Lord Moray's pleasure-ground, was planted with shrubs and provided with pathways for the enjoyment of those householders who, having obtained the Earl's permission to use them, paid their share of the cost of forming the garden and undertook to contribute to its upkeep.

As a result of Gillespie Graham's bold and imaginative plan and the strict feuing conditions imposed by the Earl, Moray Place is surely the grandest achievement in the New Town. Professor Youngson, in *The Making of Classical Edinburgh* has suggested that 'it is, in the way of private building, the most splendid thing in Edinburgh'. It would undoubtedly be difficult to find anything in the city or, indeed, in Scotland to equal it. Yet Moray Place has had its critics, chiefly on the grounds that the houses of its northern sections 'turn their backs' on the view across the tree-clad valley of the Water of Leith. Well, of course they do; but their residents can still enjoy the view from their rear windows or from their 'hanging gardens' on the very edge of the valley and for the rest of us the majestic design, the severity of its massive frontages softened by the trees at its centre, is ample compensation.

Almost within hailing distance of the back gardens of Moray Place and presenting a complete contrast to it, there is a short quiet street, so hidden away on the lower ground across the Water of Leith that a visitor might never find it except by accident; but, once having found it, no visitor could fail to be charmed by it. This is Ann Street; and its houses were new just about the time that Moray Place was being planned. Ann Street is close to the old village of Stockbridge. It was built for Henry Raeburn, the portrait painter, and named after his wife Ann Leslie. The architect may have been James Milne but tradition maintains that Raeburn either designed it himself or played a large part in its design. Certainly the lightness and delicacy with which familiar Georgian characteristics are used to make up the street pattern suggest the eye and hand of an artist. But the finest features of Ann Street are the long front gardens between the houses and the pavement; the gardens are always rich in summer colours and their lush foliage brings a new dimension to the classical outlines of the house fronts, giving a rural aspect to the street which is quite different from any other in the New Town.

This little gem of a street is part of a development begun by Henry Raeburn on his own property. He and his wife lived nearby in the old mansion of St Bernard's, which stood beside the Water of Leith, a few hundred yards upstream from the bridge at Stockbridge. It was surrounded by pleasant grounds on which, partly during Raeburn's life-time and partly after his death, a whole series of streets were built.

Most impressive of these is St Bernard's Crescent, designed by James Milne in 1825, two years after Raeburn's death. Its central block has eight massive Doric columns, two storeys high, supporting an attic storey and giving a ponderous effect which is in total contrast to the delicacy of the Ann Street houses; and this, it seems to me, reinforces the view that Ann Street owed a good deal more to Raeburn than to his architect. The scale of St Bernard's Crescent is matched by a tall and aged tree among others in its central garden ground, which must be a survivor of those that flanked the avenue leading to Raeburn's home.

Elsewhere in this area other good examples of Georgian houses, outliers of the New Town, are to be found but it would be tedious to describe them all; so I leave them for each to discover for himself, an enjoyable objective for a walk through the northern fringes of Georgian Edinburgh. I leave too the New Town streets beyond the west end of Princes Street. Some, like Shandwick Place and Atholl Crescent are contemporary with the later parts of Reid and Sibbald's new town. Some, like Melville Street, followed close upon the building of Moray Place. Others, such as Learmonth Terrace and Buckingham Terrace beside the road leading to Queensferry, had to await the coming of the Dean Bridge in 1832 to provide an easy connection with the city and then waited a good deal longer before anyone would build them. Saturation point for that type of housing had been reached and there was a long lull in building. So it was that these streets and others in their neighbourhood carried the Georgian pattern, with some embellishments, far into the age of Victoria.

There is, however, one building in the vicinity of Stockbridge that I must mention because it will bring me, by a curious train of thought, back to the Calton Hill and to still another fashion among Edinburgh's architectural styles. The building is the Edinburgh Academy in Henderson Row; and the fashion to which it leads me arose from the obsession that gripped the people of Edinburgh in the early nineteenth century – their obsession with the idea that their city was 'the modern Athens' and that, therefore, public buildings and monuments should imitate Greek and preferably Athenian, originals.

Not that there is anything particularly Grecian about the Academy building apart from the Greek motto above its portico which conveys to any Greek scholar who may happen to pass by, the message that 'Learning is the Mother of Wisdom and of Virtue.' But the story of its founding, and its opening in 1824, is inextricably bound up with that of the opening of the new High School building on the Calton Hill in 1829 and nothing could be more Grecian than that.

In 1822 the High School, managed by the Town Council, was still on its old site in High School Yards, in the building at the foot of Infirmary Street to which Scott had gone from his home in George Square and to which Henry Cockburn remembered being taken, as a boy, along the wooden footpath above the newly completed arches of the South Bridge. By the 1820s the school had become seriously overcrowded and, as ever more families moved from the old town to the new, its situation was becoming inconvenient for increasing numbers of its scholars. So the Town Council began to consider building a second school for the benefit of those living on the north side of the city. The site selected was that on which the Academy was later built and William Burn (who, in due course, designed the Academy) was chosen to be the architect for the proposed second High School.

Then, however, arguments arose from two sides. A member of the Town Council objected to the idea of having two schools, fearing that, with one in the New Town (at which an entrance fee was to be charged) and one in the old town, distinctions of wealth would be introduced whereas in the past children from all walks of life had studied happily together. After some discussion his point was taken and the Town Council set about searching for a more central site on which a single school could be built to replace the old one and provide more ample accommodation.

Meanwhile, an exactly opposite point of view was being put forward by Henry Cockburn. He says:

Leonard Horner and I had often discussed the causes and the remedies of the decline of classical education in Scotland; and we were at last satisfied that no adequate improvement could be effected so long as there was only one great classical school in Edinburgh, and this one placed under the Town Council and lowered, perhaps necessarily, so as to suit the wants of a class of boys to more than two-thirds of whom classical accomplishment is foreseen to be useless. So one day on top of one of the Pentlands . . . we two resolved to set about the establishment of a new school.

Having put the idea to several of their friends, including Sir Walter Scott who 'took it up eagerly', a subscription was raised and the site at Henderson Row (unsuitable for the Town Council's new requirements) was obtained. There, on 1 July 1823, the foundation stone was laid; fifteen months later, in the building designed by William Burn, the new school was opened as the Edinburgh

Two New Town Residents – Francis Jeffrey (*1773–1850*), *on the left, a founder and editor of the* Edinburgh Review, *critic,* Advocate *and, from 1834,* Lord Jeffrey, Judge of the Court of Session; *and* Henry Cockburn (*1779–1854*) Advocate, *supporter of Parliamentary and Local Government reform but critic of many other changes; from 1834, Lord Cockburn. Both drawings are from Benjamin Crombie's 'Modern Athenians'.*

Above: 'O Felicem Diem' – Oh Happy Day. *George IV lands at Leith in August 1822 to be greeted by Bailie McFie, Chief Magistrate of Leith (on the King's right) and by many other dignitaries. The King's carriage awaits him on the left of the picture. On the extreme right, a young pickpocket has seized his opportunity. This oil-painting (12 feet by 6 feet) still hangs in Leith Old Council Chamber. It is by Alexander Carse.*

Right: Sir Henry D. Littlejohn, Edinburgh's first Medical Officer of Health. The outcry arising from the conditions of squalor revealed by the collapse of the Paisley Close tenement led to his appointment in 1862. This drawing appeared in the Edinburgh Magazine in January 1904, four years before his retiral.

Left: Bailie Fyfe's Close (107 High Street), drawn by James Drummond, RSA, in 1853. On the left is the rear wall of the tenement (entered from Paisley Close, No. 101) which collapsed into the High Street in November 1861, causing many casualties.

St Bernard's Well *in the Water of Leith Valley, near Stockbridge. This drawing, by Thomas H. Shepherd in 1829 shows the structure as designed by Alexander Nasmyth in 1789.*

A Newhaven Fishwife – *welcome vendor at Edinburgh doors well into the present century. This one, with her supply of fresh oysters for sale, was drawn by John Kay in 1812.*

Academy. Its first Board of sixteen Directors had, as Chairman, Robert Dundas of Arniston and included Sir Walter Scott, Cockburn, James Skene of Rubislaw and William Burn.

The Town Council were annoyed to find this school being founded as a rival to their own. There was, however, nothing they could do about it. A story did indeed circulate that, in selecting the site at the foot of Howe Street for William Playfair's massive St Stephen's Church, begun in 1826, the Council did so deliberately in order to block the view of the Academy which until then was admirably seen from the whole length of Howe Street. But the only possible verdict on that story is the useful Scottish one of 'not proven'.

The decision having been taken to have only one High School, the next problem was to find a central site for it. At last someone hit on the idea of using a piece of ground belonging to the Town Council known as Miller's Knowe beside Regent Road on the south slope of Calton Hill – a little too far east perhaps, but more or less equally accessible from the old and new towns. For that site, with its fine southern aspect, Thomas Hamilton, a former pupil of the school, was instructed to prepare a plan. A modest, unassuming man, he had, very recently, won wide acclaim for his monument to Robert Burns in Alloway, Ayrshire, designed in the shape of a small, circular Greek temple.

There were three reasons why Hamilton designed the new High School in Grecian style. It was a style in which he enjoyed working; secondly, the Town Council, smarting under the criticisms of the quality of teaching in their school which had been loudly voiced by the founders of the Academy, would welcome a design that would outwardly demonstrate the classical bias of the High School; and thirdly, there was the current obsession with the idea that Edinburgh was the modern Athens. So the Town Council were delighted with Hamilton's plan, as well they might be.

Its central feature, containing a great hall beautifully proportioned, is based on the Theseum that overlooks the ancient agora, or market place, beneath the Acropolis of Athens. On each side of the school's central hall, rows of pillars lead outwards to two flanking pavilions like miniature temples, with their porticos facing inwards towards each other. Because of the sloping site a maze of underbuilding, partly concealed by a massive arrange-

ment of walls and partly used as ornament, raises the whole building above the road, thus adding to its impact.

As a Greek temple it is magnificent; but as a school building it
left much to be desired. The classrooms were large and draughty
and awkwardly (albeit symmetrically) arranged at a variety of
levels; the thickness and solidity of the walls made even minor
alterations into major operations. The waste of space among
under-buildings was considerable, though in the days when pri-
mary pupils shared the building with the older scholars, those dark
passages and stairs, doing service as dungeons, caves and castles
added spice to many a small boy's play-time break. The worst
feature is that in almost the whole length of the southern frontage,
with its open outlook and fine view, there are no windows (who
ever heard of a Greek temple with windows – or a school without
them?).

However, in 1829, light and outlook were not so highly regarded.
On 23 June in that year the 700 pupils joined in a procession from
the old school to the new, 'preceded by the band of the 17th Lancers,
each class marching with a master at its head, followed by the
High Constables, the magistrates, professors of the university
and all those noblemen and gentlemen who had attended the
High School, in fours'. When they reached the new building, everyone was loud in praise of it and no one mentioned the lack of
windows facing south.

After 140 years, in 1969, the Royal High School removed, less
ceremonially, to its modern accommodation at Barnton on the
west side of the city. The Regent Road building has since been
transformed into the City of Edinburgh Art Centre. In former
classrooms the town's collection of paintings, providing a kind
of short history of modern Scottish art, is admirably displayed and
special exhibitions are often held. What better use could have
been found for Hamilton's Grecian masterpiece?

The High School building is only one, though undoubtedly the
finest, among several buildings that we owe to the city's Athenian
period. At the Mound, William Playfair's many-pillared Royal
Institution, built in 1823 (now the Royal Scottish Academy Gallery)
and his National Gallery, completed in 1845, are both impressive
essays in Grecian style. The former, as we now see it, is larger
than it was originally; and the statue of Queen Victoria

sitting so uncomfortably upon its roof, was not added until 1844.

Of the other Grecian buildings, the national monument on the crest of Calton Hill, though only a fragment of what was intended, is the most impressive. Its twelve great pillars are the beginning of a building that was to have been an exact copy of the Parthenon dominating Edinburgh as the Parthenon dominates the old part of Athens, and intended as a memorial of the Napoleonic wars. It was planned by William Playfair, along with C. R. Cockerell, and during the visit of George IV to the city in 1822 its foundation stone was laid by Commissioners on the King's behalf. Despite eloquent appeals, money came in very slowly and by 1830, with only the twelve great pillars of Craigleith stone and their architrave completed, contributions ceased altogether and the work stopped. Sad as that may have been, I have a feeling that those twelve pillars standing out against the sky are a good deal more effective than the completed building would have been.

Close to the national monument stands Playfair's Grecian Doric monument to his uncle, John Playfair, mathematician and natural philosopher. It was completed in 1826. Appropriately, in view of John Playfair's Presidency of the Astronomical Institution, the monument, which is not impressive in itself, forms a corner feature of the wall round the Calton Hill observatory buildings. The 'old observatory' at the opposite end of the enclosure is in the form of a round tower with gothic windows. Designed by James Craig of New Town fame, it was completed in 1792 and is his only surviving building in the city. The 'new observatory', a Roman Doric building in the centre of the enclosure was planned by Playfair and completed in 1818.

Prominent on a knoll to the west of the old observatory is another Grecian-style monument, also by Playfair. It was placed there in 1832 to commemorate Dugald Stewart who, in 1785, succeeded Adam Ferguson as Professor of Moral Philosophy at Edinburgh. Both it and the monument to Burns on the lower slope of the hill near Regent Road, designed by Thomas Hamilton and completed in 1830, were copied from the monument of Lysicrates in Athens.

How did all this enthusiasm for things Greek begin? According to Robert Chambers in *Walks in Edinburgh* (written before the pillars of the national monument had been built and before the High School was planned) the city's alleged resemblance to Athens was first pointed out by 'Athenian Stuart'. He was James Stuart, an eighteenth-century Londoner of Scottish descent, who made an expedition to Athens to obtain exact measurements of its ancient ruins and afterwards became a recognized authority on classical art. He was followed by Hugh W. Williams ('Grecian Williams') who had been brought up in Edinburgh and, having also visited Greece, produced many paintings of Greek scenes and views of Edinburgh showing supposed resemblances.

Carried away by these ideas, Robert Chambers exclaims that, viewed from some points on the Pentland Hills, 'the landscape is exactly that of the vicinity of Athens . . . in the abrupt and dark mass of the Castle, rises the Acropolis; the hill Lycabetes . . . appears in the Calton; in the Firth of Forth we behold the Aegean sea – in Inchkeith, Aegina; and the hills of the Peleponnese are precisely those of the opposite coast of Fife'. Others took up the notion and more writers than one have referred to the city as the modern Athens and its people as modern Athenians.

All nonsense, of course. In addition to the forced nature of the comparisons, Edinburgh's obsession with fluted pillars and Grecian porticos ignored completely the difference in quality (and in quantity) of our sunlight from that of Athens and the different texture of our Craigleith stone from that of Pentelic marble as a result of which the full effect of sharp light and shade can scarcely ever be seen on Edinburgh's monuments. Nevertheless, that Grecian craze of 150 years ago has added something special to the heritage of Edinburgh and to the character of the New Town. Without Hamilton's extended Theseum and Playfair's fragmentary Parthenon the city would be the poorer.

13 Theatrical events

One of the first public buildings opened in the New Town of Edinburgh was the Theatre Royal. It stood from 1769 until 1859 on the site of the present General Post Office, among a group of undistinguished buildings forming Shakespeare Square, some of which were demolished to make way for Waterloo Place, the rest disappearing with the theatre when the Post Office was built.

In 1769 only a few people had moved to the New Town, but David Ross, proprietor of the former Playhouse in the Canongate, was far-sighted enough to see that, before long, most of the theatre-going public would be living on the north side of the valley. So he decided to take the theatre to them but, astutely, he chose a site which was close to the North Bridge and thus reasonably accessible also from the old town. The opening of the theatre had been timed to coincide with the opening of the bridge but, a few days before the date fixed, the press announced: 'The unhappy accident of the bridge deprives the town of a convenient road to the new theatre and therefore Mr Ross cannot open it this season'; and so, for the time being, performances continued in the Canongate.

In Edinburgh, theatrical people were well accustomed to setbacks of one kind and another. In the previous fifty years they had had to struggle against the prejudice of magistrates, against religious intolerance and, often, against too much 'audience participation' in their affairs. In the 1720s Tony Aston and his players were in trouble in connection with their performances in the Skinners' Hall, in Skinners' Close. Both hall and close have disappeared. They were off the High Street between the present Blackfriars Street and South Gray's Close. Although the players appearing there were sponsored by a group of noblemen, the Bailies sought to prohibit their performances on the ground that plays 'might lead to vice and immorality'. Answering them Aston said that his company would not speak one word on stage that they had not previously spoken before Their Majesties in London and 'it is indecent and disrespectful to call those things immoralities which are patronized by Their Majesties in the metropolis of the kingdom'. Events conspired, however, to give the Bailies the last word. Lady Morrison whose house was situated, very inconveniently, underneath the Skinners' Hall complained that the performances 'bended her roof too much'. So the Bailies had the building inspected by 'fifteen sworn men, the most skilful in building in this city' and then ordered the performances to cease on grounds of safety.

Allan Ramsay, poet of *The Gentle Shepherd*, opened a theatre in 1737 in Carruber's Close, High Street but after only six months, under an Act of Parliament for the restriction of stage plays, it had to be closed, causing him considerable loss. Not long before that, a petition had been presented to the magistrates by a group of citizens protesting against plays as tending 'to debauch the morals of those who attend them, being filled with impure and vile jests, immodest representations, horrid imprecations and oaths, blasphemous reflections on Providence and many other immoralities which cannot but pollute the minds of men; yea, in some of them they have the boldness to act some of the most awful and terrible works of God, such as thunder and lightning etc., which is too daring for creatures to imitate and cannot be done without great guilt....'

A few years after the closing of Allan Ramsay's theatre, someone awoke to the fact that the Act under which it had been closed could be circumvented by including musical items in each programme and advertising the entertainment as a concert, for which the tickets would be sold, the play being performed as an extra.

Under that convenient arrangement, plays were regularly staged in the Tailors' Hall in the Cowgate and, after 1746, in the Canongate 'Concert Hall' or Playhouse. Its site is commemorated by Old Playhouse Close and Playhouse Close, near Moray House, but no vestige of the theatre remains.

It was in that theatre, in 1756, that scandal was caused by the performance of 'A New Tragedy called *Douglas* written by an ingenious gentleman of this country'. The ingenious gentleman was the Rev. John Home, minister of Athelstaneford in East Lothian and therein lay the scandal – that a minister of the gospel had not only written a play but had arranged with actors for its performance. He had to resign his charge, of course; and several fellow-ministers who had gone along to see the play were severely dealt with by the Church authorities. But one of them, the Rev. Thomas Whyte of Liberton, was let off lightly because, although he had attended the performance, he had had the good grace to conceal himself as best he could behind a pillar, 'so as not to give offence'.

No one now thinks very highly of Home's *Douglas* but at the time it was hailed as a masterpiece and not only by the unknown member of the audience who, unable to restrain his excitement or his patriotism at the end of one of the more purple passages, called out: 'Whaur's yer Wullie Shakespeare noo?' Such men as David Hume and Henry Mackenzie also commended the play despite the fact that, in London, Garrick had said that it was 'totally unfit for the stage'.

As for audience participation in theatrical matters, that was carried to extraordinary lengths not in the sense of the audience taking part in the action of the play but in the direct action they sometimes took against the management or the programme or the players. There was an evening in 1749 when some army officers in the audience called upon the band to play the tune 'Culloden'. This aroused the Jacobite wrath of others who promptly ordered the tune to be changed to 'You're welcome, Charles Stuart'. Whereupon the two factions set about one another with swords and sticks and whatever bits of theatrical furniture readily came to hand. Next day, a notice appeared intimating that, in future, the orchestra would play only what the management instructed.

A few years later another riot took place when footmen and other servants whose masters were in the audience and who, by custom, were given free places in the gallery took exception to the performance of a farce called *High Life below Stairs* which they regarded as insulting to them.

In 1766, Allan Ramsay (artist son of the poet) published anonymously a pamphlet in the form of a *Letter from a Gentleman in Edinburgh to his Friend in the Country* in which he described yet another riot caused by the omission of a hornpipe which had been advertised to be danced during a performance of *The Beggar's Opera*. This seemingly trivial omission, it appears, had come after a period of growing dissatisfaction with the management on account of miscasting and last-minute changes in casting, of which the audiences disapproved. One excellent actor had been given minor parts while another, being a favourite of the managers, was given the leading roles although 'he is actually unfit for anything but inexplicable dumb show'; an excellent actress was turned out to make way for one who 'has actually lost her looks, her voice, her teeth . . .' and so on, through a catalogue of complaints. The quarrel had culminated, on the night of the missing hornpipe, in the ladies being allowed to leave the theatre, after which 'scenes, sconces, boxes and benches were quickly tore to pieces and a deal of mischief performed'. Such were some of the ways in which, in those days, Edinburgh audiences showed their displeasure.

Fortunately, by the time the Theatre Royal was opened in the New Town the situation had improved. Under legislation introduced in 1767 the theatre was officially licensed and the old pretence that the play was a mere appendage to a concert was no longer necessary.

On Saturday, 22 May 1784, one of the great events of Edinburgh theatrical history took place in the Theatre Royal in Shakespeare Square: Mrs Sarah Siddons made her first appearance in Scotland. In the previous year she had, in the words of one writer, 'burst upon the astonished Londoners in the zenith of her tragic greatness' and now here she was in Edinburgh. According to all accounts the theatre was besieged during her visit by eager would-be playgoers. People sent their servants to queue all night for tickets; on one day over 2500 applications were made for 630 places. When it was announced that doors would be opened at 3 p.m. (for a 6.30 p.m. performance) queues began to form at 11 a.m. and military help had to be called in to control the crowds. The crush was so great that one lady with no intention of going to the theatre who just happened to be passing as the doors were opened found herself carried, willy-nilly, into the pit. It is doubtful whether any theatrical occasion in Edinburgh ever again caused such excitement until the era of pop-concerts came upon us. To see Sarah Siddons people came from as far afield as Newcastle (a two-day coach journey then) and it was said that pickpockets travelled from London to reap from the throng a harvest of watches, snuff-boxes, purses, hats and even wigs.

On her first night in Edinburgh Mrs Siddons played one of her most famous roles, that of Belvidera, the only female character in Thomas Otway's highly dramatic and gory tragedy, *Venice Preserved*. Two stories are told of that first evening. One concerns an Edinburgh lawyer, by no means a regular theatre-goer, who had been persuaded on this special occasion to accompany his daughter to the play. Having obtained seats with great difficulty he remained silent through the first two acts then turned to his daughter and, much to her embarrassment, asked loudly: 'Which was the woman Siddons?'

The other story demonstrates that, despite the excitement outside the theatre, even the histrionic genius of Sarah Siddons could not easily break through the reserve which by this time had begun to characterize Edinburgh audiences. Having declaimed a dramatic speech in her most dramatic style she paused, expecting a thunderous round of applause. Instead, the speech was succeeded by stony silence. Then one voice was heard exclaiming: 'That's no' bad.' The ice was broken. There was a roar of laughter followed by enthusiastic applause. The theatre-goers of Edinburgh had taken Mrs Siddons to their hearts. After that came the final accolade of acceptance. The General Assembly of the Church of Scotland rearranged their time-table of meetings so that they would not clash with her performances – a change of attitude which must have caused some astonishment to the Rev. John Home.

Mrs Siddons remained in Edinburgh for three weeks appearing in seven different plays, including Home's *Douglas*. Of her appearance in *Venice Preserved* the *Scots Magazine* wrote:

It is impossible for words to do justice to the merit of this inimitable woman. Her natural qualifications are very uncommon. The symmetry of her person, the wonderful expression of her countenance which is at once bold, dignified

L

and beautiful, the strong penetration of her eye and the plaintiveness of her voice captivated every auditor. . . . In several scenes her powers were astonishing indeed – the last occasioned several ladies to faint.

As Isabella, in Southerne's tragedy *The Fatal Marriage*,

she melted the audience at one time with pity and at another harrowed up the soul with terror . . . and threw many, both gentlemen and ladies into faintings and histeria. She is too powerful in this character for most people's feelings and she had well-nigh made a real tragedy in the house.

During her three weeks in the city Mrs Siddons was believed to have cleared £1000; and before she left, a group of Edinburgh gentlemen presented her with a silver vase on which was engraved 'As a mark of esteem for superior genius and unrivalled talents, this vase is respectfully inscribed with the name of Siddons – Edinburgh, 9th June 1784'.

In the next thirty years or so Sarah Siddons paid several visits to Edinburgh and was always received with enthusiasm. Meanwhile her son Henry and his wife became well-known theatrical figures in the city. In 1809, sponsored by Sir Walter Scott and others, Henry Siddons obtained a theatre licence and operated under it, not in Shakespeare Square but in a 'new' Theatre Royal beside Leith Walk; 'formerly the Circus and subsequently concert-rooms [it] has been fitted up with tolerable neatness, although somewhat in the "gingerbread-work style".' It stood near the large modern roundabout at the junction of Leith Walk and Broughton Street. For its opening strict traffic rules were prescribed. Carriages were to come by way of Leith Street or York Place; only sedan chairs being permitted to approach by St James Square. The internal arrangements of Henry Siddons' new theatre, however, were unsatisfactory and before long he moved back to the old Theatre Royal.

There, on 13 March 1812, Sarah Siddons, then aged fifty-seven, made a farewell appearance at which 'the whole of the rank and literature of Edinburgh were present'. As on her first appearance the theatre was thronged to overflowing. 'Many hats, shoes, shawls etc. were lost in the scuffle, but', said the *Evening Courant*, 'we rejoice to say no serious mischief occurred. The play was *Henry the VIII* in which Mrs Siddons sustained the part of Queen Catherine with indescribable effect.' At the end, 'she spoke a poetical adieu to the audience in a style that suffused every eye with tears. . . .' However, in the manner of many theatrical celebrities, she came back three years later to make her second final farewell.

In the years that followed, Mr and Mrs Henry Siddons made many friends in Edinburgh. Though Mrs Henry Siddons never aspired to the heights of tragedy reached by her mother-in-law, she was acclaimed for her portrayal of gentler characters and in Edinburgh she was much respected for 'the brilliant example of respectability she gave to her profession', as well as for the skill and charm of her acting.

Though theatre-going was a popular pleasure among many of the well-to-do families who lived in the New Town about the time of Sarah Siddons' farewell visits and in the years that followed, neither that nor concerts nor assemblies could fill all their leisure hours. So an intricate pattern of social visiting and entertaining developed on a scale that had not been possible in the crowded conditions of the old town. To understand its finer points – whom to visit at what hour of the day and whom to invite to tea or dinner or supper parties and with which other guests – must have required a continuing study of the unwritten rules of etiquette; continuing, because the rules were always changing. The accepted time for a dinner-party, for example, moved in course of a few years from three o'clock, to four, to five and finally six o'clock; and to make it even more difficult, some households always lagged behind the general change so it was necessary to know, at any given time, which families were 'with it' and which were not. No doubt the servants had an intelligence network of their own about such matters which would often be helpful.

Several who took part in all this socializing wrote their memoirs in their old age. Usually these were intended only for family reading and not, initially, for publication and so they contain gossipy items of information, trivial in themselves, which add up to a more vivid picture of their times than would emerge from a formal history. The *Memoirs of a Highland Lady* written by Elizabeth Grant of Rothiemurchus is one of these. Her family, like others who had country homes, rented different houses in the city from time to time, overcoming the furnishing problem, if the house was not a furnished one, by hiring the necessary items from Mr Trotter's furniture warehouse in Princes Street.

In 1815, the Grants stayed 'in the most disagreeable house possible; a large gloomy No. 11 in Queen Street, on the front of which the sun never shone'. In 1816, they took Sir John Hay's house in George Street, 'an infinitely more agreeable winter residence than Lady Augusta Clavering's very gloomy old barrack in Queen Street'. Later, they moved to Charlotte Square, 'a house I found the most agreeable we ever lived in in Edinburgh'; and then, for three years, her father took a lease of No. 8 Picardy Place which she did not like at all – 'down in the fogs of Leith, far from any country walk, away from all our friends'. The house in Picardy Place, only a short distance to the east of Queen Street, could not fairly be described as being 'down in the fogs of Leith' but after the amenities of Charlotte Square one can see what she meant.

Elizabeth Grant's memoirs explain also the social groupings of those days not, of course, through the whole social spectrum but among those who were at or near her own level. She says:

It was a bad system that divided us all into small coteries; the bounds were not strictly defined, and far from strictly kept; still, the various little sections were all there, apart, each small set overvaluing itself and undervaluing its neighbours. There was the fashionable set, headed by Lady Gray of Kinfauns. . . . Within, or beyond this, was an exclusive set . . . a literary set, including college professors, authors and others pleased so to represent themselves; a clever set, with Mrs Fletcher; the law set, strangers and inferiors. All shook up together they would have done very well. Even when partially mingled they were very agreeable. When primmed up, each phalanx apart, on two sides of the turbulent stream of politics . . . there was really some fear of a clash at times.

Mrs Fletcher of 'the clever set' also eventually wrote her autobiography, one of the most illuminating of these curious publications. Her husband, about twenty-five years her senior, was a Whig advocate, a close friend of Henry Erskine and of Francis Jeffrey. Soon after their marriage in 1791, he had acted gratuitously on behalf of members of the 'Friends of the People' at the sedition trials. Though he was not himself a supporter of all the aims of that organization, the fact that he had befriended them was enough to make him unpopular among some of the other social sets in the city and to cause him, for a time, to lose many briefs that might have come his way.

Mrs Fletcher's memoirs throw further light on the customs of her day. Writing of 1811 she says:

The society of that time was delightful. . . . Large dinner parties were less frequent. . . . In their place came large evening parties, sometimes larger than the rooms could conveniently hold, where card-playing generally gave place to music or conversation. Tea and coffee were handed about at 9 and the guests sat down to some light, cold refreshment later on in the evening; people did not, in these parties, meet to eat but to talk and listen. There, you would see a group (chiefly of ladies) listening to the brilliant talk of Mr Jeffrey; in another part of the room, perhaps another circle amongst whom were reverential-looking students lending their ears to the playful imaginative discussions of Dr Thomas Brown, while Professor Playfair would sometimes throw in an ingenious or quiet remark that would give fresh animation to the discourse. On other days, old Henry Mackenzie would enliven the conversation with anecdotes of men and manners gone by.

In those days, when conversation was still regarded as an art, or at least an accomplishment, I wonder if the interesting discussions always seemed to be going on, as they do at parties nowadays, in the group at the opposite end of the room? Probably they did, except that in the company named by Mrs Fletcher it would be difficult to imagine any dull conversation. Francis Jeffrey, then aged thirty-nine, living at 92 George Street and practising as an advocate, was still editor of, and prolific contributor to, the *Edinburgh Review* of which he had been one of the founders in 1802. 'His mind,' it was said, 'was always full of excellent matter, his spirit was always lively; and his heart was never wrong. He had no exclusive topics. All subjects were welcome; and all found him ready, if not in knowledge, at least in fancy.' There lies the secret; for good conversation it is the play of ideas, not the uttering of facts, that counts.

Dr Thomas Brown was a close friend of Jeffrey and the Fletchers and was also associated with the *Edinburgh Review*. He lived at 79 Princes Street and had recently succeeded Dugald Stewart in the Chair of Moral Philosophy at Edinburgh. Then aged thirty-three, it was claimed on his behalf that at the age of four he had undertaken a critical comparison of the four gospels. John Playfair, who was sixty-three, had been Professor of Natural Philosophy at Edinburgh for six years. He lived mainly in Burntisland, across the Forth and, according to Jeffrey, he was devoted to books – and to ladies.

Henry Mackenzie, whom we have met before, was now aged sixty-six and was living at 6 Heriot Row. It is, perhaps, significant

that he was present 'on other days' for the other persons named
were predominantly Whigs and Mackenzie supported the Tory
side in politics; though, in fact, the charm of his conversation and
his fund of stories made him a welcome guest in many different
companies until the end of his long life in 1831.

Another favourite pastime of New Town families was to indulge
in amateur theatricals in their own homes. When the Fletcher
family lived at 51 North Castle Street they had as neighbours, just
round the corner in Queen Street, Lady Williamson and her
daughters. These two families often combined to put on performances for their relatives and friends and they did not hesitate
to tackle serious drama. Lady Williamson's house was the larger
and there, says Mrs Fletcher, 'one of the drawing-rooms was
converted into a little permanent theatre during one winter,
when the play of *Douglas* and some of Joanna Baillie's dramas were
got up with great effect and large audiences gave their applauses
con amore' – those last two words suggesting that the applause may
have had more to do with the affection of the audience for the
players than with the merit of the performance.

Such amateur productions continued to be a favourite household pastime for a good many years and in another book of mem-
oirs there is an account of performances given at 52 Queen
Street, when it was the home of Professor (later Sir) J. Y. Simpson,
discoverer of the anaesthetic qualities of chloroform. As the
Professor and his wife did not live there until 1845, the performances
must have taken place soon after that. The tale is told in Lady
Eliza Priestley's *Story of a Life-time*. She was a daughter of Robert
Chambers and in the 1840s lived with her parents at 1 Doune
Terrace, near Moray Place. There she had met and become engaged
to William Priestley, Simpson's young assistant, who lived with
the Simpsons and proved such an able pupil of his master
that he later became a royal obstetrician and was knighted in
1893.

At the time when Simpson was experimenting with chloroform
there had been much coming and going between the two households and Lady Priestley recounts how he used to try out his
discovery on her, her sister and their friends at Doune Terrace:
'With some of the liquid simply poured on a handkerchief he
would have half-a-dozen of us lying about in various stages of

sleep. Our mother feared nothing and was only too delighted to sacrifice, if unavoidable, a daughter or two to science.'

In addition to the rather dangerous 'entertainment' provided by that kind of research, the two households also indulged in play-acting. Despite the eminence of some of the performers they seem not to have attempted plays of the calibre of those put on by the Fletcher–Williamson company. On one evening, the dramas performed were *Bluebeard* and *The Babes in the Wood*. In *Bluebeard*, Professor W. E. Aytoun of the Chair of English Literature at Edinburgh played the title role while Eliza Chambers took the part of Fatima 'and appeared in a superb oriental costume picked up at a sale by my mother'. She complained that, while she and the other characters learned their parts in advance, Professor Aytoun insisted on leaving his words to the inspiration of the moment, sometimes with disastrous results.

In the other play, the 'Babes' were impersonated by Professor Simpson and Dr Lyon Playfair (then Chemist to the Geological Survey and later Professor of Chemistry at Edinburgh). 'They were dressed in white muslins with short sleeves and they sucked oranges as they wandered through the wood. They did not say much, but looked everything and fairly brought down the house.' Anyone who wonders why that should seem so funny need only look at the statue of Sir J. Y. Simpson's burly figure seated in his chair near the west end of Princes Street and then try to imagine the scene.

That kind of recreation was enjoyed in many households in those pre-television days. There was, however, one Edinburgh lady who seems to have been alone in carrying her acting ability into real life. She was Miss Stirling Graham and in 1860 she issued privately her little volume of *Mystifications* in which she gave details of impersonations which she had performed in Edinburgh some forty years before and which had provided her and some of her friends with a good deal of merriment. Sometimes, in the guise of an old lady newly arrived in the city, she would be introduced at a dinner-party or other social occasion at which a few of those present were 'in the know' and enjoyed helping to carry on her pretence. At other times she carried out the deception less publicly. Always, she claimed, it was done without malice.

Francis Jeffrey was one of those who were taken in, though it is hard to believe that he can have been deceived for more than a few minutes and one suspects that he may, after all, have been 'playing her along'. She did claim, however, that 'the cleverest people were the easiest mystified. . . . Indeed children and dogs were the only detectives.' Although Miss Graham was not yet thirty years old the favourite character in which she chose to appear was that of a litigious and rather cantankerous old lady, the fictitious Lady Pitlyal. On an afternoon in 1821, made up to look as aged as possible and along with an accomplice posing as her daughter, she arrived at 92 George Street and demanded to see Mr Jeffrey. She then told him a complicated story about a barn and other farm buildings in the County of Angus which she had inherited and which had been burnt down through the carelessness of neighbours whom she now wished to sue. Would Mr Jeffrey please take up the case? After a strange and quite lengthy conversation about the legal merits of the supposed case she departed, leaving an envelope on the table containing a fee of three guineas.

By all accounts, including his own, Jeffrey did not discover until the following day that the old lady had been a fiction and that he had been well and truly caught by one of Miss Stirling Graham's 'mystifications'; whereupon he laughed heartily, sent back the fee and offered to help her with any similar impersonation she might like to undertake. Well, perhaps he was deceived; for the interview took place late on an April afternoon when there would be little sunlight in Jeffrey's study. But it seems to me that, if Miss Stirling Graham was as successful as she claimed to have been, she had missed her vocation and should have been appearing with Mrs Henry Siddons at the Theatre Royal; except, of course, that no lady of quality, in those days, would have gone upon the stage.

14 Great occasions

Not all great spectacles were performed upon the stage. What could have been more spectacular than the visit of George IV to the city in 1822? For fifteen days the town was wild with enthusiasm; as well it might be for no reigning monarch since Charles II had set foot in Edinburgh. Now, George IV, of the House of Hanover, in the sixtieth year of his life and the third of his reign was visiting his northern capital. The pageantry of processions and parades, banquets and balls would really have had to be seen to be believed.

Much of the pageantry was master-minded by Sir Walter Scott. According to J. G. Lockhart, Scott's son-in-law and biographer, the Town Council had been so bewildered by the novelty of the visit that 'they threw themselves on him for advice about the merest trifles; and he had to arrange everything from the order of a procession to the embroidering of a cross'. Nor was that all. Scott's house at 21 Castle Street was besieged by Highland chieftains, several of whom had arrived in Edinburgh for the occasion, each with a rather fierce looking 'tail' as their groups of clansmen in attendance were ludicrously called. The chiefs applied to Scott on questions of precedence which they sought to settle on the basis of the relative positions their clans had occupied at the battle of Bannockburn, a matter on which, it seems, they regarded Scott as an expert.

The fact was that the authorities had been given exceedingly short notice of the impending visit. Rumours of it had circulated for some time, but it was not until 24 July that the Lord Provost reported to the Town Council that he had just received a letter from Lord Melville intimating the King's 'gracious intention to visit this metropolis as early as the 10th or 12th of August'. That gave them just sixteen days to make all the necessary arrangements – though, in the event, they had twenty-one days because the King did not arrive until 14 August and did not land from his yacht until the following day.

So it is not surprising that the Council were in something of a flurry. In fact, they coped well with the situation cutting red tape and placing everything, immediately, in the hands of a committee of fourteen members with full powers to act as they thought best. That committee, headed by the Lord Provost, no doubt consulted Sir Walter Scott informally on many matters, as Lockhart suggests; they also co-opted him to two of their four sub-committees, each of which dealt with a particular aspect of the royal programme.

That Scott worked prodigiously hard on his part of the planning and organizing cannot be doubted. That he revelled in it and relished every moment of the events as they occurred is equally certain. The pomp and the ceremony, the kilts, the plaids, the skirl of the pipes and the cheering crowds all appealed immensely to his romantic spirit; to say nothing of the opportunities the occasion brought him for meeting with the highest in the land. It is evident that he and the committee of Council members played their parts well for, to judge by contemporary accounts of the visit, everything happened without a hitch; apart from the landing of the King at Leith which was delayed for a day by torrential rain.

It was estimated that 300000 people watched the King's ceremonial entry to the city, and that at a time when the population within the Edinburgh census area was just over 112000. Crowds had flocked from all over Scotland; every house and hotel was crowded and many who could not find rooms camped out, some in Holyrood Park and on Calton Hill. The highlanders who had come with their chief from Breadalbane in Perthshire lived in tents which they pitched, precariously, on the Castle bank overlooking Princes Street.

Lockhart was among those who criticized the preponderance of kilts and bagpipes in all this display. 'With all respect to the generous qualities which the Highland clans have often exhibited,' he said, 'it was difficult to forget that they had always constituted a small and almost always an unimportant part of the Scottish population. . . . But there could be no question that they were picturesque – and their enthusiasm was too sincere not to be catching.' It was so catching, in fact, that the King himself donned highland dress for one appearance, adopting the Royal Stewart tartan. Said Lady Dalrymple Hamilton when the propriety of such garb for a King was questioned: 'Oh, I don't know. If he's to be here so short a time, the more we see of him the better.'

For those who did not aspire to the wearing of a kilt, the Town Council had issued the edict that, on His Majesty's advent everybody was to be 'carefully well-dressed, black coat and white trousers if at all convenient'. How many ordinary citizens, one wonders, could afford to rig themselves out in that fashion? For many, it must have been beyond all possibility. One who declined to do so was Thomas Carlyle. Having read the edict he 'resolved rather to quit the City altogether and be absent and silent in such efflorescence of the flunkeyisms'. So he took himself off to Dumfriesshire for the duration of the royal visit. Even there, he found that no one talked of anything else and that the papers were full of it; and perhaps that served him right.

The whole programme can fortunately be seen through the eyes of several who were there. We can see it in paintings by such artists as Alexander Carse, Sir David Wilkie and James Skene and a number of English artists, including J. M. W. Turner who came to Edinburgh specially to record the visit; and we can see it, also, through several written accounts. Foremost among these is Robert Mudie's narrative, *A Historical Account of His Majesty's Visit to Scotland*. Published within a month or two of the event it describes in minute detail every incident, almost every wave of the King's hand, from the moment – 12.20 p.m. on Thursday 15 August – when he stepped ashore at Leith until, at 3.10 p.m. on Thursday 29 August, he embarked at Port Edgar, just west of Queensferry and set sail for London.

A more personal and endearing picture of the various events emerges from a different source, the letters of two young ladies

from Inverness-shire who had come to Edinburgh with their
father and brother for the great occasion. They were Jane and
Mary Grant of Rothiemurchus, twenty-two and eighteen years old
respectively, sisters of Elizabeth Grant, the highland lady from whose
memoirs we have already gained some knowledge of Edinburgh's
social life of those times. Unhappily for Elizabeth, she and her
mother were both indisposed at the time of the King's visit and so
were unable to come to Edinburgh; but this is fortunate for us as,
otherwise, there would have been no need for her sisters to write
their lively letters home conveying so much of their excitement
and delight.

On the first day, after the ceremonial welcome at Leith, the
King drove in procession up Leith Walk, the whole way lined with
representative groups and crowded on each side with cheering
citizens. At the junction with Picardy Place, just at the point where,
now, there is a wide traffic roundabout and a tall, modernistic
device of coloured light-tubes, an ornamental city gate had been
erected. There the cavalcade paused to enable the Lord Provost
and Councillors to present the King with the keys of the city which
in time-honoured fashion he returned to them for safe-keeping.
The ceremony was watched by huge crowds at windows, on roofs
and on wooden stands built in front of almost every house. From
two different houses the two Grant girls watched. 'The procession
was beautiful,' wrote Mary. 'I think the King's carriage splendid;
he was very gracious and each lady in our houses declared he gave
her a particular bow.'

Through York Place the procession went, into St Andrew Square
and then by Waterloo Place to Regent Road below the Calton
Hill, the slopes of which were black with cheering people ('How
superb!' exclaimed His Majesty) and so to Holyroodhouse. After
a short ceremony there, the King drove on to Dalkeith House
where he stayed, during his visit, as the guest of the Duke of
Buccleuch, the palace at Holyrood being used only for some of
the formal functions.

These functions included a 'drawing-room' at which more than
500 ladies were presented, all resplendent in dresses with flowing
trains requiring careful management. Among them, as eager and
anxious as any, were Jane and Mary Grant. Their good friend,
Mrs Henry Siddons, had supervised their dressing and their coiffure

for the event and she had also taught them (who better?) how to curtsey gracefully. Jane, more composed than her sister, carried it off well. 'The ease of his manner gave you confidence,' she wrote. 'Some ladies said they got no kiss at all and one was heard to say she was not satisfied, but he gave *me* a kiss'; a discriminating monarch, obviously.

Mary was more than a little nervous. She had slight difficulty with her train, which upset the timing of her approach. 'I scarcely saw the King,' she wrote. 'I don't think I even made a curtsey. I have not an idea of his face.' However, a few days later they were both made very happy when a former footman of their family sought them out specially to report that acquaintances of his who had been on duty at the drawing-room 'had heard the gentry saying they saw no one better dressed, nor who looked better, or did better, than the two Miss Grants of Rothiemurchus'.

To describe all the events and incidents of this memorable visit is impossible. In Mudie's account they filled over 300 pages. So a summary must suffice. There were two great balls in the Assembly Rooms in George Street – one given by the Peers of Scotland and one by the Caledonian Hunt – and although the King did not dance at either, 'no part of the entertainment amused his Majesty more than the reels which he stood upwards of half-an-hour to observe'.

There was a state procession to the Castle – the most splendid procession of all – with the regalia of Scotland, sword of state, sceptre and crown, carried before the King. It was only four years since these symbols of Scotland's nationhood had been discovered, in a lockfast chest in the Castle, which had been opened on the urgent representation of Sir Walter Scott and this was the first opportunity, since then, for them to be carried in such a procession. So it was, truly, a momentous occasion.

There was a banquet in Parliament Hall, given by the Town Council; a review, on Portobello sands, of cavalry and yeomanry regiments, 3000 strong, and also a contingent of several hundred highlanders; and there was a church service, attended by the King, in the High Kirk of St Giles.

On the evening of 27 August, the Theatre Royal was crowded to the roof for a royal command performance of *Rob Roy*, based on Scott's novel, with Mrs Henry Siddons as Diana Vernon and

Charles Mackay as Bailie Nicol Jarvie, the pawky and preposterous Glasgow magistrate; a part that Mackay had made so much his own that, off-stage, it must at times have been difficult to know whether one was speaking to the actor or the Bailie. The King greatly enjoyed his performance and when Bailie Nicol Jarvie exclaimed to Francis Osbaldistone 'Nane o' your London tricks here', His Majesty 'gave a hearty and sonorous laugh, such as belongs only to the most frank and generous natures'.

Throughout the whole visit every building and every house had its illuminations. With such a multitude of candles, transparencies, lamps and gas-jets it was a miracle that no serious fire occurred. At that time, there was a gas-works in Canongate with a chimney more than 300 feet high which was the centre of much criticism for many years. Even it was pressed into service, with a crown at its summit brightly lit by gas, which could be seen for miles around.

The members of the Grant family and their friends, who included Francis Jeffrey, joined the throngs in the streets and nearly wore themselves out tramping hither and thither in the late August evenings, to view the illuminations. 'Imagine if you can,' wrote Jane, 'every spot as light as noon-day, each house illuminated with splendour. But of one extraordinary fact you can form no conception. The admirable behaviour of the people. Not a drunken or an uncivil man among them. With their clean, best clothes, the common people seem to have put on their politest manners. In the most fashionable assembly, I have seen those who think themselves gentlemen push forward more rudely to procure an ice than did these honest people to satisfy their natural curiosity' – a graceful tribute to the ordinary folk of Edinburgh.

Royal visits, like all other things, come to an end. On 29 August the King, in a plain four-horse travelling carriage, with an escort of Scots Greys, drove through the city and westwards through the fine parkland of Lord Rosebery's Dalmeny estate where the procession was joined by Lord and Lady Rosebery in their carriage. At the Royal Burgh of Queensferry in the rain the Provost and Town Council and the townspeople 'in their best attire, hailed the King's appearance with the most joyous acclamations'. The bells in the tolbooth and the kirk of the burgh peeled out as the King passed through the little town, 'bowing in his usual polite and gracious manner'.

At Hopetoun House, the Earl of Hopetoun's palatial mansion about two miles west of Queensferry (designed in part by Sir William Bruce of Kinross and in part by William Adam) the King, as well as a company of archers, yeomanry and Hopetoun tenants nearly 1000 strong, was entertained to lunch by Lord Hopetoun. There the final ceremony of his Scottish visit took place. 'The name of Mr Henry Raeburn, the celebrated portrait painter, was called; and upon the appearance of that gentleman, the King took in his hand the sword of Sir Alexander Hope [who was standing nearby] when Mr Raeburn knelt – and arose, Sir Henry Raeburn.'

Almost immediately afterwards the King drove to the nearby harbour of Port Edgar and was rowed out to his yacht, the *Royal George*. His Scottish visit was over – except for the sound of the cheering crowds on the pier at Leith which was wafted out to him as the yacht, with her escort vessels, sailed past the city towards the open sea.

The visit of the King had been a right royal occasion and the people had entered into the spirit of it with verve and enthusiasm. Sir Walter Scott, as one of its chief organizers, had revelled in it. Rather less than five years later, there came another great occasion for him; brief, less elaborate and unpremeditated but, this time, an occasion in which he played the leading role.

It was the theatrical fund dinner, held in the Assembly Rooms in George Street on 23 February 1827. This was an inaugural dinner to mark the founding of a fund for retired and needy actors, and for it, 300 people were seated in the great ballroom – all gentlemen, of course; ladies did not yet attend public dinners. On the invitation of William Murray, Theatre Manager, who organized the event, Sir Walter Scott was there as chairman, supported by several of his friends, including Robert Dundas of Arniston, the Earl of Fife and Sir John Hope of Pinkie. Another of his friends, Lord Meadowbank, had come at short notice and, at the last moment, was asked to propose the toast of 'the Chairman'.

As speakers in such circumstances have to do, he cast around urgently in his mind for something suitable to say; and the inspiration that came to him was to announce that the author of the Waverley novels was none other than their Chairman for the evening. A quick whispered conversation with Sir Walter followed, in order to obtain his consent. Then Lord Meadowbank proposed

the toast of 'the Great Unknown . . . to whom, as a people, we owe
a large and heavy debt of gratitude. . . . He it is who has conferred a
new reputation on our national character and bestowed on
Scotland an imperishable name.' Lockhart, in his *Life*, adds that,
long before the learned Lord had finished speaking, the storm of
applause had become deafening and 'the company had got upon
chairs and tables' which says much for their enthusiasm but little
for their manners.

When the cheering ended, Sir Walter, obviously relishing every
moment, declared himself now to be on trial before Lord Meadowbank. 'If I chose to defend myself against the charge of authorship,'
he said, 'any impartial jury would surely bring in a verdict of not
proven.' But he did not so choose; he was prepared to plead
guilty to the charge of being author, and he meant total and un-
divided author, for his novels, he said, contained not one single
word that was not derived from himself alone.

When the renewed cheering had died down, Sir Walter turned
to the actor, Charles Mackay, and proposed 'the health of my
friend Bailie Nicol Jarvie' whereupon Mackay, in the voice of the
Bailie (he never could escape from that character) replied: 'My
conscience. My worthy faither could never have believed his son
would hae sic a compliment paid to him by the Great Unknown.'

Among those present at the dinner was Miles Fletcher, son of
Mrs Fletcher (of 'the clever set') whose autobiography has already
provided us with some glimpses of her times. When he arrived
home he told her that Sir Walter had publicly declared himself the
author of the novels. His mother's comment was that the fact
was 'already as well-known as if he had proclaimed it at the market-
cross ten years before', which was true because, in acknowledging
the toast in his honour, Scott had said that the secret had previously
been 'communicated to more than twenty people'. Such a secret
told to twenty people was unlikely to remain a secret long and this
one had soon become an open secret.

The Fletchers, of course, did not much admire Scott. Though
he had been a near neighbour in Castle Street, they belonged to
an opposite political set. Once, when someone had offered to give
them a plaster cast of a bust of Sir Walter by the sculptor Chantrey,
they had declined the offer and had asked to be given instead one
of Sir Samuel Romilly, the social reformer whose principles, they

explained, were more in keeping with their own. While believing Sir Walter to be 'an excellent private character, as well as a man of consummate genius', Mrs Fletcher considered that he was 'one of those great men who have an undue estimate of the pride of life and, though he did not care for money, he cared too much for baronial towers and aristocratical distinction'. However, the theatrical dinner was the first public function Sir Walter had attended since financial disaster had engulfed him a year before and, however superfluous his acknowledgement of authorship may have been, to begrudge him those moments of vociferous acclamation would have been churlish indeed.

Two more great events, neither royal nor literary, followed a few years later in 1832 and 1834. Both were occasions of great public rejoicing and demonstration in Edinburgh. The reason for the first was the passing of the Parliamentary Reform Act; for the second, the triumphal visit of Earl Grey who had recently retired from parliament and who, when Prime Minister, had been largely responsible, by his statesmanship and energy, for the successful passage through parliament of that Act and also of the Burgh Reform Act which followed it in 1833.

Why did the passing of these two Acts – dreary bits of legislation as they may seem to be – mean so much to the people of Edinburgh, and of Scotland generally? For the answer to that question it is necessary to put oneself briefly in the position of the ordinary citizen just before the Acts were passed.

Neither in the election of his member of parliament nor in that of his town councillor did he have any say whatever. County members of parliament were elected by a few well-to-do landowners; burgh members, representing royal burghs only, were, except in Edinburgh, elected for groups of burghs, four or five of which might share one member of parliament appointed not by the people but by the Town Councils who themselves were not democratically elected. Edinburgh alone among all the burghs had its own member of parliament, shared with no other town, but he, too, was appointed by the Town Council. As for the Town Councils, until 1833, they were more or less self-perpetuating, their members elected by an elaborate but wholly undemocratic procedure (ritual would be a better word) which was gone through annually in October, accompanied by a good deal of junketting.

M

So, when the Reform Acts gave a say in the choice of MP and Councillor to every man who was of full age and who was also qualified as a '£10 ratepayer', these were undoubtedly occasions for rejoicing even although many were still left without a vote. Forty years before, Lord Braxfield had eagerly sentenced to transportation leaders of the 'Friends of the People' who, rather clumsily and brashly perhaps, had sought to gain reforms along these lines. During those forty years others, wiser and more sophisticated in their approach, had carried on the struggle – Jeffrey, Cockburn and Alexander Fletcher among them. So, when the Reform Act was passed in 1832, the Whigs and others who were liberal-minded, as well as the ordinary man in the street, were all naturally exultant. Success having crowned their long effort, it was natural to think it a time for public rejoicing.

Within four weeks of the passing of the Act a great demonstration was organized in the city by the Trades Council and the many trades organizations. The *Scotsman* reported that the procession which assembled on Bruntsfield Links 'for numerical strength and magnificent display immeasurably surpassed any pageant of the kind ever witnessed in Edinburgh'; and at that point their reporter, obviously overwhelmed by the general excitement added; 'or perhaps on the face of the yet-discovered globe'.

His last phrase can be discounted as a piece of hyperbole, excusable in the circumstances, but the pageant does seem to have been something quite out of the ordinary. The number marching in the procession was said to be 15000 and the *Scotsman* estimated the crowd assembled on the Links at 80000. In addition, said their reporter, 'the trees were crowded with urchins, root and branch'.

The programme opened with '"Rule, Britannia", sung by upwards of fifty professional gentlemen' scarcely enough, one might think, to be heard by all the 80000 but perhaps many others joined in to augment the professional choir. Then, several loyal resolutions were passed. Together with the choice of song, the purpose of the resolutions presumably was to emphasize the constitutional nature of the triumph that was being celebrated and to allay any lingering fears among the Tories of Edinburgh that this might be a subversive demonstration.

Eventually, the procession moved off. It consisted of contingents from seventy organizations vying with one another to display the most ornate and elaborate banners. Some represented groups such as the Caledonian Youths, the Highland Societies and the Cramond Trades; but most represented single crafts – masons, joiners, hatters, saddlers, blacksmiths, brewers, shawl-makers, to name just some chosen at random; and among them, there was a contingent of sedan-chairmen. The *Scotsman* report, showing some partiality, gave more space to the display of the letter-press printers than to that of any other trade.

The route taken by the long crocodile, with bands playing and banners waving, was by Lothian Road, Charlotte Square and Princes Street; then down Leith Walk to the toll-bar near the Leith boundary to meet and exchange greetings with a smaller Leith procession. On the return journey to Bruntsfield Links, the route included the Canongate and parts of the old town, making a round trip of fully six miles.

Two years later enthusiasm was not diminished. Earl Grey retired from parliament in July 1834 and immediately arrangements were made to honour him in Edinburgh. For his visit on Monday, 18 September, two functions were arranged. In the afternoon, in the Waterloo Hotel, Waterloo Place, the Freedom of the City, and addresses from other towns in Scotland as well as from trades organizations were to be presented to him and in the early evening a great public dinner was to be held.

There had been a ceremony in the morning in Dalkeith, and soon after lunch time the Earl and Countess in a carriage-and-four, followed by other carriages carrying distinguished visitors, arrived in the city. They were met near the boundary by a procession of trades representatives with scarves and banners and drove to Waterloo Place through streets lined with spectators. It was re-ported that every shop was closed and nothing was to be heard but congratulation and rejoicing.

For the Freedom ceremony only a limited number of people could be accommodated in the hotel ballroom to see the Lord Provost, the Rt Hon. James Spittal present the burgess ticket, in a richly ornamented gold box which was inscribed to the Earl, in testimony not only of his splendid talents and virtues but also of gratitude for his eminent services as Prime Minister and, 'above all for the great measure of Parliamentary Reform which, while it was of inestimable benefit to the empire at large, was peculiarly gratifying to the people of Scotland, as bestowing upon them the political weight and consideration due to citizens of a free state'. They would also see addresses presented by the Councils of thirty-seven other burghs, from Wigtown in the south-west to Dingwall in the north-east and on behalf of the inhabitants of eleven other populous districts, as well as several trade and mercantile bodies.

For the dinner, the aim had been to enable everyone to attend who wished to do so. No hall was large enough and so Thomas Hamilton, architect of the Royal High School at Calton Hill had been hurriedly commissioned to design an immense dining-hall of wood and canvas to be built, for this one occasion only, in the playground of the school. In record time it was designed and built: 113 feet long and 110 feet wide, sufficient to accommodate at least 1500 diners, and 1000 more to hear the after-dinner speeches. Its interior decoration was by David Roberts, one-time scene painter at the Theatre Royal and later a Royal Academician. For lighting, the great gas chandelier from the Theatre Royal was borrowed and gas was laid on to it and to four smaller ones fitted up at the corners of the pavilion. These lighting arrangements unexpectedly upset the programme because the Duke of Hamilton, who was to have been in the Chair, suffered from an eye complaint and could not face the brilliance of the lighting. So his place was taken by the Earl of Rosebery.

Admission to the Grey Pavilion as it was named, was thoroughly organized. Holders of white tickets (1500 or more) were instructed to form themselves into groups of thirty persons each in the school playground whence they would be led to their tables by stewards. The holders of 800 buff tickets would dine 'as best they could' in the classrooms of the school and would join the main party in the pavilion after dinner; in addition (and this was quite an innovation), space would be reserved for ladies to come in to hear the speeches. When that time came 'a brilliant cluster of 240 ladies' attended. They included the Countess Grey who was seen to be 'much affected' by the great cheering which followed the drinking of her health, proposed by the Marquess of Breadalbane.

At this point it gives me pleasure to hand over the task of describing the occasion to a young journalist who, having only recently joined the staff of the *Morning Chronicle* in London, had been detailed to cover the Earl Grey dinner in Edinburgh. He was Charles Dickens, then twenty-two years old and unknown. His *Sketches by Boz* and *Pickwick Papers* and all his other brilliant novels were yet to come. Along with his friend and fellow-journalist, Tom Beard, he arrived by sea at Leith a few days before the event. It was his first visit to Edinburgh and he was much impressed. It was also his first sea trip, the sea was rough and he did not greatly enjoy that.

In the *Morning Chronicle* of Thursday, 18 September 1834, the account of the Earl Grey celebrations sent to the paper by the two young reporters fills more than ten closely-printed columns. Almost all the space is devoted to verbatim reports of the many laudatory speeches that were made, but there are a few short passages of description on the subject of the dinner which, from their style and witty observation, must surely have been written by Dickens. Here they are.

It had been announced that the dinner would take place at five o'clock precisely: but Earl Grey and the other principal visitors did not arrive until shortly after six. . . . A gentleman who, we presume, had entered with one of the first sections, having sat with exemplary patience for some time in the immediate vicinity of cold fowls, roast beef, lobsters and other tempting delicacies (for the dinner was a cold one) appeared to think that the best thing he could possibly do, would be to eat his dinner, while there was anything to eat. He accordingly laid about him with right good will; the example was contagious and the clatter of knives and forks became general. Hereupon, several gentlemen who were not hungry cried out 'Shame!' and looked very indignant: and several gentlemen who were hungry cried 'Shame!' too, eating, nevertheless, all the while, as fast as they possibly could. In this dilemma one of the stewards mounted a bench and feelingly represented to the delinquents the enormity of their conduct, imploring them, for decency's sake, to defer the process of mastication until the arrival of Earl Grey. This address was loudly cheered, but totally unheeded: and this is, perhaps, one of the few instances on record of a dinner having been virtually concluded before it began. . . .

[After Earl Grey and the principal guests arrived] The Chairman entreated the assembly to postpone the commencement of the dinner for a few moments. The Reverend Mr Henry Grey was in attendance for the purpose of saying grace; but he was outside the room and the crowd was so great, that he could not get in. Under these circumstances, the Chairman entreated them to pause for a few minutes. As the major part of the company had already dined, they acceded to the request with the utmost good humour. The Rev. Gentleman arrived; grace was said; and the same ceremony was repeated at the conclusion, which soon arrived. . . .

Another trifling delay was occasioned by the arrival of the gentlemen who had dined in the school-room with the buff tickets, for whose accommodation seats were hastily placed in the spaces which had been previously occupied by the waiters. The Chairman enquired of the stewards whether all the company were yet seated? Several stewards replied in the negative; and various gentlemen corroborated the assertion, by exclaiming that it was entirely impossible they could sit down anywhere.

As he wrote those paragraphs it cannot have entered Charles Dickens's mind for a moment that, less than seven years later, in June 1841, he himself would be the guest of honour at a dinner in Edinburgh, attended by more than 300 people and, a few days afterwards, would receive the Freedom of the City: 'in testimony of the sense entertained by the Magistrates and Council of his distinguished abilities as an author'.

For the time being he was a young reporter on what was probably his first assignment for his paper. The speeches were going on interminably in the stuffy atmosphere of the Grey Pavilion, taxing to the full his very considerable skill and speed as a shorthand writer. There were at least twenty-four speeches and many toasts, interspersed by songs and orchestral items, selected with more or less apt reference to the toasts immediately preceding them. The selection of a glee, 'He has made the people free', was not inappropriate to follow the toast to Earl Grey who, besides his reform achievements in home affairs had also played a large part in the abolition of slavery in the British colonies. It may be open to doubt whether Sir John Dalrymple, whose health was next proposed by the Earl was pleased when the toast was followed by a song, 'I'll clout my Johnny's grey breeks'.

The two reporters obviously carried out their task conscientiously and well but, having read through all the speeches, as long, laudatory and repetitive as speeches on such occasions tend to be, one cannot help wishing they had devoted less space to them and more to the kind of light-hearted description of the proceedings with which their report of the dinner began. That being so, it is a relief to turn to the previous day's issue of the *Chronicle* and to find there a paragraph by 'Our Own Correspondent' which Charles Dickens must have written on the previous Saturday, just after he arrived in Edinburgh. It deals, not with a great occasion but with one kind of little occasion popular in the city in those days. It must have been a very sunny September day, for this is what he wrote:

A promenade took place this morning in St Andrew's Square, for the benefit of the Blind Asylum, the Deaf and Dumb Institution and the House of Refuge: it was most respectably attended, but a lamentably dull affair. A marquee was erected in the centre of a parched bit of ground, without a tree or shrub to intercept the rays of a burning sun. Under it was a military band, and around it were the company. The band played and the company walked about; and when the band was tired, a piper played by way of variation and then the company walked about again; and when the piper was tired, such of the visitors as could find seats sat down and those who could not, looked as if they wished they had not come.

With a flash of that feeling for the less fortunate which later played so large a part in his novels, his report went on:

The poor blind-school pupils, who occupied the warmest seats in the enclosure were very hot and uncomfortable, and appeared very glad to be filed off from a scene in which they could take little interest and with which their pensive, care-worn faces painfully contrasted.

Although Charles Dickens found the promenade 'lamentably dull', his view was not shared by the local press. The *Edinburgh Evening Courant* reported, a few days later, that 'the Grand Promenade held in St Andrew Square last Saturday (the last for the season) was by far the most splendid for beauty and fashion that ever took place in Edinburgh, there being upwards of 2000 present'. The *Courant* went on to say that the nett proceeds which had been handed over in equal portions to the three charities mentioned had amounted, in total, to £90.

15 Social problems

While the families in the New Town were entertaining in the comfortable drawing-rooms of their spacious houses and enjoying their conversations and card-playing and other social occasions, conditions in the old part of the city were going from bad to worse; and, although that aspect of Edinburgh's story is not a pleasant one, it has to be looked at if anything approaching a balanced view is to be seen. It was partly because the comfortable, better-off citizens did not look at that other side of the picture, in many cases did not admit or even know it existed, that conditions became so bad; until, one November night in 1861, a disaster occurred that revealed conditions of squalor and crowding to which they could no longer turn a blind eye.

It would be unfair to imply that no one had cared. A few people, mainly clergy and medical men, had been preaching, writing and working for years in an effort to improve the lot of the poor and the underprivileged. To give even a faint notion of what they were up against I must turn to figures; but I promise to keep this statistical bit to the briefest and, in return, all I ask is that the figures be seen not just as numbers on a page but as families of men, women and children crowded into the tall, dark and in some cases tottering tenements of the old town.

I will take just one example out of many: the building known as Middle Mealmarket Stairs in the Cowgate. Not long before its demolition in the 1860s to make way for extensions of the Law Courts it was said that 'for filth, poverty and overcrowding it was not surpassed in the city'. On its five flats it accommodated fifty-six families, totalling 248 people, with neither sink nor water-closet among them; a state of affairs that existed, in varying degree, in many other buildings.

To turn from the particular to the general, a report on the census of 1851 showed that in the fifty years since 1801 the number of people living in the old town had grown from 20 000 to 30 000, an increase of 50 per cent. During that period of fifty years there had been no corresponding increase in the number of houses. So it was only by a process of division and sub-division that additional dwellings had been provided for the increased population – if, in fact, a single room in a crudely sub-divided house can be called a dwelling. So the figures meant that, in the old town generally, in the mid-nineteenth century, at least thirty people were living where only twenty had lived before and those twenty, it will be recalled, had already been pretty tightly packed together.

Some part of the rise in numbers would be due to natural increase – the excess of births over deaths – and some would be due to the general drift from country to town although that was less marked in Edinburgh than in Glasgow and other industrial centres. In addition, the author of the 1851 census report attributed a large part of the increase to the growth of the railways which brought from Ireland, to work on their construction, many who afterwards settled in the city.

Whatever the causes, the poverty and the overcrowding became intolerable. In such conditions, the death rate was high and sickness was rife. Yet the authorities did little about it except in times of epidemic. In the years 1831–2 there was a country-wide epidemic of cholera. To combat this in Edinburgh, a local board of health was set up consisting of medical men, Town Council representatives, clergymen and others, totalling thirty-five. Fortunately for them the disease gave some warning of its approach. It had started in the south of England and it seems to have moved northwards along the main coaching routes, carried by travellers from the south. Turning the pages of newspapers for the last weeks of 1831 and the first few weeks of 1832, it is fascinating in a grim kind of way to follow its progress. First, there are reports of cases at Grantham and, a few days later, at York; then at Newcastle . . . Berwick . . . then Haddington; and, on 28 January 1832, the headline in the *Edinburgh Evening Courant* is: 'The cholera has reached Edinburgh.'

The breathing space provided by that steady progress of the disease gave time for the Edinburgh board of health to make plans and, during the course of the epidemic, they organized a kind of mini-health and social service in the city although no one then thought of it quite in that way. It was known that dirt, undernourishment and lack of warmth and proper clothing all helped the disease to do its worst, so the efforts of the board were directed against these conditions.

First, streets must be cleaned and the closes and houses in the poorest districts whitewashed, so staff were employed for that work. Then the practice of keeping pigs in the ground-floor rooms of houses which, astonishingly, was still prevalent in some areas, must be stamped out. This, with the help of the police, the board managed to achieve before the disease reached the city.

To provide nourishment and warmth, soup kitchens were opened and donations of coal, clothing and food were collected for distribution to the poorest families. Because the danger of infecting other patients was too great, the Infirmary would not admit persons suffering from cholera and so four special cholera hospitals were opened in buildings hastily adapted for the purpose.

In this combined operation many private citizens helped in different ways. It was reported of Duncan McLaren, who much later became Lord Provost and, afterwards, a member of parliament for the city, that as a young man during the epidemic he had carried patients to hospital on his back and had been fortunate not to contract the disease in doing so. Without all these efforts, the ravages of the outbreak would undoubtedly have been much greater. As it was, the records show that, in 1832, 1886 persons in Edinburgh contracted the disease, of whom 1065 died.

Here, one might have thought, was an opportunity to retain some form of permanent organization to improve conditions in the poorest quarters of the city; but after the 1832 epidemic and a lesser one following it, the board of health was disbanded, the temporary hospitals were dismantled and the whole organization of help for the poor lapsed.

There was, of course, the Charity Workhouse (it stood where Forrest Road is now) in which Robert Fergusson had died in 1774; and both Canongate burgh and the parish of St Cuthbert's, which covered a wide country area west of the Castle, had their poor-houses in which, in the last extremities of poverty or old age, the very poorest could find shelter. But otherwise poor relief was minimal and its distribution haphazard. In Edinburgh, two men at that time led two opposing factions seeking to improve the situation. Both sincerely sought to ease the circumstances of the poor but the conflict between their opposite views undoubtedly helped to delay progress for several years.

One was the Rev. Thomas Chalmers whose statue stands in George Street at the Castle Street crossing. After nine years' work in a poor Glasgow parish and six years as Professor of Moral Philosophy at St Andrew's University he had come to Edinburgh in 1828, at the age of forty-eight, to be Professor of Divinity. He was one of those who at the 'disruption' in 1843 led the procession of 470 ministers and members out of the General Assembly of the Church of Scotland in St Andrew's Church, George Street, to Tanfield Hall at Canonmills to found the Free Church of Scotland. He became first Moderator of the Free Church Assembly and first Principal of the Free Church College. That, however is a different story.

The other leading figure in the struggle to improve conditions was a medical man, Dr William Pulteney Alison, of whom you will find no statue. He was born in Edinburgh in 1790 and lived all his life in the city, almost the whole of it in Heriot Row. Though he held, at different times, three professorships in the Faculty of Medicine at the University he is, deservedly, remembered mainly for his efforts to improve the lot of the poor.

Not long after he had become a doctor there had been opened at 17 Thistle Street (less than ten minutes' walk from his home) the New Town Dispensary, supported by charitable donations, the object of which was to provide medical advice and attention for needy persons in their own homes and he immediately became one of its two physicians. His work for it gave him a deep insight into the way in which the poorest of Edinburgh's citizens then lived. Toiling up long stairs and groping into dark and crowded cellars he gave the same care and attention to the most wretched

of the dispensary's patients as to those who could pay him well.
Indeed, it was said that what could have become for him a lucrative
practice among the wealthy never developed because of his pre-
occupation with the poor.

Dr Alison was among the first to draw attention to the close
relationship between poverty and disease and, in his annual
reports on the work of the dispensary, he set out to demonstrate
that connection. He also wrote numerous pamphlets in which he
insisted that only a system of compulsory assessment and an
officially organized arrangement for distributing poor relief could
ease the problem of poverty and its attendant diseases – diseases
which, he was careful to point out, might start among 'the lower
orders' but could not be relied upon to limit their effects to any
one stratum of society.

In putting forward his case William Alison was moved not only
by his first-hand experience of conditions in the back streets of
the city and his medical knowledge, but also by a deeply held
religious belief. Yet, strangely, his sternest opponents in his efforts
for reform were men of equally deep religious feelings. Foremost
among them was Thomas Chalmers who preached and wrote
uncompromisingly that charity was a Christian act which must be
voluntarily undertaken and not imposed through a system of
compulsory assessment. Compulsion would deaden the heart of
the giver and encourage the recipient to think he need not try
to help himself.

So Thomas Chalmers urged that all assistance to the poor must
be voluntary and freely given. Any officially imposed system was
anathema to him. If the voluntary method did not work then,
presumably, the poor must simply grin and bear it. What William
Alison could never understand was why it must be assumed that
a spirit of Christian goodwill could not accompany the payment of
an officially collected poor rate as readily as it might accompany
a coin placed in a church collecting-box. But the possibility that
it might do so was something which Chalmers and his colleagues
could not or would not accept.

Eventually, a Royal Commission came down firmly on the side
of Dr Alison and the Poor Law Amendment (Scotland) Act of
1845 was passed, bringing about almost all the reforms for which
he had agitated for so long. Though the system of poor relief

introduced by that Act fell far short of present-day ideas of social
security, it was, in its time, a considerable step forward.

William Alison was by no means the only medical man in
Edinburgh who went out of his way to help the poorest of patients.
There have always been those who would do so as a matter of
course. Sir J. Y. Simpson, at the height of his fashionable fame,
would willingly journey from his Queen Street home to a garret
in the Canongate to bring the benefit of his skill to a patient who
needed it. Like Alison, he also was distressed by the conditions he
saw on such visits and missed no opportunity of pointing out the
need for reform.

In 1829, at just about the time that Simpson had begun his work,
James Syme, one of the most famous of Edinburgh's many famous
surgeons, opened a hospital of his own with twenty-four beds, in
Minto House, a mansion which stood in what is now Chambers
Street. Admittedly, he did so partly – perhaps mainly – for his own
benefit. Through a difference of opinion with colleagues he had
been denied facilities in the surgical wards of the Infirmary. Then
thirty years old, he was laying the foundation of his great reputation which earned him the unofficial title of 'the Napoleon of
Surgery' and he needed access to beds and patients, in order to
develop his skills and pass them on to his students. But the fact
remains that, in the first four years' existence of the little Minto
House hospital, some 8000 patients were treated there. Most of
them were poor and more than half the cost of their treatment
and maintenance was met by Syme himself, the remainder coming
from students' fees and donations.

Among leading churchmen who strove, in the middle of the
nineteenth century, to improve the sordid conditions they saw
around them in the city were Thomas Guthrie and James Begg,
both Church of Scotland ministers who, like Chalmers, seceded
to the Free Church. Guthrie's chief concern was the plight of the
homeless and neglected children who then roamed the streets. For
them, in 1847, he founded schools where they were given food,
instruction in reading, writing and arithmetic and, if they were
old enough, training in the rudiments of a craft. Religious training,
also, was part of the daily programme but, with a broad-minded-
ness rare in those days, Guthrie did not insist on this if a child
had parents who could show that he received such teaching from

them even though it might be in the tenets of another denomination.

The first of Guthrie's schools was opened in Ramsay Lane, close to the Castle esplanade, where the building it occupied can still be seen with a carved stone bible above the door displaying the text 'Search the scriptures'. With that peculiarly Victorian combination of sympathy and insensitivity, he named his schools the 'Edinburgh Original Ragged Industrial Schools'. His *Plea for Ragged Schools* was widely read and led to the establishment of many similar schools. Today, direct successors of his first school still bearing his name (but happily not now 'Ragged') play their part in the provision made, in Scotland, for the care and training of children who are in need or have been in trouble.

While Thomas Guthrie was pioneering work among deprived children, James Begg was concerning himself with the daunting problem of housing. His sermons and writings on the subject were collected in a booklet which he called *Happy Homes for Working Men* and his special achievement lay in the formation of co-operative building societies for those who, being in employment, were not in abject poverty but yet could not find the means to provide themselves and their families with decent homes.

The Edinburgh Co-operative Building Society, founded by Begg, provided several schemes of 'model working-class dwellings'. One of the best of these, built in the 1860s and known as 'the colonies' is at Glenogle Road near Stockbridge, where eleven short parallel terraces, at right angles to the Water of Leith, still provide good accommodation in surroundings which retain something of the rural character which must originally have been a feature of the scheme. At the ends of six of the terraces are small, attractive, stone carvings depicting the tools of the trades involved in their building – the mason's mallet, the carpenter's saw, the blacksmith's anvil and so on. These carefully executed little carvings reflect the pride with which the original occupiers must have seen their homes completed.

The men whose efforts on behalf of their fellow citizens we have just seen were among the few who thought about such problems at that time. In contrast to the 'social mix' of the previous century when, as Robert Chambers put it in his *Traditions of Edinburgh*, 'gentle and semple living within the confines of a single close or even a single stair knew and took an interest in each other', it was now as though a curtain had dropped between the New Town and the old. For many of the families living in the comfortable houses of Queen Street, Great King Street and Moray Place, the crowded 'lands' of the High Street and the Cowgate were not only out of sight but also out of mind. The opposite applied too. An old woman living in the High Street who had not been in Princes Street for many years was asked why this was so. 'Och,' she replied, 'Princes Street's no' for the likes of us'; and she seemed to regard that as a perfectly satisfactory answer.

Then, as I said at the beginning of this chapter, a disaster happened. Just after one o'clock on Sunday morning, 24 November 1861, there occurred, in the words of a contemporary press report, 'one of the most calamitous and heartrending occurrences which it has ever been our duty to record'. The whole seven-storey tenement at 101 High Street 'fell with a tremendous crash and in an instant was swallowed up in a cloud of dust and rubbish'. All the floors from top to bottom had given way and the front wall had fallen outwards, leaving only the back wall standing.

The fire brigade and other rescue workers were quickly called out and their work of rescue and search among the ruins went on for several days; on one of these they were visited by 'a very eminent stranger at present in our city, Mr Charles Dickens, who showed the liveliest interest in the scene and story of the calamity'. At one stage, as the workers were struggling to lift heavy joists and debris a boy's voice was heard calling from beneath the rubble: 'Heave awa' chaps, I'm no' dead yet.' Eventually he was pulled to safety; and a year or so later, when a new tenement was built on the site, at Paisley Close, a carving of the boy's head was placed above the entrance, surmounted by a scroll bearing his words of exhortation to his rescuers. There it can still be seen, on the tenement which has been known ever since as 'Heave awa' hoose'.

The boy himself lived for many years to tell the tale. He was one of the lucky ones. The building, belonging to seven different owners, had been occupied by twenty-five families, several of whom kept lodgers and it was said that nearly 100 people had been sleeping in its many rooms when the disaster occurred. Of these, thirty-five were killed and many gravely injured. It was this disaster and its

dramatic revelation of the conditions in which people were living
that shook the smug citizens out of their complacency. Within a
day or two both Begg and Guthrie had addressed public meetings
pointing out that the disaster had illustrated, all too vividly,
points they had been making for years about the urgent need for
better living conditions for the poor.

More public meetings followed and within a year, as a direct
result of the catastrophe and the public concern it had belatedly
aroused, the Town Council decided (though even then only
by a majority of one vote) to appoint Edinburgh's first Medical
Officer of Health, with an immediate remit to report on the sanitary condition of the city and propose measures for improvement.

A searching technical inquiry was also held at which many
witnesses were examined. The inquiry found that the strength of
the tenement which was said to have been more than 200 years
old, had depended on a great central wall rising from foundation
level to the chimney-stack, seventy feet above the ground. Several
years before, openings had been made in that wall by the owner
of the ground flat shop without any official inspection or approval.
A boiler had also been inserted, the heat from which had tended
to disintegrate the mortar in what remained of the wall. Gradually
it had weakened till breaking-point was reached. The immediate
result of that disclosure was to tighten up the enforcement, by
the Dean of Guild Court of the city, of the regulations then govern-
ing the construction of buildings; the longer-term result was the
development of a thorough and effective system of building
inspection and control.

The strangest disclosure from the evidence given at the inquiry
was the long period during which there had been obvious signs
that the building was likely to collapse. Only one man had recognized the signs and no one had heeded his warnings. He was
Gavin Greenshields, a working joiner. For many weeks he had been
employed by the owners to adjust doors in the tenement which
repeatedly jammed as the building settled. About a month before
the disaster, he told the inquiry, he had been taking his barrow
down Paisley Close when it stuck, where it had never stuck before,
against a bulge in the wall. In the following weeks he found the
bulge increasing steadily, so he told some of the tenants 'who only
laughed'.

Later, he called on one of the owners at his comfortable home in the suburbs and warned him of the danger; but that owner afterwards told the inquiry that 'he did not think Greenshields' opinion entitled to any weight'. When a large block of stone fell into the close on the day before the final crash Gavin, greatly alarmed, hurried off to report the matter to his employer. If he had gone instead to the police or the city superintendent of works the outcome could have been very different. But he went to his employer who told him brusquely to mind his own business. Even when events had so disastrously proved him right, the only reason his employer could give for not having heeded him was that 'Gavin was a peculiar man, always talking nonsense'. On this occasion it was found, too late, that his nonsense had been sound sense.

The appointment of Medical Officer of Health also made sound sense. The man selected to be the first MOH, not first in Edinburgh alone, but in all Scotland, was Dr Henry Duncan Littlejohn. He was then thirty-five years old and had been police surgeon in the city for about six years, a post which had given him a special know-ledge of conditions in the least salubrious districts. He was energetic, forthright, a humanitarian devoted to his cause and unlikely to be a respecter of anyone who might seem to be putting obstacles in his way. He held his appointment as Medical Officer for forty-six years retiring in 1908, at the age of eighty-one. For forty years he was a lecturer in Forensic Medicine at the University and was appointed Professor in 1897. His knowledge in that sphere and his experience as police surgeon led to his being much in demand as an expert witness in cases where medical evidence was required and it is said that because of his reputation for giving sharp and witty answers under cross-examination, his students used to flock to the court when it was known that he was to be in the witness box.

During all his years in office Sir Henry Littlejohn made many innovations, sometimes against strong opposition and there can be few aspects of health administration today which do not owe something to his insight and initiative. It can truly be said that, because of him, Edinburgh became a better city in which to live.

N

16 Health pioneer

Sir Henry Littlejohn's service as police surgeon and Medical Officer of Health spanned more than two-thirds of the long reign of Queen Victoria and four-fifths of the short one of Edward VII. So his life and work provide a frame within which to view changes and developments that carried Edinburgh through the nineteenth century and into the twentieth. Some of the most far reaching of these were improvements for which he was largely responsible.

He had begun his official career in 1856, just when the area over which the Town Council held sway had been extended to include the burghs of Canongate and Easter and Wester Portsburgh and suburban areas as far west as Coltbridge (beyond Donaldson's Hospital), as far south as Newington and as far east as Meadowbank, increasing the size of the city at one stroke from 600 acres to 4500. The duties of Medical Officer of Health extended over the whole of that area. At the same time, there had been an administrative change, the Town Council of forty-one members taking over responsibility for police, lighting and cleansing and a few other functions from a separate body of ninety-six commissioners of police which had been evolved, under a cumbersome system of dual control, on the pattern of those original southern district commissioners who were so concerned about the bickering of boys in the streets around George Square.

The change had not been brought about without argument, in course of which one bold commissioner of police suggested that the Town Council should be abolished and their functions transferred to the police commissioners. He did not thereby endear himself to the Lord Provost, Bailies and Councillors, ever conscious of the centuries of tradition they represented and, in the event, it was the mundane and merely functional body of police commissioners who disappeared from the scene. Now, in 1975, the Town Council have also gone, but a Lord Provost remains at the head of the new Edinburgh District Council to carry on some of the old traditions.

As first Medical Officer of Health, Dr Littlejohn's immediate remit was to produce a comprehensive report on the sanitary condition of the city. For that daunting task he was allocated a staff of one clerk and one police constable. In 1974, when Edinburgh's seventh and last Medical Officer of Health, Dr J. L. Gilloran, transferred to the new Lothian Health Board to continue, as the Board's first Specialist in Community Medicine to care for the health of the city along with that of its surrounding area, a staff of more than 500 transferred with him, many of them highly qualified in branches of the medical, nursing and allied professions. That comparison sharply illustrates the growth of public health care in little more than a century. It is a growth to which Sir Henry Littlejohn made an impressive contribution.

In producing his report, Dr Littlejohn was helped not only by his staff of two but also by three or four other city officials and, it is said, also by Dr J. Y. Simpson who, as we have seen, was deeply concerned about conditions in the poorer areas. For the purposes of this report, Littlejohn divided the city into nineteen 'sanitary districts' for each of which he painstakingly collected facts and figures to show living conditions, work patterns, death rates among adults and children and the incidence of diseases. Then, by comparing the facts for one district with those for others, he was able to demonstrate what now needs no demonstration but then had to be hammered home, that proneness to disease and high death rates are directly related to the conditions in which people live and work.

When it was published in 1865, the report created something of a sensation. Never a man to mince words, Dr Littlejohn had been outspoken about the conditions he had uncovered and he called for regulations to control all manner of things, from building standards and property maintenance to the conditions in underground bakehouses and the way in which the city's 2000 cows were housed and looked after. He called urgently for regulations which he could enforce to prevent the sale of unsound meat and contaminated milk; and his criticism of those engaged in such trades upset quite a number of people whose vested interests might be affected.

Undoubtedly the most important part of his report and the part that made the greatest visible impact on the city was the chapter dealing with the need for the clearing of slum areas. The fact that his recommendations on that subject were quickly and vigorously followed up was due only in part to their obvious urgency. It was due much more to the chance that the right man to help him appeared in the right place at the right time. He was William Chambers whom we last met as a young man delivering books to residents in the sanctuary of Holyrood. In 1865, a prosperous publisher in partnership with his brother Robert in the firm of W. & R. Chambers, he became Lord Provost; and he proved to be just the ally Dr Littlejohn needed. Between them, they carried through the first great slum clearance and improvement scheme Edinburgh had seen. Previous schemes, such as the building of Waterloo Place in 1815, the construction of Johnston Terrace and George IV Bridge in the 1830s and the building of Cockburn Street by the Railway Access Company about 1860 had been primarily for the improvement of communications, any slum clearance that resulted being only a by-product. This time, the whole purpose of the project was the improvement of housing conditions.

According to William Chambers' own account, it was his interest in the housing problem that led him to accept the Lord Provostship. He said: 'I entertained the conviction that the insalubrity, vice and misery that prevailed were traceable, in great measure, to that wrong system of house construction which consists in narrow courts and alleys. If I could possibly obliterate the hideous results in these quarters, a good deal would be done.'

Only a month or so after becoming Lord Provost he said, in a speech to the Town Council:

Almost every day since I was elected I have perambulated the closes of the old town. I have scrutinised every one of them from Old Fishmarket Close to St John Street. Besides looking into every accessible hole and corner, I have gone to the tops of the taller buildings to get a good bird's-eye view of the whole concern. So far as I have gone I can fully bear out the published opinions of Dr Littlejohn as to the absolute necessity for opening up the closes. The great question is, how are they to be opened up; for that lies at the basis of all sanitary reform.

He went on to explain that the aims should be to widen some of the old closes so as to form new streets (in that way, St Mary's Street and Blackfriars Street were formed) and, in other cases, to build new streets cutting across the old closes, as was done with Jeffrey Street which, curving round on its line of diminishing arches, intersected fifteen crowded alleyways. In all, fifteen new streets were provided by this great scheme. They included a wide thoroughfare leading from South Bridge to George IV Bridge which replaced the narrow, squalid North College Street, alongside the University Old College. In justifying this new street, William Chambers said, 'The Government has laid out £50000 on building the Industrial Museum [now the Royal Scottish Museum]; as a matter of gratitude and good policy, as well as contributing to sanitary reform, the Town Council should sanction this general plan.' They did, and in gratitude to him, they named it Chambers Street. Twenty-five years later they placed a statue of him by John Rhind at its half-way point.

The Town Council also approved of the whole improvement plan, though not without the usual grumbles about cost from their more reactionary members; and the necessary Act for the Improvement of the City of Edinburgh, under which the Council were named as Improvement Commissioners, received the royal assent in 1867. In view of present-day concern about the importance of public consultation before important decisions are taken and the impression one is apt to have that such consultation is something new, it is interesting to find that when this scheme was in preparation a great deal of trouble was taken to involve the public and public bodies in discussions about it.

Nine influential organizations were consulted. It would be

tedious to give all their replies but some are of interest. The Royal
College of Physicians welcomed the improvement scheme 'with
peculiar satisfaction' because it was on lines they themselves had
advocated and they helpfully added a few suggestions of their own.
The University congratulated the Town Council on the scheme
but 'did not propose to offer active co-operation to any other part
than that which involves improvement of streets in the neighbourhood of the University'. The City Parochial Board made a careful
distinction between the parts of the scheme concerned with
strictly sanitary improvement, which they fully supported, and
those concerned with amenity which they thought should be
postponed. The Secretary of the Chamber of Commerce had a
ponderous style. He said: 'While giving the scheme their cordial
support, the Chamber desire the plans to be subjected to the
ordeal of public and professional opinion in order that they may
be rendered as conducive as possible to the object in view.'

The method adopted for consulting the opinion of the general
public was to encourage the holding of a ward meeting in each
of the thirteen municipal wards into which the city was at that
time divided. Meetings were held in twelve of the wards and all but
one of the meetings declared themselves against the scheme,
the odd supporter being Canongate Ward. The ratepayers in the
New Town wards were strongly opposed to the whole project,
mainly because they had been involved not long before in considerable expense to improve the drainage of their own part of the
town and they did not see why they should pay rates to improve
other people's living conditions.

The public view having thus been tested, a majority of the
Town Council, inspired by their Lord Provost and their MOH
and supported by most of the public bodies, wisely decided that
they should be leaders of the public, not followers, and by twenty-
two votes to fifteen the verdict of the ward meetings was ignored
and the scheme was approved.

For the first time, provision was included in the Improvement
Act requiring the authorities to provide new houses for a large
proportion of those who would be displaced by the clearances,
the remainder being expected to find other accommodation for
themselves. Two buildings bear an inscription testifying that each
was the first building erected to re-house those displaced by the

1867 Improvement Scheme. One, in Blackfriars Street, built 'by the Blackfriars Building Association of 24 working men', claims to contain 'the first dwelling-houses erected to provide accommodation for the industrial classes on the site of those demolished by the city authorities under the Improvement Act, 1867'. The other, near the top of St Mary's Street, claims to be 'the first building erected under the Improvement Act 1867 – The Rt. Hon. William Chambers of Glenormiston, Lord Provost'. In fact both were right, one building being the first put up independently, the other being the first built under the auspices of the Town Council.

Dr Littlejohn's next great contribution to the cause of public health came twelve years later. He had been much concerned about the problem of infectious diseases such as scarlet fever, diphtheria, smallpox and cholera of which there were frequent outbreaks; and he pointed out that he could hope to exercise some control of these outbreaks only if he could be sure that his department would be informed of cases as soon as they were discovered. So he sought to obtain statutory powers to require doctors to notify him immediately of every case of infectious disease occurring in their practices. This produced a storm of protest and opposition from the medical profession who considered that any such requirement would cut across the confidentiality which, they said, had always existed and must always exist between doctor and patient. Dr Littlejohn, however, considered that there were circumstances in which the public interest had to come first; and he was not a man to be easily put off. So, in 1879, when the Town Council were promoting a parliamentary bill for other purposes, he urged them to have a clause included requiring doctors practising in the city to report to the Medical Officer of Health, within twenty-four hours, the name and address of every patient diagnosed as suffering from any one of eight specified infectious diseases; and authorizing payment to the doctor of a fee of 2s. 6d. for every such case in which the diagnosis was afterwards verified.

Despite the opposition, the clause was inserted, the Act was passed and Edinburgh became the first area in the United Kingdom in which notification by doctors of infectious diseases was compulsory. The certainty this gave of obtaining prompt and reliable information was a vital factor in enabling Dr Littlejohn to develop measures for checking the spread of disease in the city. Not until

ten years later did a general Act of Parliament make similar compulsory powers available to any local authority choosing to adopt
the Act and a further eight years passed before the Public Health
(Scotland) Act of 1897 made compulsory notification universal;
so here was one important aspect of community care in which
Edinburgh was ahead of the rest of Scotland by eighteen years,
thanks entirely to one man's persistence.

The control of tuberculosis was another field in which Dr
Littlejohn played an important part and, as with his housing
improvement measures, he did so in collaboration with a forceful
Edinburgh figure who appeared on the scene just at the right
moment. He was Dr (later Sir) R. W. Philip, who had made an
intensive study of tuberculosis and who opened a clinic in an
upstairs room in Bank Street in 1887. The place is marked, and the
story is told, by a round blue plaque on the building, placed so
high up that you almost need a telescope to read it. There, Dr
Philip's scheme to combat tuberculosis began – a scheme which
became the prototype for many elsewhere and, in 1912, was adopted
by the government as a model which all local authorities were
advised to follow.

In the 1880s, tuberculosis was not generally recognized as an
infectious disease. It was scarcely recognized as a disease at all but,
rather, as something that just happened. Little was done except
to sympathize with the victim; and when something *was* done, it
was usually the wrong thing, like closing windows instead of
opening them. Then the connection of the disease with infected
milk was not understood; and in 1888 Dr Littlejohn published a
long report dealing with that aspect of the problem. From that
time on, he and Dr Philip worked together on the development
of their scheme, the essence of which was co-operation; co-
operation not only between one medical man and another but
also between medical man and administrator, between home and
clinic, hospital and health department.

One major problem was to persuade apparently fit members
of a patient's household to submit to examination; any suggestion
that they might have contracted the disease without knowing it
was likely to be dismissed as new-fangled nonsense. It was in
obtaining the co-operation of such contacts and in teaching the
public generally about the disease and its treatment that Dr Little-

The Old Town Today – the Canongate. *On the right is the Canongate Tolbooth, dating in part from 1591 and now used as an annexe to Huntly House, the City Museum, opposite. Beyond, on the right, are new and reconstructed 'lands' and, in the distance, is the Tron Church.*

The New Town Today – Charlotte Square, *west side, and the dome of St George's Church, now West Register House. Between 1813 and 1848 Lord Cockburn lived in No. 14, the third house from the right. From this corner of the Square he listened, on summer evenings, to the sound of corncrakes calling in Lord Moray's fields.*

Arthur's Seat, the Castle and the sharp skyline of the Old Town,
seen from the south. This photograph was taken from Blackford Hill.

Duddingston Village and Loch and Holyrood Park. *A picture spanning
many centuries. It shows all the features described in Chapter 20, from the ancient
hillside terraces to the modern school. For good measure, Holyrood Palace can be
seen in the distance and almost the whole circuit of the sanctuary of Holyrood can
be traced.*

Cramond Village, *at the mouth of the River Almond – until 1975, the western extremity of Edinburgh. The village houses restored in the 1960s, are in the foreground.*

Princes Street, Old and New. *Two of the original eighteenth-century Princes Street houses can be recognized, one on each side of the Frederick Street opening; and several eighteenth-century houses are also seen on the right-hand side of Frederick Street. A preview of the twenty-first-century face of Princes Street appears in the new blocks, with walk-ways at first-floor level, towards the left- and right-hand sides of the picture. The slim spire of St. Andrew's Church, in George Street, completed in 1787 is in the background.*

Queensferry – *the ancient Burgh, between two modern bridges across the Firth of Forth where ferries plied for centuries. Queensferry is within the new City of Edinburgh District, the western boundary of which only just includes the harbour of Port Edgar, seen to the right of the road bridge. In the foreground is the Fife village of North Queensferry with its old ferry slipway.*

john's public health department played a major part in the combined operation. All this work was much helped when, partly
through his efforts, tuberculosis was added to the official list of
notifiable diseases in 1906; and out of all that work came, within
quite recent memory, a dramatic drop in the ravages of tuberculosis.

There were other subjects on which Sir Henry Littlejohn held
ideas well ahead of his time. Take this, for example, from an
article he wrote in 1900: 'I have observed for some years past, with
great regret, the custom that prevails among the boys of our cities
of smoking cigarettes. . . . Much is said at present as to the increase
of cancer and its causes; but there can be little doubt that the use
of cigarettes must have a most pernicious effect'. That was sixty-two
years before the Royal College of Physicians produced their famous
report on the connection between smoking and cancer.

In a city such as Edinburgh, with a medical school that had
been famous for centuries, it was entirely fitting that the first
Medical Officer of Health should make a name for himself as a
pioneer figure in community health. It was not, however, only as a
health administrator that Littlejohn was well known. He was a
brilliant and successful lecturer on forensic medicine. His long
experience as police surgeon gave him ample opportunity to
describe real cases and actual incidents in the course of his lectures
and this he seems to have done with much wit and effectiveness.
When, after forty years as a lecturer he gave his inaugural lecture
as Professor, he remarked that 'as one not altogether unknown in
University circles' he had found 'that the magnetism of daily
intercourse with so many young and ardent spirits had constituted
an admirable training for the duties of the Chair'. The fact that
his appearance in the crowded classroom was greeted by the
students 'in their customary fashion, singing and whistling to the
accompaniment of their walking-sticks on the floor and bench'
signified not so much an unruly class as a class full of affection for
their new Professor whom they already knew so well.

He was, it seems, a dapper, brisk, small man, always dressed
in frock-coat, striped trousers and top hat. From 1866 until his
death in 1914, he lived at 24 Royal Circus and was a well-known
figure in the streets as he made his way to his office which, for
long, was in Parliament Square. Despite his brusqueness he was

kindly and was regarded as a friend by many of the slum dwellers whom he met on his official rounds of inspection. He had an interest too, in the history of the old town and, when he met a group of tourists consulting their guide-books, nothing pleased him more than to appoint himself their temporary guide.

As an expert witness in court he was in his element, answering questions decisively and firmly, sometimes too sharply for the comfort of those by whom he was being cross-examined. One famous case in which he appeared was the trial of Eugene Chantrelle for the murder of his wife by poisoning, on New Year's morning 1878, in their flat at 81 George Street. Chantrelle was a Frenchman who had lived in Edinburgh for a good many years, teaching French in several private schools. At one of these, Newington Academy, he had seduced a fifteen-year-old pupil, Elizabeth Dyer. Her excessively prim parents had insisted on marriage as the only way to avoid what, in their circle in Victorian Edinburgh, would have been a scandal too great for the family to bear. The wedding duly took place in 1868.

Chantrelle, it seems, was a thoroughly bad character, though not without some superficial charm. Not only did he frequently ill-treat his wife during their nine years of marriage but he also became, quite openly, a regular patron of certain houses of ill-fame which in those days were a well-known feature of Clyde Street and adjoining lanes in the area now covered by the St Andrew's Square bus station, within convenient walking distance of his home. Several times his wife returned to her mother, threatening to stay there; but always her mother persuaded her to go back for fear of what friends and neighbours would say if she was seen to have deserted her husband. As a result, the unhappy girl became a victim of middle-class Edinburgh morality.

In October 1877, Chantrelle insured his wife's life for £1000, payable in the event of death by accident only. On New Year's eve the poison was administered; and in the morning when his wife was taken ill and her doctor had been called, Chantrelle fractured a gas pipe in her bedroom so that the smell of gas would give the impression that her death was an accident caused by gas poisoning. He might just possibly have got away with it but the doctor, anxious to have a second opinion, sent for Dr Littlejohn who, besides his many other attributes was something of an amateur detective. 'What's all this?' he is said to have exclaimed in his usual brusque manner as he walked into the room.

Having attended briefly to the patient, who was then removed to the Infirmary (though without avail), he turned to examining the gas pipe. From its appearance, he suspected that it had been deliberately broken – a suspicion shared by the gas engineer who was called to the house later in the day. Then Dr Littlejohn questioned the maid who assured him there had been no smell of gas when she first entered the room in the morning. All of which he duly reported to the proper authorities. Taken along with his more strictly expert evidence regarding medical tests which he had made it was more than enough to convict the unpleasant Monsieur Chantrelle of the crime. On 31 May 1878 he had the doubtful distinction of being the first person executed inside Calton gaol, all previous executions having been carried out in public, latterly at the south-east corner of the crossing of Lawnmarket and George IV Bridge, where three brass plates in the roadway mark the spot.

The powers of observation and deduction which Dr Littlejohn displayed in the Chantrelle case and which he was fond of demonstrating to his students from time to time, led the writer of an article in the *Edinburgh Magazine* in 1904 to suggest that Littlejohn, as well as his contemporary Dr Joseph Bell, may have been in the mind of Conan Doyle when he invented the character of Sherlock Holmes. There is little doubt that Conan Doyle would have attended Dr Littlejohn's lectures as well as those of Dr Bell who is usually accepted as the Holmes prototype. So it is quite likely that the character and genius of the famous detective owe something, not to Joseph Bell alone, but also to Henry Littlejohn.

17 Into the twentieth century

The fifty-two years during which Henry Littlejohn, as police surgeon and Medical Officer of Health, supervised the health and well-being of the city were years of rapid change, and nowhere more so than in the field of transport. When he was appointed, sedan chairs were still in use in the city and only fourteen years had passed since Edinburgh had seen the first steam train setting off to Glasgow from the original terminus at Haymarket Station. Until that day in 1842 no one in Edinburgh had ever travelled faster than a horse could carry him. But Sir Henry continued in office well into the age of the motor-car. In the year after his retirement Blériot flew across the English Channel and, two years later, the first aeroplane crossed the Firth of Forth. The age of aviation had arrived.

So, into less than seventy years was packed the history of travel; and the history of travel in Edinburgh, in those years, calls for a brief examination, if only for the sake of some of the more eccentric forms it took. Among these were two different types of two-wheeled, one-horse vehicles, the 'Noddy' and the 'Minibus'. Here is what one of Dr Littlejohn's early contemporaries thought of them:

The Noddy and the Minibus seemed to have embodied in them all the possibilities of discomfort to the traveller. The Noddy was well-named. It exhibited on the steep hills of Edinburgh an almost animal tendency to throw the occupant out on to the horse's back and if the horse made even a slight stumble when going downhill, go the passenger must. . . . The Minibus was a sort of infant representation of an omnibus – square, with side seats, and entering from the back. The driver, when he reached his fare's destination, turned the minibus with its door to the pavement and backed it into the gutter. Human ingenuity could scarcely have devised a vehicle more capable of giving the acme of discomfort to horse, driver and passenger. The driver was cramped up between horse and vehicle. The horse had its shafts jumping up and down. Luggage could only be carried by being put inside before the passenger entered and when ascending a hill a lady's box would require all the owner's efforts to prevent it from crushing her. . . .

On the whole, the Stockbridge bus seems to have been more comfortable. Henry Littlejohn must often have used it on his way from home to office, for it plied from the village of Stockbridge up the steep climb through Royal Circus and Howe Street to Princes Street and thence by North Bridge to Newington. Because of the steep hill it was drawn by three horses. There were seats inside and out, those outside being reached by an iron ladder at the rear; and, in cold weather, for the greater comfort of the inside passengers a liberal supply of straw was strewn upon the floor.

Horse tramcars did not arrive in the city until 1871 in which year the Edinburgh Tramways Act authorized the provision of tramcars to be worked 'by animal power only'. The first route was from Haymarket, along Princes Street and down Leith Walk to Bernard Street, near Leith Docks. Starting with only twenty cars the system spread until, by 1891, there were 300 cars and over 1000 horses. Many are the tales told of the trace-horse boys who were employed to provide extra horse-power on some of the steeper gradients. Amateur jockeys all, they delighted in galloping their steeds downhill to pick up the next car, to the great alarm and danger of the lieges.

The very steep streets of the New Town, however, were unsuitable for horse cars and so the Stockbridge bus and similar vehicles continued to serve the north side of the city until someone had the idea of installing cable-cars. Two routes were provided, both cables being driven from a power station in Henderson Row, near the Edinburgh Academy. One route, opened in 1888, ran down Hanover Street and Dundas Street to Canonmills and Goldenacre. The other, opened in 1890, took over the northern section of the

Stockbridge bus route. For simple routes like these with no sharp bends and no junctions the system, though slow and noisy, worked well enough. Trouble came later as the network of routes grew.

In the closing years of the nineteenth century it had become clear that some form of public transport other than that provided by animal power was called for if Edinburgh was to move into the age of technology. Electric trams were becoming fashionable but, in Edinburgh, Princes Street posed a problem. The erection of unsightly poles and wires in what they regarded as 'the world's most beautiful street' was something that neither the Town Council nor the public would countenance. The cable system was working well on the north side of the city; why not extend it? So, in 1898, the decision was made to undertake 'the cabling of the tramways' – and for twenty-four years the cable system, with its many failings, provided transport for the citizens; and provided also an endless source of fun for music-hall comedians in the city's theatres.

Eventually the system – the fourth largest of its kind in the world – extended in an intricate network through the city, with four power stations driving fifty-two miles of cable, serving a twenty-six mile network of routes beneath the streets. To these cables each tramcar was attached by a 'gripper' suspended through a slot between the rails. To stop the car the driver had to release the gripper and apply the brakes. To change cables at a junction was a trickier operation for then he had to release one cable and grasp another, a manoeuvre requiring careful timing as his car approached the junction. If he bungled the operation, a cable was liable to break and when that happened the whole system served by it came perforce to a standstill until a repair or replacement could be completed.

Despite its disadvantages those of us who remember the cable-cars do so with some sense of nostalgia. The rhythmic banging of their four pairs of wheels over the rail-joints; the smell of their gas lighting at night; the sound of the warning bell which the driver clanged above his head and the constant rattling of the cable in its underground channel – all these are inextricably mingled in one's mind with a host of other childhood memories. And just to prove that these extraordinary vehicles were not, after all, a figment of childish imagination but really did exist, you will find, carefully preserved at the Princes Street end of Waterloo Place, a short length of cable-car track complete with its cable-slot between the rails.

Not the least of the inconveniences of the system was the fact that, as early as 1905, Leith Town Council had replaced their horse cars by electric trams, precluding the possibility of through-running between the two towns. As a result, everyone travelling between Edinburgh and Leith (more than nine million passengers every year, it was said) had to change trams at the burgh boundary at Pilrig, a procedure which came to be known as 'the Pilrig muddle'. The Edinburgh authorities did, in fact, urge Leith to adopt the cable system for the sake of uniformity. But, said a local paper of that time, 'Leith is a live little town. It does not wish to adopt prehistoric methods of locomotion within its bounds.' Still, in the end Edinburgh had the advantage. In 1922–3, when the Edinburgh system was converted to electricity (with centre poles in Princes Street painted a comely grey) it was possible to adopt the most up-to-date ideas in tramcar comfort, in marked contrast to the austerity of the out-of-date vehicles that were being used in the former Leith area.

Among events that the horse-trams had helped to bring about was the opening up of West Princes Street Gardens to the public, though it would be far-fetched to suggest that they were solely responsible, since the movement to have the gardens opened had begun twenty years earlier. But the coming of the trams and the greater mobility they provided, undoubtedly enabled more people than ever before to come easily into the centre of the city to see the gardens for themselves (through locked gates) and to realize what a boon it would be to have them opened to the public.

Just as the valley at the east end of Princes Street was saved for the future by David Hume and his neighbours, so we owe the formation and preservation of the gardens at the western end to the foresight of the proprietors of the original houses at that end of the street, known generically as 'the Princes Street Proprietors'. In 1816, to their eternal credit, they obtained an Act of Parliament prohibiting building in the western half of the valley. They then acquired the ground on a long lease, partly from the town, partly from the Crown, as owner of the Castle bank, and partly from other lesser proprietors. Thus they effectively preserved, for their own delight, the impressive view of the Castle and the old town ridge from their windows.

What they had acquired was, largely, the muddy bed of the old Nor' Loch and its drainage proved to be a difficult problem; but in a year or two that was successfully accomplished and the proprietors set about landscaping and planting their new pleasure-grounds. In planning the layout they had the assistance of James Skene of Rubislaw, whom we earlier met as a mischievous youngster on the stairway of James Court and who, by now, was well known for his water-colour sketches of old Edinburgh scenes. In January 1822 he reported that 'considerable advance has been made in laying out the grounds'. Shrubs, flowers and garden ornaments had been received from several sources. Henry Raeburn had presented carved stones from his estate at Stockbridge and Lord Moray gave trees from his grounds of Drumsheugh. An eccentric antiquary and collector of bric-à-brac, Charles Kirkpatrick Sharpe, who lived at 93 Princes Street, gave an old bell to be rung at the closing of the gates.

Perhaps the strangest gift of all was that of the Scottish Society of Antiquaries. It was a massive runic burial monument which had been brought from Vestmanland in Sweden some twenty years earlier and which Skene, with some difficulty (for it weighed over two tons) placed high on the Castle bank where it still stands, just below the esplanade. It bears a design and an inscription interpreted as meaning: 'Ari set up this stone in memory of his father. God rest his soul.' Who Ari was, and why the stone he had erected with such filial piety above a distant Scandinavian grave should have been thought suitable as a garden ornament at the heart of Edinburgh, are not explained. Perhaps such a bulky monument was an encumbrance to the Antiquaries who were glad to seize this opportunity to dispose of it gracefully.

With the gardens laid out and 'embellished', the proprietors paid for and obtained their keys. A few distinguished people were given complimentary keys – among them, Sir Walter Scott. His letter of thanks is preserved in Lady Stair's House museum, between the Lawnmarket and North Bank Street. It is dated 21 May 1827 and in it he expresses his thanks to the Committee of the garden 'for an accommodation which circumstances and my increasing infirmities render extremely agreeable to me as my health requires exercise which I can take much more easily and agreeably in its beautiful walks than along the public street'.

Strict rules of conduct were laid down for those using the gardens. Dogs were not admitted, cricket might not be played, even by small children, and perambulators were prohibited. Only after much agitation would the committee allow persons in bath-chairs to enter the gardens and then only on presentation of a doctor's certificate showing that the ailment from which the invalid suffered was not contagious. Smoking was regarded as 'an offensive nuisance' and was strictly forbidden. Admonishing an offender, the clerk to the committee said: 'Whilst it is seen that gentlemen smoke cigars in the grounds, that is used by others as an excuse for smoking even more offensive tobacco. . . . The complaints of ladies and others are numerous against the nuisance and many are frequently obliged to leave the grounds or to turn to other walks therein by people smoking.'

When the plans to build a railway through the gardens were first mooted in 1836, they were vigorously opposed by James Skene on behalf of the proprietors and their opposition continued for several years. But by 1840 Skene was living abroad and several of the Princes Street houses were being replaced by shops and hotels whose owners were less opposed to railway development. So, in 1845, work on the railway was begun, most of the proprietors having been satisfied with an assurance that it would be enclosed by six-foot-high walls and by a mound of earth and shrubs which would effectively conceal the trains from the drawing-room windows of the Princes Street houses. The first train ran through the valley in August 1846.

To the strict rule of privacy occasional exceptions were made. On days when regimental bands stationed in the Castle were invited to perform in the gardens it was the practice sometimes to admit not just key-holders but also 'other persons of respectability' to enjoy the music. These occasions must have been dreaded by the gardeners who had the unenviable task of manning the gates and distinguishing between 'persons of respectability' and others.

When the movement to have West Princes Street Gardens opened to the public began, it came first from a surprising source. The Scottish Association for Suppressing Drunkenness asked that the gardens should be thrown open during Christmas and the

o

New Year 'with the object of keeping parties out of the dram shops'. Not surprisingly, that application was refused; but a similar request, more tactfully worded, was made a year later and it was then agreed to open the gardens to the public on Christmas Day, New Year's Day and one other day.

The ground having thus been broken, negotiations were begun for the transfer of the gardens to the Town Council. The negotiations dragged on for a long time because of legal difficulties arising from the terms of the 1816 Act. Eventually, agreement having been reached, a new Act authorizing the transfer was obtained under which the Town Council were required also to widen Princes Street and to undertake some improvements in the gardens. To show their goodwill, the proprietors contributed £500 towards the cost of a bandstand, handing over to the Royal Infirmary the balance of £83 remaining in their fund. In October 1876 the gardens were permanently opened to the public.

The debt owed by citizen and visitor alike to the Princes Street Proprietors for transforming and preserving the Nor' Loch valley for posterity is immeasurable, for it cannot be denied that it is the deep green valley at its heart that gives the city centre its character. If the valley had been filled with buildings as, in the early-nineteenth-century craze for building, might easily have happened, neither the Castle on its rock nor the old town on its ridge could have had the impact on the eye that both now have. As it is, the Castle rising so strongly from the valley proclaims the solid dignity of the capital city of Scotland. The theatricality of the old town roofs and spires, soaring above the gardens, aptly symbolizes Edinburgh's role as festival city.

According to William Maitland, first historian of Edinburgh, who wrote in 1753, Edinburgh had been recognized as the capital city of Scotland since at least as early as 1456. Although no longer in Maitland's day the seat of parliament the city never displayed more worthily and whole-heartedly the character of a capital city than it did in the years following his lifetime – the 'golden age' that spanned the late eighteenth and early nineteenth centuries. In those years, despite the social shortcomings of the time, the city was not only renowned in literature and the arts but was renowned also, as a capital city should be, for the vision and imagination of its civic projects.

The great venture of the New Town; the imposing design of the University building (now the 'Old College') fronted by six huge monoliths of Craigleith stone which could so much more easily have been transported and built in sections but for a flamboyant eagerness to impress; the grand sweep of Regent Road; and the curving line of Johnston Terrace, suspended between Castle and Grassmarket – all these were civic schemes, proudly executed and worthy of a capital city. But after them, for a century or more, you would be hard put to it to find a civic project comparable to any of them for breadth of vision, boldness or imagination.

The former city fathers having had their financial fingers burnt, their successors in office were naturally wary. It is true, also, that in those hundred years the city carried out many important and useful municipal projects, William Chambers' improvement scheme among them. But these schemes were no more than any self-respecting municipality ought to have been undertaking in those times. Through all those years, as with the formation of Princes Street Gardens, the creation of the finest buildings in the city – those that contribute so much to its character as a capital – was left to the initiative of private benefactors.

There is Fettes College at Comely Bank, designed by David Bryce in the gothic likeness of a French château and built in 1870 from the fortune left by Sir William Fettes, an early-nineteenth-century Lord Provost; looking down on it from Queensferry Road there is Daniel Stewart's College, all towers and turrets, designed by David Rhind and built in 1853 under the will of Daniel Stewart, an Exchequer official who had died in 1814; and there are several others.

Most spectacular and, I think, by far the most successful of all these great Victorian buildings that enhance the city is St Mary's Episcopal Cathedral whose three spires – the tallest 275 feet high – so sharply and effectively mark the western end of Melville Street. Its two smaller spires are named Barbara and Mary in memory of the Misses Walker on whose estate the surrounding streets were built and who bequeathed their fortune to found the cathedral. It was built between 1874 and 1879 and was said at the time to be 'the largest and most beautiful church that has been erected in Scotland, or perhaps in Great Britain since the Reformation'. Designed by

Sir Gilbert Scott as an essay in church architectural history, it embodies features borrowed from many medieval churches and abbeys, blended to form a building of great beauty.

Throughout the later nineteenth and early part of the twentieth centuries, Edinburgh as a city, basking in the reflected glory of these great buildings, confined its attention to necessary but more mundane municipal developments. Then, suddenly and unexpectedly and at what might have been thought a quite inappropriate time, there emerged a scheme, the like of which for boldness and vision Edinburgh had not seen for more than a hundred years. This time it was not a building that was created but something vastly more imaginative: the Edinburgh International Festival of Music and Drama.

The year was 1947. To create such a Festival in Edinburgh at any time would have been remarkable. To do so in the midst of the austerity of those immediate post-war years was an astonishing act of faith. The Lord Provost of the day, Sir John Falconer, eagerly accepted the idea, pursued it with vigour against all doubts and criticisms and insisted that only the highest standards of performance would suffice. His successors in office, and the Festival Society he founded, have since seen to it that these high standards have been maintained. In doing so they have shown that Edinburgh in the twentieth century, no less than in the eighteenth, can act in a manner worthy of a capital city.

18 Water of Leith

As a capital city, there is one thing that Edinburgh lacks –
a great river. London has the Thames, stately and important; Paris has the romantic Seine and Rome the mighty Tiber. Edinburgh has the Water of Leith. Stately, romantic, mighty are none
of them words you could with honesty apply to it; yet it has
interesting associations, it provides some pleasant riverside walks
and for centuries, it played an important part in the life of the
city. For long it must have been one of the hardest-worked rivers
in the country. According to the first Statistical Account of Scotland, published in the 1790s, there were then seventy-six mills for
which the Water of Leith provided motive power.

Of the river's twenty-mile length, just over ten miles have been
within the city since the boundary was extended in 1920, taking in
the villages of Colinton and Juniper Green. Only the first four
miles from the source of the river, high on the north-west edge
of the Pentland Hills, are outside the bounds of the new City of
Edinburgh District. So now we need discount only those first
few miles which do not even bear its name on the map, to regard
the Water of Leith as truly Edinburgh's river.

It must once have been a clear and sparkling river. An Act
of the Scottish parliament in 1617 decreed that the standard pint
jug was to contain 'three pounds seven ounces troy of clear run-

ning water from the Water of Leith'. Later, it fell on evil days. As
the New Town grew and villages outside the city extended, it
became too convenient as a ready-made drain and rubbish dump.
As the nineteenth century wore on, complaints about this became
more numerous until, eventually, Acts of Parliament were obtained to authorize the construction of sewers down the length
of its valley and these relieved the over-burdened river of much
of its unpleasantness. Thanks to those Acts, to the more recent
endeavours of the Lothian River Purification Board and to the
occasional activity of groups of young volunteers, the Water of
Leith, though not yet as sparkling as a highland burn, is reasonably
clean. Less than a mile from Princes Street, you may fish in it for
trout and sometimes catch one.

It is a moot point whether it is better to explore a river from
source to sea, enjoying at each turn an expanding vista; or from
sea to source, to be rewarded as one goes by changing glimpses
of the river itself and its immediate surroundings. My preference
is for the upward journey, so I propose to start where the city's
river meets the sea at Leith. For centuries, its small estuary was the
only harbour Leith had. It was the right to control that harbour
that was confirmed to the early burgh of Edinburgh by the Charter
of Robert the Bruce in 1329. The great docks that have grown around
it were not begun until the first years of the nineteenth century.
So for five centuries the mouth of the little river of Leith was
Edinburgh's gateway to foreign lands and foreign trade. The
river-side where that original harbour was is still known as the
Shore and its massive stone-built quayside and cobbled road still
carry something of the tang and character of an ancient port.

Just below the bridge at Bernard Street, on the edge of
the quay, you will find a moulded iron crown with the legend
'Geo IV – O Felicem Diem'. It was placed there, on the first anniversary
of the event, to mark the exact spot at which the King's foot had
first touched Scottish land, in August 1822. Below the crown,
on the face of the quay, is a larger plaque giving details of
the landing and of the dignitaries who greeted the King. It is so
placed as to be readable only from a boat and so, out of consideration for landlubbers, the Leith Civic Trust in 1967 affixed a briefer
notice of the occasion to the wall just across the roadway from
the quayside.

When His Majesty stepped ashore here, every vantage point was crowded including the roof and ledges of the custom house which you can see on the opposite quay. It had been built ten years before from a design by Robert Reid. The bridge across the harbour was then a lifting one as can be seen in Alexander Carse's painting, between pages 152 and 153. Stands, crowded with spectators, were provided at the ends of the bridge, while sailors manned the rigging of every vessel within sight. For His Majesty's benefit a floating landing stage was provided, to rise and fall with the tide. Now, such a thing would be unnecessary, for it is always high tide here since a sea-lock was constructed in 1969 at the harbour entrance to admit ships of up to 24000 tons to the docks.

It was also at this point, or perhaps a little further upstream, that Queen Mary landed on that damp and misty day in 1561. After she came ashore, it was reported, 'she remanit in Andro Lamb's hous be the space of ane hour'. Five minutes' walk from the quayside you will find Lamb's House with corbelled stair-tower and crow-stepped gables, beautifully restored and used as a busy and active day-centre for old people. But any notion that Lamb's House Day Centre is 'Andro Lamb's hous' in which the Queen rested is dispelled by the experts of the Royal Commission on Ancient Monuments who say that 'it has all the appearance of dating from the second decade of the seventeenth century'.

For a mile or so upstream, the river lies among factories, work-shops and yards and is not readily approached; nor is there any-thing very pleasing to see if you do approach it. But at Bonnington Bridge, where Newhaven Road crosses the river, it is worth while looking around. Nearby, along a cobbled lane east of the bridge is Bonnyhaugh House, now given the number 71 in Newhaven Road. It was built three and a half centuries ago by the Town Council of Edinburgh for Jeromias van der Heill, a Dutchman whom they had invited to come from Holland to teach the craft of dyeing. Close to it are a few remaining cottages of old Bonning-ton village and derelict mill buildings which once stood in a wide expanse of cornfields. Recently, other red-tiled mill buildings which were used latterly as a skin works have been demolished, leaving only the ancient weir across the river, a sturdily-built sluice and a dried-up mill-lade to show that here was once a thriving riverside community. Even the railway embankments and bridges nearby, built when the weir and the lade were already centuries old are themselves derelict and partly demolished.

The first bridge for vehicles at Bonnington was built in 1812. Before then there was a ford with stepping stones which, at some time, were supplemented by a footbridge. From the ford a bridle track ran through cornfields to Newhaven. The track was known as the Whiting Road and was much used by fishwives carrying their creels of fish for sale to the housewives of Edinburgh. In the middle of the eighteenth century the track was the subject of a right-of-way dispute between the owner of Bonnington mills, who used it as a road for his carts, and the adjoining landowners who claimed that it was a right-of-way for horses and foot traffic only.

According to the evidence in the case, the ford sometimes provided a tricky and dangerous crossing. One witness remembered seeing a post chaise coming that way with two ladies in it who narrowly escaped drowning as the driver struggled to negotiate the river. Another said that smugglers' carts sometimes passed that way in the night time. Not long before, one of these carts had stuck fast in midstream and the barrels it carried had had to be taken off by boat.

As to what the smugglers' cart was carrying, there is no information but some possible light on the question comes from a Town Council minute of 1744. On that occasion, the Council had been considering what they called 'the scandalous and prevailing practice of smuggling brandy, tea and other foreign commodities' and they lamented the fact that fishermen at Newhaven and elsewhere seemed to prefer smuggling to fishing. No doubt the fishermen found it more lucrative; especially as there is reason to believe that highly respected merchants and shopkeepers in the city (Sir William Fettes, allegedly, among them) had long made extra profits by dealing in smuggled goods. On this occasion the action proposed to be taken by the Council was 'to discourage the immoderate use of tea, brandy and all other smuggled goods'. How they proposed to discourage their use without incurring the anger of some of their merchant colleagues and friends is not clear; but they took the opportunity to record their displeasure at 'the growing number of people of the very lowest rank who use tea and brandy in place of ale and home made spirits'.

A mile or so above Bonnington the river flows past Powderhall, now dominated by a modern refuse disposal plant and a grey-hound racing track. Water from the river is used in the disposal process at about the point where once it drove a snuff mill and a pepper mill. Of these no traces remain, nor of several country houses that once stood amid attractive gardens near here. To these eighteenth-century Edinburgh folk came in summer for the benefit of the country air, a commodity not much in evidence around Powderhall nowadays. But from the featureless green open space of St Mark's Park, beside the river, you can enjoy one of the best views there is of the old town outline against the sky.

Canonmills was the next village upstream but practically nothing of its village character remains. Here, in the twelfth century were mills granted by David I to the monks of Holyrood; and to these mills the bakers of Canongate were 'thirled'; that is to say they were bound to deal with no other mills. Here, too, was once a paper mill where a certain Peter Bruce produced the paper he required for the manufacture of playing-cards of which he held a monopoly. In 1682 he complained to the Privy Council that one of his neighbours, Alexander Hunter, had 'conceived some prejudice and malice against him'. Under silence and cloud of night, Hunter and some accomplices 'had most maliciously broken down the mill and had diverted the water from it so that it would not work'. Worse still, and most ungallantly, he had thrown Mrs Bruce, the miller's wife, into her own mill-dam; incurring through these misdeeds a fine of £50 and a spell in the Tolbooth.

Across the bridge at Canonmills are two attractive outliers of the new town – Howard Place (a part of the main road) where at No. 8 Robert Louis Stevenson was born in 1850; and Warriston Crescent, a curving cul-de-sac whose houses have gardens running down to the river, with hawthorn bushes, lilacs and laburnums over-hanging the water. At No. 10, Frederick Chopin stayed when he visited Edinburgh and gave a recital in the Hopetoun Rooms, Queen Street, in 1848. Here he was bored by the genteel ladies who fluttered around him and by those who, eagerly playing the piano for his approval, kept looking at their hands and striking the wrong notes.

Between Canonmills and Stockbridge there is a riverside path bordered by dark and rather gloomy shrubs; but a walk along it may be enlivened by the sight of a swan or of a coot paddling in the reeds beside the banks. We arrive at Stockbridge by way of St Bernard's Row and the end of Raeburn Place, reminding us that much of this neighbourhood was laid out by Sir Henry Raeburn on his St Bernard's estate. Stockbridge is famous also, or should be, as the birthplace of another artist, David Roberts. He was the son of a shoemaker who lived, a few steps uphill from the river, in a house in what is now named Gloucester Street but was then Church Street, so called because for centuries it was the route taken by the villagers of Stockbridge to the West Church or St Cuthbert's Church, below the Castle rock at the western end of the Nor' Loch. The house in which David Roberts was born in 1796 has recently been renovated as a project supported by the Edinburgh New Town Conservation Committee, set up jointly by the Town Council, the government and other organizations, including local residents.

The house has, above its door, a lintel inscribed with the motto Fear God Onlye, the date 1605 and the initials I.G. and I.R. The date, however, has no relevance to the age of the house. The lintel and some of the other stones used in its construction came from a house in the Lawnmarket, demolished to make way for the opening up of Bank Street as an approach from the earthen mound.

It is said that at a very early age David Roberts showed a delight in pictures, reproducing on the whitewashed walls of the house some of the lurid drawings he used to see outside the menagerie and other booths that were clustered on the earthen mound. He was apprenticed to a house painter at the hamlet of Silvermills nearby and in due course was employed in painting mansion houses, including Craigcrook Castle, at Blackhall, which later became famous as the country home of Francis Jeffrey. There, carefully preserved by the present owner of the house, Jeffrey's study still remains, with a painting by David Roberts on a wall.

Roberts' real chance came, however, in 1815, when he was engaged to paint scenery for a travelling circus. From that, he progressed to become scene-painter at the Theatre Royal and, in 1822, at Drury Lane, London. The house in which he lived as a boy was practically on the route that Henry Raeburn followed on his regular daily walks from his home to his studio at No. 32 York

Place; and it is not improbable that on these walks Raeburn would sometimes pause at Church Street to give words of advice and encouragement to the budding young artist.

David Roberts' experience of scene-painting undoubtedly helped him to become a skilful painter of landscapes and buildings and, after making several tours abroad, he produced a series of drawings of eastern temples and biblical scenes which were engraved and published in two large volumes. In these, the influence of his scene-painting is obvious. The massive chunky masonry of the ruins in his pictures is almost three-dimensional. You imagine you could hide behind his pillars. Despite his lowly origin, David Roberts went on to achieve great fame. He became a Royal Academician in 1841, was commissioned by Queen Victoria to paint a picture of the Crystal Palace in 1851 and received the Freedom of the City of Edinburgh in 1858.

Just above Stockbridge we come into the deep Dean Valley. The houses of Moray Place are high above us on one side and those of Eton Terrace on the other, but beside the river we might be in a remote glen for all we can hear or see of the city. Here you will find St Bernard's Well, in visiting which, you will remember, Henry Erskine's friend never wearied in well-doing. The spring here was first brought to notice in 1760 when it was claimed that its waters were 'equal in quality to the most famous in Britain' and a few years later it became a popular resort. Then in 1788 it was bought by Lord Gardenstone, one of those bluff eccentric judges in which the Scottish courts seemed to abound in those days. His particular eccentricity, apart from an excessive fondness for snuff, was that he liked to keep a young pig as a house pet.

His Lordship had a new structure built over the spring, to a design by Alexander Nasmyth, based on a temple at Tivoli, Italy, and containing a statue of Hygeia, goddess of health. He installed as keeper of the well one George Murdoch, and drew up a code of rules by which the keeper was to regulate its use. He was to attend from 6 a.m. until 9 a.m. during which time only those who paid or who could produce a medical certificate were to have access to the well. From 10 a.m. until 1 p.m. anyone might drink the waters free. The charges were moderate: for adults, one penny a glass or sixpence a week, children half price. Regular devotees could buy a season ticket covering the period from May to October, for which the charge was 'at least 5s. sterling'. An important rule required those who had taken a glass of the water 'to retire immediately and walk about for at least five minutes, both as a benefit to themselves and to make way for other water-drinkers'.

Soon after these rules had been promulgated, a medical treatise on the water of the well and its quality was published by J. Taylor, M.D. Having provided a chemical analysis of the water, Dr Taylor went on to describe its taste as being 'at first unpalatable; but from use becoming pleasant and agreeable'. As one who once drank at the well many years ago I can endorse, with emphasis, the first part of that statement. Nothing would have induced me to test the truth of the second part.

In an appendix to his treatise, the enthusiastic Dr Taylor gave details of twenty-six of his patients who had taken the waters. They had been suffering from troubles varying through a whole gamut, from 'bruised leg' to 'total blindness', and he claimed that all had benefited except one; and that one, be it noted, was disappointed only because he had failed to persevere with the treatment and not because the waters were not beneficial. I like very much Dr Taylor's chapter on 'The Water of St Bernard's Well made into Coffee'. From this I learn that such coffee 'drunken after dinner is an excellent digester. The animal spirits are thereby exhilarated and, from being morose and sulky, we are all at once metamorphosed into a gay and cheerful mood.'

During the nineteenth century the well gradually fell into disuse and the temple and statue became ruinous. Then in 1887 it was given a new lease of life through the generosity of William Nelson, the publisher. He must have had faith in the well for it was his habit to walk three miles every morning from his home on the south side of the city to drink its waters. At his own expense he had the structure and the surrounding grounds refurbished and installed a new statue of Hygeia. Thereafter, for fifty years or so, the well was fairly regularly patronized. In the 1930s a firm of chemists even obtained permission to bottle the water and sell it from their shops. But in doing so they had overlooked Dr Taylor's warning that 'it is much better and more effectual to use the water upon the spot; it loses much by carriage' and their venture was not a success. In 1940 the well was closed. Sixteen years later a proposal to make its waters once more available was countermanded, on public health grounds, by the Medical Officer of Health who clearly did not share Dr Taylor's enthusiasm for their virtues.

Not far beyond the well is Thomas Telford's Dean Bridge, its tall piers and graceful arches carrying the roadway 106 feet above the river. Built in 1831 for carriages, coaches and carts it serves today a stream of traffic far greater than anything Telford could have imagined. A high-level bridge here was first thought of by John Learmonth, proprietor of the Dean estate, north of the river, who became Edinburgh's last Lord Provost before local government reform in 1833 abolished the old undemocratic regime. This, however, was his private project, not a public one. He wanted to dispose of land on his estate for building and a road bridge to provide a convenient link with the town was an obvious pre-requisite. So, in conjunction with the District Road Trustees who were responsible for public roads in the area, he obtained plans for a bridge and, in 1828, invited 'builders of skill' to tender for its construction.

Learmonth was prepared to meet the cost himself, and in the event he paid for the bridge, the cost as stated by Telford being £18556. The Road Trustees met the cost of the approach roads. They had agreed to collaborate only if the design was entrusted to Telford. He was then seventy-two years old and this was almost his last work before he retired from practice as a civil engineer. From his own account of the project one quickly senses his pride in it; and it is undoubtedly one of his masterpieces. A feature to which he drew special attention was the hollow construction of the piers, saving weight and cost and, as he said, allowing every stone as it was laid to be inspected from all sides to ensure accurate bedding. He pointed out, also, the outer arches, just above each main arch, supporting the footpaths and parapets and he described as the most delicate operation of all, the gradual removal from beneath the arches of their temporary wooden supports which had to be done slowly and evenly so as to ensure that all the arches subsided uniformly to their point of permanent stability.

The contract for building the bridge went to an Aberdeen builder, John Gibb, who had been Telford's resident engineer twenty years before for the building of Aberdeen harbour and in whose ability Telford had great faith. There is a story that when progress on the bridge seemed too slow to meet the contract date, Gibb answered his critics with the quiet assurance: 'Dinna worry. Ye'll get your bit briggy on the due date.' Then having completed it before the stipulated day, he erected a gate at each end and admitted pedestrians at a charge of one penny each until the day on which his contract required him to hand the bridge over to Learmonth and the Road Trustees. The novelty of the view from the new bridge ensured that he collected a great many pennies.

The bridge was completed early in 1832 but was not opened for traffic until May 1834 when the press announced that 'the new cut of road north of the Dean Bridge is now completed'. But John Learmonth and his heirs had to wait much longer for a return on his outlay. The great Edinburgh building boom had halted and no one wanted to build houses on his land until the 1850s, when Clarendon Crescent was built. Buckingham Terrace, Learmonth Terrace and Belgrave Crescent were not begun till some time after his death in 1858.

Looking down from the west side of the bridge the scene is a strange one to find in the centre of a city for there, far below, is the Water of Leith village, now generally known as Dean Village, a jumble of roofs, lanes and warehouses, some ruinous and some recently restored. They are all huddled on the hillsides and the river banks, with an ancient bridge in their midst which for centuries was the only crossing for traffic bound for Queensferry and the North. No medieval town was complete without its mills where its baxters (or bakers) could grind their flour, and those of Edinburgh were here in the Water of Leith village. As years went on there came to be eleven mills, referred to in the town's records as 'the eleven common mylnes of this burgh upon baith sides of the Water of Leith'.

In its deep valley, the river makes an S-bend and the mills were clustered in two groups on the flat areas enclosed by the curves of the S. Those on the north side were driven from a dam above the village and those on the south from the lower dam which still provides quite a spectacular waterfall. The lade from that dam was made, eventually, to drive at least nine mills. The first was close by on the site now marked by three millstones erected as a decorative feature beside the path. Three more mills followed in quick succession. From the last of that group the water was carried in a raised wooden trough down the valley, past St Bernard's Well to St Bernard's Bridge, at one end of which can be seen the arch, now built up, through which the water flowed on to Stockbridge. There it supplied power for Kedslie's mill until 1814 when a steam engine was installed. From Stockbridge the water was carried on its way, sometimes above ground, sometimes below, to turn wheels at Silvermills and Canonmills and finally at the pepper and snuff mills of Powderhall before being returned to the river.

Among those who regretted the change from water-power to steam at Kedslie's Mill were Mr and Mrs Henry Raeburn of St Bernard's House. In 1816, along with some of their neighbours, they brought an action against the mill owners, complaining that smoke and smuts from the mill-chimney prevented full enjoyment of their gardens and made the washings hung out by their servants 'as black as before' so that they had to be washed all over again. The case was the first ever brought in the Jury Court, a new court established in that year which functioned only until 1830.

The Raeburns had Henry Cockburn as Counsel to present their case; but Messrs Kedslie had the star performer, Francis Jeffrey, on their side. He gave the first of his many sparkling performances in actions in this court. In what the press described as 'a most ingenious and humorous speech', Jeffrey jested to the jury about 'Mrs Raeburn's lily-white hand' being blemished by specks of dirt from the chimney. He also made much of the fact that a colony of washerwomen who lived and plied their trade nearby had never been inconvenienced by the smoke; and he produced, as he put it, 'a cloud of these pure and amiable females to bear witness in my favour'. His tactics carried the day and judgment was given in favour of the mill owners and against the plaintiffs.

Through the centuries there are many references in the town records to the Water of Leith mills. Their 'damheads', their wheels and their timbers repeatedly fell into disrepair and committees had to be sent to inspect them and report. Sometimes the damage was caused by floods and the seventeenth-century diarist John Nicoll has left us a vivid account of one such occasion when it was his belief that the damage caused represented no more than well-deserved retribution. In 1659, the Town Council had imposed a tax on ale sold within the burgh and, in September of that year, says Nicoll, 'no sooner was the 8d. the pint on ale begun to be exacted to the great hurt of the subjects but immediately thereafter the Lord did manifest his anger in sending doun ane unheard of and uncouth storm of wind and wet by the space of three days and three nichts whereby sundry houses, with eleven mills belonging to Edinburgh . . . with their dams, water-gangs . . . wheels and whole other works were destroyed and violently taken away by these great deluges of waters.'

An important day annually in the village was that on which members of the ancient and worthy Incorporation of Baxters came down the steep Bell's Brae for the feeing of the millers and the fixing of their wages. On such days it was the amiable custom for bakers and millers together to conclude their business by adjourning to a local tavern for food and refreshment. On feeing day in 1716 the tavern keeper's account included items for beef, veal, 'broth and other necessaries' and also for brandy, ale and 'pypes and tobacko'. A revealing feature of that account is the fact that two postscripts were added, suggesting that the company had some difficulty in deciding when they had had enough. Brandy and ale are included in the main bill, and then two lines are added: 'Item *more* to the millers for ale: £1: 12/-' and 'Item *more* for brandy and ale: £1: 3'. Those two short lines concisely conjure up a picture of the jovial company round the tavern table.

When the Dean Bridge was being built, the workmen on it, high above the village, are reported to have heard a strange sound every morning. This was 'the beating of hiemett' the long established means by which the millers sought to ensure that they and their assistants started work in good time. One of their number who could be relied upon not to oversleep was engaged to stand early each morning on the bridge in the village beating a large corn measure or 'mett' with a rolling pin to a particular tune or rhythm which, besides waking all his fellow-workers, was heard far up and down the valley.

No longer will you hear the sound of 'hiemett' on a walk through the village streets; but the baxters and the millers have left a number of signs for you to recognize as you pass by. At the foot of Bell's Brae is the building known as 'the old tolbooth', converted in 1885, to form an episcopal mission church and hall. Originally a granary, it was built in 1675 and bears the inscriptions

'God bless the baxters of Edinburgh who built this hous' and 'God's providence is our inheritance'. There is also a carved panel to be seen on which are two bakers' peels crossed, one carrying three cakes and the other a pie; suitable symbols of the bakers' craft. Across the road, built into the wall of the old bridge, another stone also displays two bakers' peels with cakes ready to be thrust into the oven.

Fragmentary traces of the old mills can still be discovered here and there and two large storehouse or granary buildings have recently been restored to fulfil new uses. One, bearing the date 1805, towers to a height of six storeys on the north bank of the river. Improbably, you might think, and yet successfully, it has been converted into flats whose occupants enjoy a modern city life-style in an old-world village setting. Opposite, and between Bell's Brae and the river, another ancient warehouse has been effectively given new life as an architects' office. These restorations and some council houses designed to blend with the old are bringing new life to a village that was very nearly derelict.

The millers' craft was not the only one that flourished here. There was a tannery, closed only recently, and a colony of weavers whose 'seal of cause' was granted in 1728 and who earned a reputation for their linen and damask work. Their cottages and work sheds, from which the clack of their looms could be heard daily, were mainly strung out along the mill-lade on the north side of the river. That part of the village in the later nineteenth century became a hopelessly crowded area where poverty and disease were rife. Then a benefactor stepped in and provided what is perhaps one of the most interesting features of the village. He was John R. Findlay, proprietor of the *Scotsman*.

He lived in Rothesay Terrace, the houses of which rise like a great grey cliff above Belford Road. From his windows he looked down across the Water of Leith on to the huddle of crowded, insanitary cottages in the heart of the Dean Village. In their place he provided Well Court, designed by an Edinburgh architect, Sydney Mitchell, on lines that were much in advance of that time. It provided flats for working people, grouped round a square and incorporated a hall for social occasions, lectures and Sunday services. The flats are of varying size to suit the requirements of different family groups and of the elderly. The whole scheme may

P

have owed something to the ideas of social planning which Patrick Geddes was putting forward so vigorously about that time. Built of a warm red stone, with a varied and interesting outline and a clock tower to provide a focal point, Well Court has been described as presenting, from J. R. Findlay's Rothesay Terrace window, 'a picture amiably reminiscent of romantic Nuremberg'. Romantic or not, it proved to be an eminently practical and successful scheme.

Above the Dean Village, for rather more than a mile, the banks of the Water of Leith are not open to the public although this length includes, between Belford Bridge and Roseburn Bridge, a pastoral valley which could form a ready-made riverside park, providing the quiet pleasures of the countryside less than a mile from the heart of the city. For more than forty years there have been plans that some day it should do so.

South of the river at this point, standing in its own extensive grounds, is Donaldson's School for the Deaf, arguably the most ornate building in the city. Designed by W. H. Playfair and completed in 1850, it is in magnificent Tudor style. It is said to have cost £100000 and was provided under the will of James Donaldson, a printer who once worked in modest premises at the foot of West Bow and who died in 1830, leaving his fortune to provide a hospital for poor children including those who were deaf and dumb. When Donaldson's Hospital was new, Queen Victoria and Prince Albert inspected it and out of their visit a story grew which, even now, is sometimes told as if it were fact. Her Majesty, it is said, was so impressed by the splendours of the building that, there and then, she offered to buy it as a royal residence. When the board members respectfully but firmly declined her offer, the story goes on to say, she was exceedingly angry and threatened never again to grace Edinburgh with her presence.

That is the story. What really happened, as reported by a former governor of the hospital, was that, after touring the building, the Queen turned to the board members who had escorted her, thanked them for their attendance and added: 'Your school is finer than any of my Scottish palaces.' Thus are legends born.

Beyond the bridge at Roseburn, the river is again more accessible. It flows past Roseburn public park beside which is the old mansion of Roseburn, a sixteenth-century tower with seventeenth- and eighteenth-century additions. Another mile and a bit upstream, the river circles round Saughton public park. The mansion here was demolished years ago but its old garden provides surely as fine a rose garden as can be seen in any public park anywhere, with 15000 blooms to delight the most knowing rosarian or just anyone who can enjoy colour and beauty.

Still following the river we come to what remains of the village of Slateford. Here the river is crossed by the Union Canal, carried sixty-five feet overhead on a sturdy stone-built aqueduct of eight arches. When the canal was opened in 1822, linking Edinburgh with the Forth and Clyde canal at Falkirk, and so with Glasgow, such an aqueduct must have seemed to the villagers a spectacular piece of civil engineering for it was before the days of the ubiquitous railway viaduct. The villagers would have more than a passing interest in the canal as many of them worked at Hailes Quarry, a mile away, and stone from the quarries along its route was an important item in the cargoes carried by the canal boats.

Passengers journeyed that way too; and it must have been a smooth and peaceful means of travel between the two cities, gliding through fields and along hillsides, often with fine views or, as here at Slateford, sailing above rooftops. You could go overnight, if you preferred, sleeping in a comfortable cabin while two horses, one ahead of the other on the narrow towpath, pulled you at speeds up to nine miles an hour. 'Many tourists,' it was said, 'especially those with families of children, prefer canal conveyance betwixt the two cities.'

Our route, though, is upwards by the river. From Slateford, a public walkway winds close beside the stream through the woodlands of Craiglockhart Dell and Colinton Dell, bringing us into the heart of Colinton village. Fifty years ago Colinton was in the country. Now it is surrounded by the city. But the suburban villas and bungalows crowding in upon it have not destroyed its village character nor its sense of being a community. The steep village street leads down to the old bridge, to the church and to the manse garden in which Robert Louis Stevenson played as a child when his grandfather, Lewis Balfour, was minister here in the 1850s. There is a Pentland Essay in which R.L.S. describes the garden and its surroundings as he remembered them, and if you read it, you will find that little has changed. The church, the manse, 'the tombstones thick on the terrace of the churchyard' are there.

So are the trees on the steep opposite hillside, 'seeming to climb to heaven'; and the little water-door leading from the garden to the river. There is still the sound of water everywhere, but no longer the sound of mills, flour mill below and snuff mill above 'with wheel and dam singing their alternate strain'.

Long before Stevenson's time, the snuff mill had belonged to James Gillespie, whose fortune later founded a home for old people and a school. While he attended to the working of the mill, the snuff it produced was sold by his brother from their shop in the High Street, near the luckenbooths. William Creech and all the frequenters of Creech's levées would be among his customers and the snuff sold so well that in 1773 James Gillespie was able to buy the house of Spylaw, a little way upstream from his mill and to extend it and transform it into a comfortable country mansion for himself. You can see it among its fine old trees in Spylaw public park where it is used now for community purposes. James, as befitted the country gentleman he had become, also bought himself a carriage, though allegedly a very plain one. Plain though it was, its doors carried, in gold paint, his initials J.G. Seeing these, Henry Erskine suggested that a coat-of-arms should be added, with the motto 'Wha would hae thocht it, that noses had bocht it?'

About a mile above Colinton is the village of Juniper Green, of no great age and with no claims to fame. But its houses are strung out pleasantly along the high ground north of the valley with wide views south to the long rolling range of the Pentland Hills. It is a good starting point for walks across these hills by curlew-haunted tracks to Silverburn or into the Tweeddale District of the Borders Region at the village of Carlops, amid scenes that have not changed much since they were the setting for the poet Allan Ramsay's pastoral play, *The Gentle Shepherd*.

As to Juniper Green, I said it had no claims to fame, but I can think of two occasions which may just qualify. It was to a cottage in the village that Thomas and Jane Welsh Carlyle came briefly after their marriage in 1826, before moving to their better-known house at Comely Bank on the north side of the city and in that cottage, Carlyle said, he had his 'first experience in the difficulties of housekeeping'. Four years later, Charles X of France and some of his household came out from Holyrood to the seventeenth-century Baberton House, half a mile from the village, to enjoy a few months' shooting on the Pentland Hills and in the nearer woodlands.

So, on the cross-section of the city carved out for us by the Water of Leith, we have reached its 1920 boundary. What lies beyond is part of the new Edinburgh and belongs to a different chapter.

19 Along the city coast

Edinburgh is not readily thought of as a maritime city. Yet since 1920 it has had as part of its boundary a sea-front of about ten miles along the Firth of Forth. That sea-front includes the port of Leith and the 'resort' of Portobello, each formerly a separate town. It includes also the village of Newhaven, long famous for its oysters, and Cramond village, at the mouth of the River Almond on the site of a Roman station. Now the City of Edinburgh District boundary takes in five more miles of wooded shore as well as the Royal Burgh of Queensferry, making up sixteen miles of sea coast of remarkably varied interest. For this chapter, I propose to stay within the old boundary, exploring the sea-front and its stories along the way from Portobello to Cramond.

For many centuries the flat expanse of land between Arthur's Seat and the sea was a desolate waste known as the Figgate Whins. The highway to Musselburgh and onwards to London passed through it and travellers were glad when this lonely stretch was behind them as it was notorious for its smugglers and highwaymen.

In 1739 the Spanish town of Puerto Bello on the isthmus of Panama, was captured by a British fleet and, a few years later, a sailor who had been in the battle came home to Scotland. He built a house on a desolate spot among the whins within sight and sound of the surf and called it Porto Bello. Its site was where the building used as a Baptist church now stands, identifiable by its clock, in the High Street east of Brighton Place.

The sailor, or maybe his successor in the house, was named George Hamilton. He seems to have found it profitable to do some saddlery and coach repairing, providing a useful service-station for travellers in trouble on the road. Soon refreshments were being sold and in October 1753 Hamilton, seeking to attract custom, advertised that a horse race would be run 'at Porto Bello, in the midst of the Freegate Whins'. So, Portobello was on the map.

Before the end of the eighteenth century two different kinds of development had begun in the neighbourhood. They were opposite and incompatible. First, extensive beds of clay were found on and near the site of the present electricity power station. These began to be exploited in 1763 by William Jameson who came to be known as 'the father of Portobello'.

Then, in 1795, intimation appeared in the newspapers that 'Mr John Cairns at Portobello begs most respectfully to inform the ladies, gentlemen and public that he has erected bathing machines upon the best construction with steady horses and careful drivers. The bathing sands are more than a mile long, perfectly smooth . . . the water clear and strong and the beach very retired.' The dilemma of Portobello had begun and it has never been resolved. Should it be a seaside resort or an industrial area?

There were extensive brickworks, bottleworks and a pottery which produced some interesting items including, in the early nineteenth century, a variety of ornaments now sought after by collectors. The last pottery firm to operate in the works at the foot of Bridge Street removed to Crieff, in Perthshire, in 1972; and two bottle-kilns, dated 1906 and 1909 on the site of the old works have been preserved because of their interest to industrial archaeologists and so that their outlines, so familiar a feature of the place, may not be lost.

Against that background of industry Mr Cairns's bathing-machines increased in popularity and Portobello became a favourite resort, in the early nineteenth century, for those who could afford to drive there or to build or rent summer homes, as many Edinburgh people did. As the summer houses increased in number and cottages and flats were built for the work people, the straggling village grew to be a compact town. Many of the houses are

charming, unpretentious examples of small Georgian domestic
building and a walk along some of the older streets between the
High Street and the sea, especially east of Bath Street, can be re-
warding for anyone with an eye for architectural detail.

In 1827, J. G. Lockhart and his family were at 37 Melville Street
(now named Bellfield Street) and were often visited by Sir Walter
Scott who was fond of walking and driving on the sands, as close
to the waves as possible. Sometimes he may have walked there
with his friend, Sir William Rae ('dear, loved, Rae' he called him).
Ten years after Scott's death, his friend, by then for the third time
Lord Advocate, was the means of saving the sands, or at least
public access to them, for posterity. In 1842, although seventy-
three years old, he was still fond of bathing. One morning as he
made his way along the pathway of turf and dry sand between
the shore and the private properties adjoining it, on his way to
bathe, he found that Mr Alexander Smith, a Writer to the Signet
who owned a villa near the shore, had extended his garden across
the seaside path and was building a wall around it against which
the sea was beating, barring further progress. Sir William was
annoyed, both as private citizen and as an officer of the Crown,
to discover this interruption of the public right of walking on the
shore of which the Crown is guardian. He immediately obtained
an interdict to have the work halted. Smith, however, protested
that his property was described as 'bounded by the sea' and could
therefore be regarded as extending to the sea's edge. At this point,
unfortunately, Sir William Rae died; but others took up the case of
Officers of State v. *Smith*.

In the Court of Session one of the judges was Lord Cockburn.
He said: 'This encroachment is bound to injure recreation and
free passage. The principle would allow the whole line of owners
to stretch their walls out to ebb-tide.' The judges were unanimous
that the wall must be removed, but Mr Smith was nothing if not
persistent and he appealed to the House of Lords.

There Lord Brougham who, as an Edinburgh man had local
knowledge denied to some of his colleagues, spoke strongly. In
his judgment, he referred to 'these very celebrated sands' and
said: 'It is quite undeniable that this act of Mr Smith's makes him
a wrongdoer. It is to the detriment and damnification of the
Queen's subjects even if no other person follow his example.'

The appeal was dismissed, Mr Smith had to remove the offending wall and the sands of Portobello were saved for the people.

About a century and a quarter later, they had to be saved again. The waves and tides, over all that time, had swept much of the sand away; to such an extent that where formerly a normally active person could have stepped down from the promenade to the beach without great difficulty, there had developed a drop of eight feet and more and the promenade and neighbouring buildings were being undermined. Unlike Lewis Carroll's walrus and carpenter who, it will be recalled, 'wept to see such quantities of sand' the Councillors of Edinburgh were grieved to see so little. In 1973 using, not seven maids with seven mops, but a large dredger and modern machinery, they scooped nearly 200 000 cubic metres of sand from the sea-bed a mile or so away and returned it all to the shore in a highly successful 'beach nourishment' operation. Thus Portobello's 'very celebrated sands' were restored to something of their former glory.

The promenade had been built by Portobello's own Town Council in the 1860s. It was the coming of burgh reform in 1833 that had made it possible for the village of Portobello to become a burgh and have its own Council, though not without initial difficulties. When the first election was planned in November 1833 'a numerous and respectable meeting of electors' decided that they had no wish to have either Councillors or officials 'because such functionaries would entail a heavy expense'. Nevertheless, the election went ahead. Fifteen electors voted and the nine candidates they had elected declined to act. So a second election was held in which 36 voted. This time, the same nine candidates were elected. They agreed to serve and the Town Council of Portobello was in business, with a Provost, two Bailies and six Councillors. Thereafter, for sixty-three years, the little town enjoyed its burgh status. After twenty years it obtained a coat-of-arms. This depicted a tower, two cannon and two full-rigged sailing ships in allusion to the rather tenuous origin of the burgh's name.

The Council served the people well and many improvements were made. The bathing machines started by Mr Cairns grew in popularity and it became necessary for the council to make bye-laws regulating their use, especially to ensure that those used by ladies were kept sufficiently far away from those used by gentlemen.

When new bye-laws were made in 1862 the Sheriff who had to confirm them before they could operate 'personally perambulated the beach to see how the bathing was conducted'; and he also wrote for information to English resorts and even to Calais and Boulogne, to ensure that the regulations would conform to the most up-to-date seaside ideas.

It was on this occasion that a press reporter remarked that the new rules 'would remove the bathing-coaches from before the houses of the Provost and one of the Bailies, but of course we do not insinuate that any such consideration has actuated them'. He went on to make some amends for his comment by complimenting the town on becoming each year, more deserving of being known as 'Edinburgh-super-Mare'.

Combination with Edinburgh, however, was still more than thirty years ahead. In the early 1890s, Edinburgh Town Council suggested amalgamation with both Leith and Portobello. Leith firmly said no; but Portobello, having taken a plebiscite among its inhabitants, in which exactly equal numbers voted for and against, agreed to the merger, on conditions. These included the requirement that, for seven years, rates within the former burgh area would not exceed 2s. in the £. The conditions were accepted and in October 1896 Portobello became part of Edinburgh.

At King's Road, so called because it was this way George IV came in 1822 to review his troops, we are at the western end of Portobello. Just before King's Road, an open-air swimming pool, described at its opening in 1939 as the finest in Scotland, nestles incongruously beneath the mass of Portobello power station. Beyond it a twentieth-century extension of the seaside promenade is flanked by a row of factories: two final examples of Portobello's dual personality.

The promenade takes us westward to Seafield where acres of reclaimed land are given over to goods yards and warehouses, for this is the edge of dockland. On the corner where the road forks is a small building with a Doric portico and a small attractive dome. It was built in 1813 as Seafield Baths, containing in those days hot, cold and tepid baths and a hotel. It must then have been a building of some distinction; and, though this may now be hard to believe, it was described when new as 'overlooking one of the finest parts of the beach'. At that time it looked out on

Leith Sands. These were renowned for bathing and Leith Races were held there, long before Portobello became popular.

Leith Races are referred to in a paper of March 1661 as 'our accustomed recreations', showing that they were older than that. Those of 1661 were not the most successful, being 'much hindered by a furious storm of wind, accompanied with a thick snow' which seems not entirely to have dismayed the competitors, some of whom carried on regardless. For long the proceedings were under the patronage of the Town Council of Edinburgh and there are many entries in their records about the provision of trophies, such as their orders to 'the deacon of the goldsmiths to make a piece of plate not exceeding £25 sterling for the horse race at Leith' and 'the Treasurer to pay the goldsmith £298:10/- Scots for making a Monteith [silver punch-bowl] for the annual horse race at Leith and engraving the town's arms thereupon'. The races on the sands came to be held for a week each year, usually in August or September and crowds travelled from all over Scotland to see them. Every morning during the week, a city officer in full uniform, carrying a pole from which hung a gaily ornamented purse, would march from Edinburgh all the way to the sands followed by the Town Guard drummer and sometimes other members of that force. As they progressed they would be joined by more and more youths until sometimes the officer and guard were lost in a motley throng, for it was a popular pastime to 'gang doon wi' the purse' to the races.

Later in the day the Town Council would go down in state and in 1735 they paid £7 13s. sterling for the hire of coaches and then '3/6 more to bring some of the Council from Leith'. Did some of their number celebrate too long and too well in an ale-house, I wonder, and miss the official coach home?

In a diary of a tour by a young man from England in 1793, there is a brief description of the races as he and his friends saw them. 'About twelve we went with the crowd to the races on Leith Sands, a vile course, but the scene is strange and literally amphibious. You see at once ships, battlements, houses, woods and waters, an immense concourse of people, carriages and horses.' Evidently it was not only the horses that interested them on that occasion, for he goes on: 'My friend Duncan thought Lady Suttie the finest woman on the Sands but I gave preference to Miss Wemyss'; a remark that seems to suggest that the race meeting was an occasion for a parade of fashion, a kind of northern Ascot perhaps. It was also an occasion for all kinds of fairground amusements, side-shows and games; as well as a great deal of thieving and damage to property.

In 1816 the races were transferred to the Links at Musselburgh but in 1836 they were back on Leith Sands though, by this time, for one day each year only. By then Leith had its own Town Council and in 1846 the Council received a long petition signed by hundreds of citizens complaining of such unpleasant accompaniment to the annual races as 'vice and profligacy', 'danger to lives', 'disgusting intemperance' and 'brutal fights', by which, they said, 'the good order of society has been disturbed, the peaceable inhabitants have been annoyed and the young, the innocent and the unwary have been ensnared'. Yet, despite the strength of their protest, ten more years elapsed before the races were finally removed from Leith.

The road straight ahead from Seafield goes through a typical dock hinterland of works and warehouses; but if instead you fork left you find yourself looking along the green length of Leith Links. The Links were an early home of golf. John Knox allegedly played golf here and on Sunday, too; but only 'after sermon' so that was all right. It was here, also, that John Patersone, partnering James VII when Duke of York, won the wager that enabled him to build his Golfer's Land tenement in the Canongate.

In 1744 'the Honourable Company of Golfers of Edinburgh' were formed and they had their club-house and meeting place on Leith Links until early in the next century. But by 1827 a writer was complaining that only occasional groups of players were seen on the Links and they were behaving 'with a gravity more suited to a funeral procession'. Twenty-five years later another recorded sadly that the Links were so little used by golfers that he had met people in Leith who did not know what golf was.

I have dwelt on the races and the game of golf because, despite the roughness that accompanied the races and the slow demise of the golf, they give some impression of gaiety and pleasure in contrast to so much in Leith's history that is grim. At the west end of the Links are two grassy mounds. They are remnants of two batteries used in the siege of Leith in 1560 when English troops, supporting the Scottish Reformers, strove hard to dislodge from the town the French troops who were holding it on behalf of Mary of Guise, Queen Regent, mother of Mary, Queen of Scots. One of the mounds, known as the giant's brae, marks the site of Somerset's battery, the other, Lady Fyfe's brae, that of Pelham's. The siege went on for many weeks, with severe losses on both sides and caused much suffering to the townspeople. Mary of Guise, seriously ill, had retired to Edinburgh Castle where, despite her illness, she watched the progress of the siege from the ramparts. In June 1560 she died and soon afterwards the siege ended.

Leith had suffered before, especially in 1544 and 1548 when the Earl of Hertford burned the town. It suffered in 1645 when the Links were crowded with huts hastily built for victims of the plague and more than half the population died; and it suffered in 1650 when Cromwell's troops occupied it. The only relic of the Cromwellian occupation that remains is the gateway to the citadel towards the cost of which General Monk persuaded Edinburgh Town Council to contribute £5000 by threatening to have their ancient privileges withdrawn. After the Restoration, the Earl of Lauderdale, who had obtained the citadel from the Crown, offered it to the Town Council for £6000, an offer which they felt it was politic to accept. So the citadel, which they did not really want, cost them £11000. The gateway, which is all that remains of it, was restored in the 1960s and can be seen in Dock Street, off Commercial Street.

One historian has said that the 'woes of Leith' began when Bruce, by his Charter of 1329, confirmed the right of Edinburgh to control its harbour. True it is that the town of Edinburgh made the most of that right and of the later powers it obtained over Leith by the acquisition in 1567 of the feudal superiority over South Leith (by far the greater part) on the south-east side of the Water of Leith and then, some seventy years later, of the superiority over North Leith, then a smaller township on the north-west bank of the river.

Through all these years and long after, restrictions were imposed by Edinburgh on trading in Leith which seem as ridiculous to us as they must then have seemed iniquitous to the people of Leith. No one was permitted to trade in Leith unless he was a freeman of Edinburgh; no freeman of Edinburgh might take a Leith resident into partnership; goods landed at Leith must be

taken to Edinburgh to be weighed and have a price fixed before
they could be sold; the people of Leith must not engage in the
making and selling of candles. There are dozens of such decrees
among the burgh records and many instances of infringement,
indicating the extent to which the rules were resented and ignored.

Other grievances stemmed from the fact that, for 266 years –
from 1567 till 1833 – the Bailies who dispensed justice in Leith were
appointed by Edinburgh and for much of that time they did not
even live in Leith. So there are entries in the Leith court books
like: 'No court this day, in regard the Bailie came not doon.' Not
that the Bailie could be entirely blamed, for the road to Leith was
a rough and muddy one and as late as 1763 the coaches plying
between the two towns, though drawn by three horses, took a
full hour for the journey. Although from time to time agreement
was reached to give the Leith people some say in the choice of
magistrates and to ensure that at least one of them lived in Leith,
these arrangements remained a recurring source of trouble.

Some credit, however, is surely due to Edinburgh for their
enterprise in building the first section of the docks. The East Old
Dock and the West Old Dock, both to the west of the Water of
Leith estuary (and both now filled in) were built by Edinburgh
Town Council between 1806 and 1817 at a cost of £300000, a sum
which formed a large proportion of the massive debt which the
old Town Council incurred. But these first two docks were the
basis from which have stemmed all the later dock extensions
undertaken by Leith Dock Commission and their successors, the
Forth Ports Authority.

Before Leith eventually became a burgh in 1833 with its own
Town Council of sixteen members, the system of administration
had become remarkably complicated. There were the Bailies, of
course; there were police commissioners appointed since 1771;
there were four incorporations – Trinity House, possibly founded
as long ago as 1380, a select company of ships' captains who still
play a prominent part in the public life of the port; the maltmen
and brewers; the trades or craftsmen and the traffickers or merchants. From 1827, there was a new hybrid body known as the
Magistrates and Masters (i.e. Masters of the four incorporations)
which lasted for fourteen years. It was they who built the handsome
Council Chamber in Constitution Street, still inscribed for all

to see: 'Erected by the Magistrates and Masters, 1828'. Later it became the Council Chamber for Leith Town Council who met in it until 1920. Their meeting room, used now by local organizations, is still furnished as they left it. It contains many portraits of former Leith dignitaries and also Carse's picture of the landing of George IV, filling almost the whole of one wall, which is reproduced between pages 152 and 153.

In the light of that short summary of the old relationship between Leith and Edinburgh, it is not difficult to understand why, after only sixty-three years of their longed-for freedom, Leith gave such a resounding 'no' to Edinburgh's proposal for a merger in 1896. Twenty-four years later, when it seemed to Edinburgh abundantly clear that two separate administrative organizations in so small an area no longer made any sense, they put the proposal again; and again the reply was a clear and unequivocal 'no'. However, this time, Edinburgh was not disposed to accept 'no' for an answer and the Bill was promoted which led to the passing of the Edinburgh Boundaries Extension Act.

Leith lodged objections, of course, but in the proceedings that followed, it was plain that these objections, based on tradition and sentiment, however understandable they might be, could not hold out against the logic of the City's proposals. There were boundary problems, as instanced by Counsel at the inquiry: 'In some places, where there were open fields, the boundary was drawn as a straight line; now it sometimes goes right through the middle of a house and the inhabitant has difficulty in knowing where he is sleeping because his head is in Edinburgh while his feet are in Leith.' There was a public house where different closing times applied at opposite ends of the same bar counter.

There were administrative problems: the Edinburgh firemaster complained that sometimes, having arrived first at a fire just within the Leith boundary, the Edinburgh brigade had been told by the Leith firemaster that this was *his* fire and they should go away. The Chief Constable of Edinburgh also had technical difficulties in dealing with criminals from the other side of the line. There was, he said, a Leith character well known as Scotch Jamie who did all his petty pilfering in Edinburgh and relied on the police boundary problems to protect him from justice.

Of course, these and other difficulties might have been solved by boundary changes and revised regulations; but there were also complicated joint trust arrangements to deal with services like water and gas supply to the two communities; and there were other problems which could not have been so easily solved. So the Act was passed and in 1920 Leith became a part of Edinburgh.

The village of Newhaven came back to the city at the same time. Since 1833 it had been within the boundaries of Leith, but long, long before that, in 1511, a charter of James IV had given to Edinburgh 'our whole new port called Newhaven'. There he had set up a shipyard for which he had great hopes, with workshops and houses for the workers and there he had built the *Great Michael*, that ship that was said to have required so much stout timber that its building had 'wasted all the woods of Fife'; though Lindsay of Pitscottie, the historian writing in the same century who coined that phrase did qualify it by excepting the woods of Falkland, where the King's palace was.

The *Michael* must indeed have been a great ship for Pitscottie's account goes on: 'all the Wrights of Scotland yea, and many other Strangers by the King's Commandment wrought very busily at her, but it was a Year and a Day ere she was complete'. When at last the ship was finished and lying off shore, the King was so confident of her strength that he had a cannon fired at her as a test. Happily, it 'did her little Skaith', after which, Pitscottie says, 'This ship lay still in the Roads and the King every day taking pleasure to pass to her and to dine and sup in her with his Lords, letting them see the Order of his ship.'

Two years later, James was killed at Flodden. His plan for a shipyard at Newhaven came to nought. Now, the name of his great ship is commemorated there only by modern name-plates on streets in the village that have been called Great Michael Rise and Great Michael Court. Not much of the old village remains intact. Its fishermen's houses with their outside stairs have disappeared, to be replaced not by mere copies of their old design nor by incongruous modern flats, but by new houses, some also with outside stairs, which have effectively translated the old village style into a twentieth-century idiom. But the old harbour is still there and the market on the quay through which the city still obtains its supply of fish; though the fish are now landed at Granton, a mile further west.

For centuries, Newhaven was famous for its oysters. The oyster scalps, opposite the foreshore of Newhaven and Leith, stretched to a point beyond the island of Inchkeith covering about ten square miles of sea-bed. They belonged to Edinburgh and the royalties derived from the fishing of them once formed a valuable part of the town's revenues. The Newhaven fishermen, however, while not refusing to pay the royalties, claimed to have an immemorial right to dredge the oysters. So when the town took to letting the fishing to others, trouble and sometimes litigation resulted; but the fishermen do not seem to have had any qualms about dredging the oysters themselves and then selling them to ships that came into the Firth for the purpose. In the seventeenth century, ships from Holland were supplied in this way, despite a proclamation against the practice; and in 1837 English ships anchored off Inchkeith while local boats took quantities of oysters out to them.

From time to time there were problems from nearer home. Fishermen from Prestonpans, beyond Musselburgh, sometimes encroached on the Edinburgh scalps and, when they did so, the Newhaven men were quick to take action. In 1788 there was a battle between boats from the two ports, waged with oars and boat-hooks. The Newhaven men were the victors and they brought the Prestonpans boat and crew back to port with them, 'after much hurt being received on both sides'.

In the first half of the nineteenth century the oyster fishings seem to have reached their peak, about the same time as the consumption of oysters in the city taverns was at its most popular. In 1836 there were over fifty Newhaven boats, each with five men, engaged throughout the season wholly on dredging oysters. In the second half of the century the oyster fishing declined. According to a Scottish Fishery Board report, six million oysters were landed at Newhaven in 1866. By 1880 the number had dropped to 200000 and in 1890 it was 2000. By the end of the century the oysters were no more and though there was talk of reviving them by bringing in supplies of 'seedlings', that was never done. Many reasons were given for the decline. The Fishery Board expert had no doubt it was due almost wholly to the over-fishing that had gone on for so long but, if that had not ruined the beds, it seems likely that pollution would soon have done so.

Q

The people of Newhaven are reputed to have been originally of Flemish or Belgian origin. For centuries, in the manner of many fishing communities, they kept much to themselves and intermarriage among them was the general rule; and they had dialect words and pronunciations of their own, some of which lingered on, among the older people, into recent years. They also had their fishwives who, in colourful costume, tramped daily through Edinburgh with heavily-laden creels, selling their fish from door to door. It is not many years since the Newhaven fishwives disappeared from the streets and the city is the poorer for their going, though no one, surely, could be blamed for giving up so arduous an occupation.

They added not only to the sights but to the sounds of the city. Their cries of 'caller herrin'' and 'caller cod' ('caller' meaning fresh) were heard daily. In the evening it was 'caller ou' (fresh oysters) that they cried. 'Wha'll buy my caller herrin'?' became the theme of Baroness Nairne's well-known song and needs no more than that to commend it. But 'caller ou', with the 'ou' stretched out in two long melodious syllables was also a beautiful sound; in support of which statement I call two witnesses who heard it many times.

First, Sir J. H. A. Macdonald, who lived in Abercromby Place in the 1850s, wrote in his *Life Jottings* of the cry of 'caller ou': 'I despair of expressing the delightful sound of it.' He added: 'How often, when it sounded, was the fishwife brought into the entrance hall to open her fresh oysters by the dozen for a delightful impromptu supper'; so perhaps his musical appreciation of the call was enhanced a little by his appetite.

My other witness is Mrs Story who, about the same date or a little later, was living in Melville Street. In her *Reminiscences* she tells of walking home in the early evening through Moray Place and 'listening, on the way, to the musical cry of the Newhaven fisherwomen who, at this time of the evening, came out with their succulent wares and sent the wild and beautiful call of "caller ou" ringing down the streets and over the roofs of the new town'. She goes on: 'Eighteen pence a hundred was the price of oysters taken just as they came, two shillings for more carefully selected ones, while the finest and largest were 2/6 a hundred.'

With that melodious cry – and those prices – in our minds, let us leave Newhaven and move on, past the site of the old chain pier, towards Granton and Cramond. Granton Harbour, built by the Duke of Buccleuch and completed between 1842 and 1850, provided an important ferry link on the railway route to the north before the opening of the Forth rail bridge in 1890. It is now a busy commercial port, and base for a fleet of trawlers. It is also the home port of the Royal Forth Yacht Club whose craft make a brave sight as they sail out through the harbour mouth on a breezy summer day.

Beyond the harbour lie gas works, oil depots and a variety of commercial and industrial premises. But persevere and soon you are at the start of the Granton–Cramond foreshore promenade where a mile and a half of broad walkway which was formed in the 1930s, curving with the shore, leads on, past attractive parkland and clumps of trees, to the village of Cramond. Until the 1930s the parkland was all enclosed as private property and the only path was a narrow rough one close to the beach.

That way in 1799 went John Stoddart, a visitor from England. And though the path was rougher then, the view he saw was not much different from the view today. Here is the gist of what he wrote.

The bay of Cramond presents a picture which has so much variety, so much sweep of view, that it cannot be passed over with slight admiration. In the bottom of the bay is the mouth of the Almond river with the village of Cramond. The Firth itself is beautifully studded by the island of Cramond and several other islands; and the distance is nobly terminated by the Highland mountains.

That is our view, too, as we reach the mouth of the River Almond which, until 1975, had been for fifty-five years the western limit of the city's coast line.

20 City of villages

*E*dinburgh is a city of villages. Within its 1920 boundary, about fifty of them can be counted. Some, like the Dean Village and Colinton which we have already visited, retain their village character. Some, like Liberton, proclaim their former separate state by the survival of an ancient tower-house, a row of old cottages and a kirkyard with weathered stones which, when you decipher their inscriptions, tell of generations for whom the village and its kirk, and not the town yonder on the Castle ridge, were the focal points in their lives. Some were hamlets of which only a rough stone wall or a street name remains as reminder of their former state. Such a one is, or rather was, Tipperlinn near Morningside, of which almost the only remnant is its name, preserved in Tipperlinn Road.

Tipperlinn was a weavers' village. Its cluster of cottages stood on ground now partly within the site of the Royal Edinburgh Hospital, between Merchiston Castle and the Jordan Burn. Parts of that castle are as old as the fifteenth century and much of it dates from the seventeenth. You will find it, restored and preserved, at the heart of the twentieth-century Napier College of Science and Technology into which it has been ingeniously incorporated. As befits the home of John Napier, inventor of logarithms, who was born in the castle in 1550, it has been preserved, not as a museum piece but as part of the administrative centre of the College in which, among a great number of other skills, the use of the tables he originated continues to be taught.

The Jordan Burn you will not find. The length of it that ran through Morningside was ignominiously buried in the 1880s when the suburban railway was constructed to serve the city's outskirts of those days. But a few years earlier, the little stream had been given a measure of fame when Sir Thomas Dick Lauder, through whose grounds of Grange it ran, gave it pride of place in the first of a series of articles (later issued in book form) which he wrote under the title of *Scottish Rivers*. He placed the Jordan Burn first, even before the Tweed and the Yarrow, and certainly as he described its course it must have been a streamlet of delight, flowing through 'arable fields which exhibit in Autumn the heaviest crops of wheat' to run beneath 'the abrupt face and green picturesque top of Blackford Hill'. The wheatfields are no more, but Blackford Hill with its larks, its linnets, its gorse bushes and its wide views across the city is there as Sir Thomas lovingly described it.

Tipperlinn gained itself a share of fame through its colony of handloom weavers. Almost every cottage in the village had an outhouse and a loom where much fine linen was woven. In the late eighteenth century Yeben Gairdner, an old weaver who lived in the village, designed and made a tablecloth with a pattern representing 'The Triumphs of Britannia'. Somehow it was brought to the notice of Queen Charlotte, the Queen of George III, who was so pleased with it that she honoured Yeben with the title of 'Damask manufacturer to Her Majesty'. After that, his business prospered and the patriotic tablecloths of Tipperlinn became a legend.

Though the village has disappeared, a short length of footpath remains, hemmed in and unattractive, replacing part of a strip of ground which, in 1586, was 'reservit for ane passage' leading from Merchiston Castle through the village, to the Jordan Burn. The 'passage' was for long used as a peat road by which the villagers brought in their winter fuel from the burgh muir, and also as the pathway down which the women of Tipperlinn took their clothes, and perhaps their patriotic tablecloths, to be washed in the Jordan Burn. The fragment of pathway that remains serves no very obvious purpose now except, perhaps, to help preserve the memory of the lost village of Tipperlinn and its weavers.

Corstorphine, on the west side of the city, is a village that is far from being lost. It is the centre of a wide suburban district whose residents take an active interest in its past and present life. About four miles from the city centre, it stood of old amid marshy land at the end of a loch, nearly two miles long, which stretched from Roseburn to the village; it was, in fact, a common practice to take goods by boat from Roseburn to Corstorphine. A lamp was provided, high on the parish church, to guide travellers coming across the marsh or along the loch at night. In recent years an electric light has been placed in the old lamp-niche to send out its friendly, but now unnecessary, message to the traveller.

The village of Corstorphine once had a castle, which stood on land acquired by Sir Adam Forrester, burgess of Edinburgh, in 1377 and held by the Forrester family for many generations. The last traces of the castle disappeared more than a century ago but its great circular dovecot remains. Built in the sixteenth century, it has more than 1000 pigeon-holes, the occupants of which must have provided many a tasty morsel for the lairds in the castle. Nearby is an aged sycamore, protected by a tree preservation order because of the beauty of its foliage and the contribution it makes to the story of Corstorphine. Beneath it, in 1679, Christian Nimmo, who was the wife of an Edinburgh merchant, slew the second Lord Forrester with his own sword because, having had an affair with her, he had afterwards said some unkind words about her. She was executed at the market cross of Edinburgh. Long afterwards on moonlit nights her ghost, clad all in white and carrying a blood-stained sword, could be seen and heard, weeping and wailing beside the dovecot. So far as I know, she has not been seen in recent years.

The parish church of Corstorphine is at the eastern end of the old main street of the village which runs parallel to, and a little to the south of the modern main road. Parts of the structure of the church belonged to the chapel built by the first Sir Adam Forrester in the fourteenth century and its architectural history through all the years since then is a complicated one. The church was drastically restored and altered by William Burn in 1828, with not much feeling for its history and again in 1905 when a genuine attempt was made to restore something of its former character. Its most striking feature now as you approach across the well-kept churchyard is the massive roof of stone slabs. Inside there are finely carved effigies of several members of the Forrester family. One, of an armoured knight, is said to represent Sir Adam who founded the original chapel. He was twice Provost of Edinburgh, showing that, even in those far-off days there was a close link between Corstorphine and the burgh.

By the eighteenth century Corstorphine had become a holiday resort for Edinburgh families. Corstorphine cream, 'prepared somewhat in the manner of the Devonshire clotted cream', was famous. There was also a mineral well, so popular that a coach ran regularly from Edinburgh 'for the express purpose of conveying passengers who wished to partake of its salubrious waters'. The well is no longer to be seen but its memory is preserved in the name of Ladywell Road and a modern office block named Ladywell House.

The village was surrounded by farms and market gardens and, with the wooded slope of Corstorphine Hill above it on the north and its wide view south to the Pentland Hills, it must have been a pleasant country retreat. Its conversion from rural village to city suburb began with the opening of the Corstorphine branch railway line in 1902 and was much hastened after the parish of Corstorphine, along with those of Cramond, Colinton and Liberton, became part of the city in 1920.

Of all the city villages, two are my favourites – Duddingston and Cramond. They are similar in that each has preserved its own identity; but their identities are very different. Duddingston, less than two miles from Princes Street as the crow flies, but protected from the city's noise and bustle by the bulk of Arthur's Seat is still a country village, although it has been within the city since 1901. Cramond, nearly five miles from the city centre has all the appearance of being a fishing community, though you will look long and fruitlessly for fisher-folk among its present-day residents. Each has a long history, made up of several chapters.

Take Duddingston, with its Norman church on a knoll above Duddingston Loch; above it a green hill-slope rises to the Queen's Drive, which encircles Holyrood Park, and continues upwards to the rocky summit of Arthur's Seat, 823 feet above the sea. On that slope, both below and above the Drive, are ancient terraces, more than thirty altogether. You can see them in the picture between pages 200 and 201; best of all, they can be seen on any sunny evening when the shadows cast by the low sun pick them out sharply along the hillside. They are the remains of cultivation terraces belonging to Anglo-Saxon and early medieval times when the ground lower down was too boggy or too thickly covered with trees and scrub to make possible the growing of crops. So the inhabitants of Duddingston and its surroundings of those days found it necessary to build these terraces and grow their crops upon them. Here and there a close inspection reveals remnants of the rough stone-built retaining walls that supported the terraces.

These terraces are not the earliest remnants of civilization to have been found hereabouts. Many years ago, bronze age implements from before the Christian era were dredged out of Duddingston Loch; and, on the crest of Dunsapie rock, above the little high-level loch of Dunsapie, there are the scanty remains of an iron age fort which might have been occupied at any time between the fifth century B.C. and the fifth century A.D. Nor are these all. At several points in the Park hollows and humps in the ground can be identified by those with an eye trained to such things, as the remains of cottages and farm buildings of varying antiquity.

Duddingston Loch is fed from springs, the famous Wells o' Wearie. As a result of drainage it is now a fragment of its former self. When Dunsapie fort was occupied and when the terraces were in use, it would be a much larger sheet of water. There was a suggestion, once, that it should be used as a source of water supply for Edinburgh but, happily, that idea was not pursued. The loch is, in fact, quite shallow – between five and ten feet deep. But what depth of mud there is beneath the water, the accumulation of silt and decayed vegetation, can only be conjectured. At one time it was regularly dredged to provide 'marl' for use as fertilizer on adjoining fields, especially those of Sir Alexander Dick of Prestonfield; and it was in course of that operation that the bronze age implements were found.

It is its setting, between loch and hill, that gives Duddingston its special charm. Although there must have been a settlement there for many centuries, the present houses belong mainly to the eighteenth century and the early nineteenth. There used to be a colony of weavers in the village producing a flaxen cloth known as 'Duddingston hardings' but the hand-loom weaving had disappeared from the village by the 1850s and the weavers' cottages, too, have disappeared. It was in a red-tiled cottage near the Duddingston Road end of the Causeway that Prince Charles is traditionally said to have spent the night before the battle of Prestonpans, while his army were encamped on the hill above. Near the opposite end of the Causeway is the Sheep Heid Inn, where the High Constables of Holyrood enjoy, every second year, their ceremonial lunch in course of their perambulation round the park. The present inn was built about the middle of last century but it replaced one said to have been established 400 years earlier than that.

The 'big house' of the village was Duddingston House (now a hotel) about half a mile away, set in pleasant parkland which now partly serves as a golf course. The house was designed for the eighth Earl of Abercorn by Sir William Chambers and completed in 1767. It has been said of it recently that 'in terms of a stylistic synthesis of Palladian forms Duddingston must surely be Chambers' ultimate villa'. Certainly it has a splendid portico, and the high-ceilinged entrance hall with its graceful staircase is impressive, though the general arrangement of the house is a curious one, only the principal apartments being in the main building while the rest are in an almost detached wing linked to the stable block. The Earl, however, was a bachelor and so lacked the commonsense advice on the lay-out of a house which a wife might have given when he was considering the plans laid before him by his distinguished architect.

The young English tourist whose description of Leith races I quoted in the last chapter dined at Duddingston House one evening in 1793. He called it a 'magnificent seat' with park, plantations and garden 'elegantly disposed'. By then the eighth Earl had died and the house was let. The visitor was told some stories of the late owner which are worth passing on. His Lordship, it seems was 'a character, all stiffness, stiff-rumped, stiff-backed and stiff-necked who was said to have made the tour of Europe without touching the back of his chaise'. On one occasion, after he had provided accommodation (at another of his houses) for Queen Charlotte, the King had thanked him, adding that he was afraid this must have given him a great deal of trouble; to which the surprising reply was: 'Yes, a great deal of trouble, sir.' On another occasion at Duddingston, the Earl had been walking in his park

one evening with Principal Robertson, of the University. By way
of making conversation, the Principal remarked how well his
Lordship's trees were growing. 'They have nothing else to do,'
said the Earl who was obviously not a brilliant conversationalist.

Duddingston Church is Norman in origin. It was built in the
twelfth century, and although much altered, some Norman
features remain, especially the richly decorated doorway in the
south wall. At the churchyard gate the watch-tower, built in the
1820s, is a reminder of the time when watch had to be kept against
'body-snatchers'. Outside the gate are two other relics of past
days. The 'jougs', an iron collar chained to the wall shows how
recalcitrants and especially 'scolding women' were once restrained.
Close by is the 'loupin' on stane', a few steps leading up to a stone
platform from which it was easy for the most aged or corpulent
parishioner to mount his horse after the church service and for
his wife to ascend decorously to ride pillion behind him.

Duddingston's most famous minister was John Thomson who
was there from 1805 until his death in 1840, but his fame was as
painter rather than as pastor; though it is only fair to add that it
was said of him that 'while not conspicuous for spiritual leadership
he was generous to the material needs of his parishioners'. There
is no doubt, however, that his principal delight was in landscape
painting and one who knew him suggested that he sought subjects
for his easel more eagerly than texts for his sermons. He had had
lessons from Alexander Nasmyth and he developed his talent with
such success that, for several years, he earned at least £1800 annually
from his painting – a considerable sum in those days. He travelled
through the highlands and to other parts of Scotland in search
of subjects for his brush and, considering the difficulties of travel
then, it is not surprising that his parish duties were correspondingly
neglected. Nevertheless, he seems to have been a popular minister.

His pictures, too, were popular. For my taste, they are too
romantic and dramatic by half; his brush could turn a wayside
copse into a dark Wagnerian forest with the greatest of ease. But
they suited the romantic taste of his day and many wealthy people
bought them to adorn the walls of their mansions. Along with
J. M. W. Turner he was commissioned to illustrate *The Provincial
Antiquities of Scotland*, the text for which was written by Sir Walter
Scott for whom Thomson's pictures had a strong appeal. Sir

Walter's brother, Thomas, was factor for the Duddingston estate and Sir Walter himself became a close friend of Thomson and a frequent visitor at the manse. In the garden there he wrote part of *The Heart of Midlothian*; and in 1806 he became an elder of Duddingston Church.

Turner also visited Duddingston several times and went on at least one sketching excursion with Thomson. But Turner's cockney speech and coarse humour had little appeal for Thomson and his circle. On one occasion he is said to have looked at some of Thomson's paintings hanging in the manse and then complimented the artist – on their frames. He did, however, compliment him also on the view from his home. As he drove from the manse door one day, Turner looked at the loch and exclaimed feelingly: 'By God, though, I envy you that piece of water.'

He might well envy him that piece of water. Duddingston without the loch would still be an attractive village in a striking setting; but it is the loch that gives the village its special appeal. It was a subject that Thomson often painted. On the shore, a few yards from the manse garden, is a small round tower built, originally, as a shelter for curlers. In it Thomson liked to sit and paint. It is said to have been named 'Edinburgh' so that, when he did not want to be disturbed, callers at the manse could be told truthfully, that the minister was 'in Edinburgh'; though friends of the artist-minister have been known to denounce the story as a fiction.

Duddingston Loch was in private ownership until 1925 when it was presented to the nation and declared, by statute, to be a bird sanctuary. Now looked after, with minimal interference with its natural state, by the Department of the Environment, advised by the Scottish Wildlife Trust, it is home, summer haunt or staging-post for nearly 100 varieties of birds. The great crested grebe and the willow-warbler nest there, the bullfinch and the chiff-chaff are summer visitors and the loch is the winter home of pochard duck, 8000 of them in 1969 and over 3000 in almost any year. What other city can claim a nature reserve like this, so near its centre.?

Just across the main road from the village and the loch, Holy Rood Secondary School was opened in 1972. Far from being an intrusion, the school has brought a new dimension to the village. Its pupils are interested in the bird sanctuary and they join in activities of the Society for the Preservation of Duddingston Village which, in co-operation with the City Planning Department seeks to ensure that Duddingston retains its character – an encouraging combination of youthful enthusiasm, local interest and official support.

Along the south side of the loch runs the track of an old railway line, disappearing into a tunnel near the Wells o' Wearie and beneath the curious rock formation known as Samson's Ribs. This was Edinburgh's first railway, opened in 1831 to provide transport for grain, stone and coal – especially coal. It ran from the Marquis of Lothian's coal pits, south of Dalkeith, to St Leonard's coal depot just beyond the Holyrood Park boundary and, later, it had branches to Fisherrow, near Musselburgh, and through Portobello to Leith. Not long after the opening of the line its possibilities for passenger traffic were recognized and during the 1830s and 1840s a trip on the Dalkeith Railway became a popular recreation; and a pleasant leisurely trip it must have been, in horse-drawn carriages, along beside the loch. The line was known as the 'innocent railway' because, in those early railway days when steam trains elsewhere were claiming many victims, it never had an accident in which a passenger was killed.

From the station at St Leonard's the carriages ran gently down through the tunnel (there was a steam engine to pull them up by rope on their return). At the lower end of the tunnel the horse was attached and the train went on its leisurely way beside the loch, the guard blowing a coach-horn at intervals. On the city's 'fast-day' holidays held annually in April and October, the railway's resources must have been fully stretched. After the April holiday in 1842, it was reported that 'the immense number of 6660 passengers passed along the line being, we are assured, nearly 700 more than ever before.'

The fare for the whole journey to Dalkeith was 8d.; to Duddingston it was 4d. Tickets were not issued, and the reason for this given by the general manager to a parliamentary committee on railways in 1839 has fascinated me ever since I came across it, years ago, in a report of the committee's hearings. 'We do not use tickets,' he said, 'because we have always found that many passengers would not tell, or did not make up their minds, where they were going which causes great confusion in using tickets.' A railway whose passengers did not know where they wanted to go sounds too good to be true; as good, in its own way, as the railway in Lewis Carroll's *Through the Looking Glass,* on which Alice was advised to 'take a return ticket every time the train stops'. In fact, the trains would pick up and set down passengers anywhere and, in the absence of tickets, passengers were counted at the start of the journey and again at the half-way point. These easy-going ways, however, were out of keeping with the age that had already begun. In 1844, the line was bought by the North British Railway Company and by 1848 passenger trains no longer ran beside the loch, though coal traffic continued until 1968.

In those early 'innocent railway' days, I wonder how many holiday passengers, uncertain where they wanted to go, looked out from the trains and, seeing the village perched so invitingly between loch and hillside, decided that Duddingston would be their destination.

As with Duddingston, so with the village of Cramond – its charm and character are derived from its situation. When in 1799 John Stoddart reached the end of his walk along the shore by Granton and Silverknowes, he turned his gaze away from the Highland hills beyond the Forth and set out to visit Cramond and the valley of the River Almond. 'Here,' he said, 'were combined the characteristics of a miniature port, with the most pleasing rural objects: the tranquil river flowing from between its high-wooded banks into the sea: the cottages irregularly scattered here and there: and the boats drawn up on the shore or launching out into the deep.' It is still much the same, except that the cottages are tidier and the boats are not the sloops and fishing craft that he would see but yachts and dinghies belonging to members of the Cramond Boat Club.

Like Duddingston, Cramond has a long history as a place of human settlement. Its sheltered creek at the mouth of the River Almond probably attracted the very earliest voyagers in their cockleshell boats. It was certainly used by the Romans. Their fort at Cramond is the only Roman find of any consequence within the city. A large part of the village is built over the fort; and the church, the tower of which belongs to the fifteenth century, stands on the site of its headquarters building. If you look closely at the lower courses of masonry on the north side of the church you will see, here and there, stones on which distinctive chisel marks bear witness to the Roman workmen by whom they were first shaped.

The fact that there was once a Roman fort at Cramond had long been known. Often, when foundations for village houses were being prepared or gardens were dug, Roman coins, pottery fragments and other relics were turned up; but, as the eighteenth-century former schoolhouse and several modern houses, as well as the church, are built over it, no full exploration of the fort is possible. Now and then, however, house owners have allowed their gardens to be trenched and from these detached excavations a general impression of the fort was obtained. Then in 1961 students of Moray House College of Education, helped by workmen supplied by the Town Council, undertook a thorough excavation in the vacant ground north and east of the church.

It was found from these digs that the fort had first been built near the middle of the second century A.D. Among the finds pointing to that date were coins, fragments of Samian ware from Gaul, cookery-pots from Britain south of Hadrian's Wall, wine jars, brooches and iron implements. That dating led to the conclusion that the fort might have been connected with the Antonine Wall, a ditch and rampart of earth and stones which was built between Forth and Clyde about 140 A.D. The Wall began from Bridgeness, only about eleven miles further along the coast, so Cramond with its natural harbour would be a good point at which to off-load supplies intended for the garrison on the Wall. This conclusion was supported by the discovery that the fort was bigger than might have been expected and had contained three large granary buildings. The students' excavation established, also, that the fort had been vacated and then reoccupied towards the end of the second century and had been finally reoccupied during the period of the Emperor Severus' campaign in the third century A.D.

But no one should go to Cramond expecting to see even part of the fort laid open to view. Through the centuries its walls, with their ready-dressed stones, must have been an inviting quarry for those in need of building material and the remnants uncovered by the archaeologists, though interesting, were scanty. So only one small section of wall has been left exposed as a sample. The rest of the excavated area has been covered over with turf to form a public garden with the outline of the buried walls marked out on the surface. To appreciate Roman Cramond today, therefore, requires some effort of imagination.

In that first phase of its history, Cramond would be a busy frontier post with boats unloading troops and supplies at the harbour, heavily laden waggons setting off along the track to Bridgeness and the Wall and messengers coming and going between Cramond and the fort at Inveresk, near Musselburgh; though the whole length of the road they would use through what is now the city has never been traced with any certainty.

After the departure of the Romans at some time in the third century came the dark years about which little can be traced, but during which the civilian settlement that had grown up just outside the fort may well have lingered on and become the nucleus from which the village grew. For tangible evidence, however, one has to take a leap across the years to a fifteenth-century tower, the crumbling remains of which still stand close to the north-east corner of the fort. It belonged once to the Bishops of Dunkeld in Perthshire who owned a part of the manor which, consequently, was known as Bishops Cramond to distinguish it from Kings Cramond, a little to the south. Near the east side of the fort is the mainly eighteenth-century mansion house of Cramond which remained in private occupation until the 1950s and is now used as a community centre.

Despite these varied features of Cramond through the centuries and despite the acres of modern villas and bungalows spreading inland from them, it is of the cluster of white-washed cottages on the steep slope above the river mouth that one thinks when one thinks of Cramond. In the 1950s they had fallen into a sad state of disrepair and were in danger of complete decay when the last private owner of Cramond House arranged to restore them at her own expense. But in 1959 she died, before being able to carry out her plan. Her public-spirited gesture, however, had not been in vain, for it inspired the Town Council to acquire the cottages and undertake their restoration. So the character of Cramond has been preserved, though perhaps a trifle self-consciously. Its cottages somehow seem to be just a little too tidy and white to be true.

Once they housed fishermen, sailors – and iron-workers. For, surprising though it may seem, there was a phase in Cramond's history when it was a thriving centre of the iron industry and, if you follow the footpath along the bank of the Almond as far as Cramond Bridge, you will find traces of several iron mills by the way. In 1794, John Philp Wood, a local resident, wrote this about his village, then known as Nether Cramond:

Nether Cramond is a thriving village, containing 87 families and 343 individuals, chiefly iron workmen, sailors and day labourers.... The harbour has belonging to it seven sloops of from 22 to 80 tons burthen, measuring in all 288 tons and navigated by 23 men. These are chiefly employed in the importation of lime for manure, coals and iron for the mills and in exporting steel and wrought iron from thence.... The sea flows no farther than Cockle Mill about a quarter of a mile above Cramond, being stopped by the dam there. The common size of vessels brought up to the mill is from 40 to 50 tons, but the navigation is reckoned dangerous on account of the rocky bottom; which lays the ship-masters under the necessity of procuring three or four experienced men from Cramond to assist in hauling them up and to show the channel and windings of the river.

As for the fishing he said:

The fisheries are at a low ebb. In particular the oyster fishery has greatly declined since 1740 when eleven large boats belonging to Cramond were constantly employed during the season in dragging for that delicious bi-valve . . . but no more than four or five boats are now employed and even those only occasionally.

Looking, nowadays, at the river and its muddy bed, it seems impossible that boats of fifty tons, even though they were hauled 'by three or four experienced men from Cramond' could ever enter it; to prove that they did so you will find, about 500 yards upstream, the sturdily-built dock into which they were hauled and at which their cargoes of iron ore were unloaded and their fresh cargoes of iron goods were taken aboard. Cockle Mill was close beside the dock, but all trace of that mill has gone and only a few boulders remain of its dam, by which the tide was stopped. But a little further on, you come to Fair-a-Far (otherwise known as Niddry's) Mill. Just enough of that building survives to indicate its size and shape and on one wall there can be seen the scraping made by its wheel which must have been about thirteen feet in diameter. The great dam of Fair-a-Far Mill remains intact and the constant rush of water over it is a pleasant accompaniment to this riverside walk.

In John Philp Wood's day there were four iron mills on the east bank of the river within a mile or so from its mouth. Cockle and Fair-a-Far Mills had first been used for iron-working some forty years before he wrote. Both were acquired by the founder of the Carron Iron Company and these mills continued to be worked by that company until they removed to Stirlingshire in 1770, to become world famous. The mills at Cramond were then acquired by William Cadell whose name survives in Caddell's Row, a group of former iron-workers' cottages beside the river. About 1882, all references to ironworks in the area disappear from local directories so it seems that Cramond's venture into industrial activity lasted for only about 130 years. During that time the village must have greatly widened its horizons for a lot of the iron used came from Sweden and Russia and much steel produced at Cramond was sent to India.

When Wood wrote his book, and five years later when John Stoddart visited the village, the iron industry there was at its peak. Stoddart was much impressed. Of Fair-a-Far Mill he said: 'Continuing our walk, we reached the large mill of the Cramond Company, in which a manufacture of bar iron is carried on. One of the forge hammers weighs, as we were told, seven-hundredweight and is moved by a water-wheel, and makes 160 strokes a minute.'

The Cramond mills were specially noted for producing nails and spades. For a time, about 12000 spades were produced annually, this branch of the industry having been introduced by a 'worthy and industrious workman, Richard Squires of Newcastle, who was greatly superior to any in that line in Scotland'. Spades made by him were easily recognizable and were in demand as far away as London.

Apart from that short venture into the iron-making business and some fishing, Cramond was always an agricultural parish. Like many another rural area it had once had its own time-honoured seasonal custom. This was known as the Lammas Feast and it seems to have had some affinity with the 'bickers' indulged in by the boys of George Square; except that the rural version was only an annual event, and instead of being a free-for-all, it was so highly organized as to become, in time, almost a ritual.

R

The parish extended on to the northern slope of Corstorphine Hill and over Leny Hill (near Turnhouse Airport). On 1 August each year the 'herds' of the parish (the lads who looked after the farmers' cattle) would gather in two groups, one on each of these hills. Each would build a tower of turf and a number of turf tables at which, says Wood, 'they feasted on cream, butter and cheese'. Each side had a tablecloth for a standard, gaily decorated with ribbons provided by the girl-friends of the 'herds'. Then each party, with standard held aloft and a piper leading the way, marched to meet the other on Cramond Moor, between the hills and the village. If the two groups were unequally matched, the weaker side usually lowered their standard and submitted, after which races were run, with picked runners from each side; but if neither side submitted, a battle of stones and cudgels followed. Afterwards each group returned to their own 'tower' and spent the evening in ball games, running races and general jollity. When or how this annual ritual had begun no one can tell; but as the enclosing of farmlands progressed, less opportunity remained for such events and in August 1758 the Lammas Feast at Cramond was held for the last time.

21 Western extension

*A*n important purpose of the local government reorganization of 1975 was described as 'the marriage of town and country', a marriage designed not just to extend the town for its own benefit, as so often in the past, but to bring together for mutual advantage burgh and rural interests which, inevitably, are already linked by the mobility of modern times. So, to Edinburgh there have been added, on its western side, more than fifty square miles of country, almost exactly doubling the city's area; though increasing its population by only 5 per cent. Included in this western extension are five more miles of coast; and also the Royal Burgh of Queensferry, to which we will be coming later.

The new area covers country of varied interest. For those to whom walking is a pleasure and to whom the countryside without added tourist attractions is still the best kind of countryside, there is a good deal of scope for enjoyment within this rural extension. There is hill and moorland at its southern edge, along the range of the Pentland Hills; there is the track of the old railway line winding through the trees of the Water of Leith valley beyond Juniper Green, which we reached in an earlier chapter, to the hillside villages of Currie and Balerno – though, as housing developments grow around them, these two are rapidly losing their village character. There are paths beside the River Almond and alongside the Union Canal to the point near the outer edge of the new District, where canal crosses river in a well-wooded glen; and there is the shore path along the edge of Lord Rosebery's estate of Dalmeny, an estate which William Cobbett, on one of his tours, described, when he drove past it in 1832, as 'one of the finest estates of Scotland'.

From Cramond village, for a small charge, one may on most days cross the mouth of the Almond by a ferry boat which has long been maintained, through the goodwill of the estate owners, to enable walkers to go by the shore path to Queensferry. It is a pleasant walk through woods and fields with the sea at hand all the way and changing views of the coast of Fife to be enjoyed. On the shore, not far from Cramond, is the Hunter's Craig or 'Eagle Rock' which has, on its east face, a rough and badly worn sculptured figure, protected as an ancient monument. It has some vague resemblance to an eagle (or, it has been suggested, the figure of Mercury) and is possibly a Roman emblem in some way connected with the Roman fort at Cramond. But even as long ago as 1794, John Philp Wood wrote of it: 'All traces of that figure are now worn away, the stone of which the rock is composed being of a soft friable nature'; so now, after nearly two more centuries of wind, sun, rain and salty spray it is not surprising that details of the sculpture in its rough niche cannot be identified.

A mile or so further on, Barnbougle Castle stands superbly on a little promontory above the shore, with the waves lapping against it. It is an ancient square tower which had fallen into decay until it was rescued and repaired in the 1880s by the fifth Lord Rosebery, who was Liberal Prime Minister in 1894-5. It has been said that it may have been in the library at Barnbougle, looking out across the Forth, that he was inspired to write some of his great speeches; but the family mansion stands a little way back from the sea. From Barnbougle the path, rounding Hound Point, leads on to join the public road, where Queensferry begins, four miles or so from Cramond.

Dalmeny Estate lies between the sea and the road to Queensferry. Long over-burdened with traffic hastening constantly to and from the ferry crossing, that road is now a quiet byway while traffic for the north speeds past on the dual carriageway of the

Forth Road Bridge approach. Between these two roads lies the village of Dalmeny with its cottages attractively spaced on two sides of a wide green. Here is a Norman church; in the words of the late Ian G. Lindsay, whose knowledge of Scottish antiquities was unsurpassed, 'the most complete example of Romanesque architecture remaining in the country'. Dalmeny Kirk, Lindsay continued:

has been altered from time to time, but the walls as they stand today would be plainly recognisable to their 12th-century builders and to the hosts of others who have passed near it on their way to the Queen's Ferry. Pilgrims to the shrine of St Margaret at Dunfermline, the Kings of Scots progressing to their palace there or at Falkland, must have seen the same Dalmeny Kirk at some time or another.

The tower of the little kirk was built in 1926, replacing the original one which had collapsed 450 years before, and at the same time late additions were removed from the interior which was then restored as nearly as possible to its early state. Outside, apart from the tower, the walls are little changed and most splendid of all is the ornate Norman doorway in the south wall with carvings of birds, animals and strange creatures from the bestiary, that curious product of medieval imagination. Truly, in Dalmeny church the City of Edinburgh District has an ancient monument of the first importance and, better still, one that can be enjoyed for its simple beauty by any passer-by without any need for expert knowledge.

There is another ancient church at the village of Kirkliston, not far away. It stands more prominently in the landscape, on a ridge of rising ground. It, too, has a richly ornamented doorway, of fourteenth-century date, but the church has been a good deal altered and the doorway has suffered badly through the years.

Dalmeny and Kirkliston villages are on the edge of an area that contributed quite a different kind of chapter to the story of the Lothians. It was a chapter that lasted for only a little more than 100 years but left behind it scars that are slow to heal. It was the period of Scotland's first oil boom. John Young, known as 'Paraffin Young', was a Glasgow cabinet-maker turned chemist who discovered how to distil oil from the beds of shale that lay in a broad belt beneath the fields of West Lothian and the western end of Midlothian. In 1850, he took out a patent and opened a small plant

near Bathgate in West Lothian. By 1913 more than fifty such plants
in the area were producing a total of three million gallons of crude
oil annually. By 1962, the last of them had closed; but their russet-
red bings of waste material remained and, here and there, the
derelict cottages of their miners. These bings can sometimes be a
striking feature of the landscape as they are picked out in a sunset
glow; generally, they are an eyesore and it is fortunate that, in
recent years, a use for their debris has been found. One massive
bing, close to Dalmeny village, is now much smaller than it was,
its contents having been transported to provide bottoming for
the dual carriageway road that runs close to its base and for the M8
and M9 motorways that pass not far away, carrying traffic smoothly
and speedily to Glasgow and Stirling.

It is not easy to explain why man-made coal and shale bings
are unsightly, while natural mounds and hillocks are not, but
so it is; and, as we go southwards towards the Pentland Hills, we
come to two small outliers of that range, close together. They
are Kaimes Hill and Dalmahoy Hill. Only about 800 feet above sea
level, they are prominent because of their isolation and, for the
same reason, they are good viewpoints. Unhappily Kaimes Hill,
the more westerly of the two, is rapidly being eaten away at its
western end by a quarry and the quarrying operations are destroying, along with the hill, the traces of a prehistoric settlement
upon it. An area of about ten acres on the summit of the hill was
enclosed, on three sides, by walls which must once have been about
twelve feet thick though now no more than grass-covered mounds.
On the fourth side, towards the north, the steep rocky slope would
provide protection enough. Here and there are gateways in the
walls, some of which have been protected outside by pointed
stones set into the ground to make approach, to say the least,
uncomfortable. Within the walls there were traces of at least
thirty hut circles, before some disappeared with the quarrying;
and there are traces of a well, so the supply of water for the population on the hill, whether permanently resident or seeking temporary protection, would pose no problem.

Kaimes Hill may have been occupied in the iron age, just before
or during the earliest years of the Christian era. The neighbouring
Dalmahoy Hill has remains of what may have been a rather later
occupation. Traces of crude walling can be found around its

summit with at least one gap that is recognizable as an entrance
gateway. These two hill-tops would be occupied, I suppose, at
about the same time as early habitations began to appear on the
slopes of Arthur's Seat and on the Castle rock which can be clearly
seen from here. That being so, it is a curious thought to play with
that, given a different turn of events all those years ago, the city
of Edinburgh, instead of being built along the castle ridge, might
have grown around these two hills of Kaimes and Dalmahoy.

The view from either of these hills embraces the whole of the
western extension of the city. If what I have written so far has given
the impression that that area consists mainly of a miscellaneous
assortment of ancient monuments, the view will soon dispel that
impression. It will be seen that almost all the country between these
two hills and the sea is well-cultivated farmland with occasional
woodland and a golf course or two for good measure. Except round
Newbridge on the Almond, there is very little industry; but it is
obviously a thriving and well-kept countryside, clearly not just
living in the past.

Three miles east of Dalmahoy Hill and just outside the former
city boundary are the woodlands of Riccarton estate which has
taken on a new and modern role. In the late sixteenth and early
seventeenth centuries it belonged to Sir Thomas Craig, a distinguished advocate who wrote a treatise on Scottish land law which
was reprinted as recently as 1934 and is still an important legal
source book; a fact which may be interpreted, according to your
choice, as demonstrating either the soundness and permanence
of the principles of Scots law or alternatively its antiquated nature.
One story about Sir Thomas is worth telling. While he was still a
practising advocate his son, Sir Lewis Craig, became a judge of the
Court of Session and it was said that when the father was pleading
in court, the son on the bench would 'uncover his head and
listen to his parent with the utmost reverence'. Could filial respect
be carried further?

After Sir Thomas, Riccarton had a long line of owners, many
of whom were distinguished in the legal profession and played
their parts in the story of Edinburgh. But recently the estate entered
upon its new phase as the site of Edinburgh's second university.
Though the Heriot-Watt achieved university status only in 1966,
its history began in 1821 when it was founded, in a rented hall in

Edinburgh, as the School of Arts; a name that seems misleading nowadays as the first subjects taught were Chemistry and Mechanical Philosophy. In 1854 the School entered its first new building in Adam Square and took the name of Watt Institution and School of Arts, in memory of James Watt of steam-engine fame. With the construction of Chambers Street, nearly twenty years later, Adam Square was swept away and the Watt Institution moved into new premises in Chambers Street where, in 1885, it was taken under the wing of the George Heriot Trust and became the Heriot-Watt College, the name it continued to bear until it became the Heriot-Watt University, just over eighty years later. On that occasion, the close association between the Heriot-Watt and the city was celebrated by the presentation to the new university by the Town Council of a handsome silver mace which had been made by an Edinburgh craftsman and which bore, in gold, the coats-of-arms of Edinburgh and of its new university.

The problem, then, for the Heriot-Watt University was to find a campus, a problem that was solved when the County Council of Midlothian made the estate of Riccarton available, although there was some regret that this new university, with its roots so firmly in the city, was about to remove beyond the city boundary – a situation that has since conveniently resolved itself. As the buildings of the Heriot-Watt continue to rise above the trees of Riccarton it can, with truth, be regarded as the second University of Edinburgh.

From modern university to ancient burgh – if we turn northwards from our view of Riccarton we can see, some seven miles away, the two great bridges carrying rail and road across the Firth of Forth where it narrows abruptly to a width of only one mile. Between the two bridges is the burgh of Queensferry. Its site, at this natural crossing place, clearly explains the burgh's existence. Its seal and coat-of-arms aptly illustrate the origin of its name, the Queen's Ferry. They show Margaret, Queen of Malcolm Canmore (St Margaret after her canonization in 1249), about to step from a small boat on to a gangway of planks leading to a rocky shore. The rocks represent the Binks, near the west end of the burgh. It was there that the Queen is said to have landed on those frequent journeys of hers across the Forth, between Dunfermline and the Castle of Edinburgh during the twenty-four years from 1069 until 1093 when her husband and she were King and Queen of Scotland. It was there, too, that the ferries still landed their passengers long afterwards, except when the state of wind or tide dictated otherwise.

To leave no doubt that the solitary figure in the boat is indeed a queen, the design shows her wearing a crown and carrying a sceptre in her right hand. To show that she is no other queen than Margaret, her left hand grasps her much-prized book of the four gospels. According to her contemporary biographer, Turgot, Prior of Durham, she dearly loved that book which was ornamented with gold and jewels and in which the figures of the evangelists were richly illuminated. When it was lost on one of her journeys she was deeply distressed. Then after much searching the book was found at the bottom of a stream which she had forded and into which her attendant must, unknowingly, have dropped it. When found, the book was lying open, 'its leaves kept in constant motion by the action of the water'. Yet, says Turgot, it was taken up, free of damage 'except that, on the margin of the leaves, some trace of the water could with difficulty be detected. . . and, as for me, I am of opinion that this miracle was wrought by our Lord because of his Love for this venerable Queen.'

When Margaret made her crossings of the Forth, Queensferry was not yet formally a burgh. But at this obvious crossing point there must have been a settlement of some kind from the very earliest times. When she passed through on her journeys it would already be a small township; and, about the end of the sixteenth century, it became a burgh of regality (not quite the same thing as a royal burgh). It was Charles I, in the year 1636, who granted the charter that declared Queensferry to be 'ane free Royal Burgh and ane free Port, Haven and Harbour' with all the liberties, privileges and immunities of such a burgh and port.

Some of these liberties, privileges and immunities were challenged by Linlithgow, eight miles to the west. It was already a royal burgh, and its Council, jealous of their rights, did not like to see their neighbour gaining ground in this way. But in 1641 the Charter was confirmed by Act of Parliament. From then on, Queensferry could take its place equally with Linlithgow and with Edinburgh as a royal burgh; now, it has become a part of Edinburgh. Strictly, it was only a small central area of the present town of

Queensferry that was within the 'royalty' but, although this still has some significance for those who live within that area, it is a detail with which we need not be concerned.

In a short chapter, one might be forgiven for beginning the story of the burgh from no earlier than the date of Charles's charter; but that would leave out the Carmelite friars who first came to the town in the fourteenth century and the remnant of whose fifteenth-century monastery, between the main street and the shore, is one of the most interesting of the town's buildings. In 1889 what remained of the monastery church was restored by the Episcopal Church in Scotland and is still in use by that Church. The building consists of the original chancel, with a curiously high-pitched vault, the tower and the south transept. The site of the nave is part of a small grass plot. In it in recent years a small herb garden has been maintained in which herbs such as the monks of old may have used are grown and a board nearby gives their names and uses – a simple, imaginative idea that adds to the interest of the old building and seems almost to bring to life the monks who worshipped in it and went out from it to tend their garden and till their fields. Here, among others, are periwinkle, for cuts and wounds; red sage, for sore throats, sweet cicely, to restore the appetite; and rosemary, a heart tonic and insecticide – surely a curious combination of uses.

The site of the monastery had been given to the monks in 1441 by James Dundas of Dundas. His massive fifteenth-century tower still stands in the midst of the Dundas estate, a mile or so from the town. Close against it, in 1818, the present-day castle of Dundas was built, a gothic edifice designed by that architect we have met several times already, William Burn. His output seems to have been endless.

Where the High Street of Queensferry narrows to become Hopetoun Road, the cause of the narrowing is Plewlands House, a seventeenth-century mansion of three storeys and garret with a projecting stair tower. In the 1950s the house came within an ace of being destroyed to make way for traffic, but, after much argument, it was acquired by the National Trust for Scotland and renovated. Its demolition would have been a serious loss for it is a fine example of the domestic architecture of its day.

The story of the building of Plewlands House can be traced in the burgh records. Samuel Wilson was a man of some standing in Queensferry, a merchant burgess and a Councillor; and he was making a comfortable living by importing timber from the Baltic and wines from Bordeaux. So he decided to build a house that would match the position in life which he and his wife, Anna Punton, had attained. No vacant site could be found within the newly designated royal burgh and so, as the next best thing, he bought some waste ground immediately beyond its bounds. There in 1641 he built his house. On the lintel above the door he put the initials S.W. and A.P. for himself and his wife, the motto *Spes Mea Christus* (My Hope is Christ) to declare his piety, and an anchor, to show his standing as a shipmaster. Soon afterwards, he was in trouble with the Council for refusing to pay certain dues. 'Why should I?' one can hear him say. 'My house is outside the "royalty".' His burgess-ticket was withdrawn and his stock of timber was seized upon for debt. But in 1649, after a court action, the burgess-ticket was returned to him, he was reconciled with his Council colleagues, and he lived on happily, one hopes, in Plewlands House until his death in 1658.

At about the time that Plewlands House was being built Queensferry's trade was prospering. Ships belonging to burgesses of the town were sailing to many European ports, bringing home timber, wine and general merchandise. In order to build up the 'common good' fund of the burgh, the shippers agreed to pay to the town treasurer 2 per cent on the sales of their cargoes; payment to be made 'as time and tide and the elements allowed'. But soon came depression; in 1666 the minutes record that, because of the 'truble and war with Holland, the merchant ships of the burgh are destitute of employment'.

Much later, herring fishing became an important business of the town. In 1792 great shoals of the 'silver darlings' appeared in St Margaret's Bay, opposite Queensferry. The burgh had no herring boats then, but that was soon remedied; and, a few years later, twelve boats, each with four or five men for crew were reaping a rich harvest every winter. There was a time when soap-boiling was the principal industry. It started in 1770 and by the 1780s there were four works in the town employing thirty men. According to the first Statistical Account of Scotland in 1791, it was here that the making of brown soap had been 'brought to its present high state of perfection'. Now it is whisky for which the town is famous. Its first distillery was opened in 1841 and today the great square red-brick building on the hill towering above the old town sends fifteen million bottles of a famous blend every year to all parts of the world.

In recent years the town has spread to the west and over the high ground to the south, increasing its area from 250 acres in 1948 to 700 acres and its population from 2500 to 5400 people. But its High Street still has the authentic 'feel' of a small Scottish east coast burgh that has been the home, for centuries, of a busy tight-knit community of merchants, sailors and craftsmen. The crow-stepped gables and ornamented dormer windows of Black Castle, a tenement built in 1626; the tolbooth, with its pointed steeple, clock and outside stairs; 'the Terraces' along the High Street, with shops below and a pedestrian way above (however modern that idea may seem to be) all combine to give the town its character. If the street is too narrow for modern traffic, then modern traffic must adjust itself to suit. As a matter of fact, it is not only modern traffic that has caused problems, as can be seen in the burgh records for 1703 when the Council were already concerning themselves about pedestrian safety. 'No horse hirer,' they said, 'or any other inhabitant shall gallop horses through the High Street under penalty of 20s. Scots.'

The Town Council minutes are full of such glimpses. In 1706 there was alarm about 'the looseness of the time' and about wandering vagabonds and idle persons who, in the darkness of night, broke into workshops and robbed the townsfolk of their goods and gear. Ten years later, it was the behaviour of some of the townspeople that worried the magistrates. At the request of the Kirk Session, they fixed a fine of 20s. to be paid by those who, having their own allotted seats in the parish church, preferred to sit 'in dark corners of the church in order, as may be presumed, to their more convenient sleeping or idle talking'. Truly, in those days, there were few aspects of a citizen's life in which the magistrates did not take an interest.

They were not concerned only with the private citizen. In 1739, the Council addressed themselves in no uncertain terms to the question of the morality of members of parliament. The member who represented the group of burghs of which Queensferry

was one, very considerately asked the Town Council to give him
some guidance on the line they would like him to take in parliament on matters of the day. He must, I think, have been surprised
by their reply.

We are all thoroughly persuaded [the Council said] that the most effectual
means for securing the Dignity of the Crown . . . and the honour and reputation of Parliament would be that the members of that honourable body
would sincerely and uprightly labour for the real interest of their Country
with an unflexible resolution not to deviate from it upon the account of any
private lucrative consideration. There has been too much reason for a long
time to think that many of the Gentlemen sent to Parliament have not been
free from undue influence . . . while, like a deluge, corruption has overspread
vast numbers of the electors . . . and to this is owing the present unhappy
situation of our Country. . . .

Two years later, the Town Clerk announced to the Council
that an Act had been passed 'for the more effectual preventing
of briberie and corruption in elections'. No doubt the member
for Queensferry, remembering the strictures of his constituents,
was among those who voted for its passing.

Annually, in late July or early August, the Ferry Fair was held.
For the occasion, the High Street and every nook and cranny
near it were crammed with stalls and booths. Crowds came from
all the countryside around to see the wonders on display and take
part in the games. Much official activity took place. The town
drum had to be repaired in readiness. The Town Officer had to
ride to Edinburgh to buy some necessary goods including 'an ell
and a half of ribbon to deck the Bailie's saddle'. For the annual
'burgh race' a pair of boots had to be bought as the prize; and, of
course, a stoup or two of wine must be in readiness.

The Ferry Fair is still held, in the second week of August.
Roundabouts and showmen's stalls crowd, not the High Street,
but the car park between Newhalls Road and the sea. A school-girl
queen is crowned and men of the town run in the burgh race with
a pair of boots as prize – though, now, the boots are exchanged
afterwards for something more acceptable. But in this sophisticated age the Fair has somehow lost its glamour.

There is, however, one Queensferry custom that has gone on
unchanged for centuries. No one knows how it began, or when
or why. It is the procession of the Burry Man, on Friday in the

second week in August. The Burry Man is a youth clad from head to foot in flannels, face and all, with slots for his eyes and mouth. The flannels are 'stuck all over with the adhesive "burr" of the burr thistle' which has to be sought for in fields and copses near the town. In each hand the man carries a staff adorned with flowers and he wears a headdress of roses. The process of dressing him up in this way begins in the early morning. That process completed, he calls at the Provost's house to be sustained with a glass of whisky. (This, however, may be a fairly recent addition to the ritual.) Then, throughout the day, he must perambulate the town, a task that increases yearly as the town expands. As he goes on his way he receives coins and greetings from the householders. The ritual demands that, all this time, he must keep his arms outstretched sideways, with the floral staves clutched in his hands. Because of this, he is provided with two attendants who collect the gifts of money and also help to support his arms. By tradition, the money collected is spent by the three, at the Fair. Walking all day in that garb, I would say the Burry Man earns every penny of his share.

That this curious custom has gone on for many centuries is strange enough; that it persists into the late twentieth century is stranger still; that no one knows its origin or meaning is strangest of all. Many have tried to find the answer, without success. Some think the Burry Man may represent the spirit of vegetation and be related to the 'little leaf man' of central Europe, transferred from May to August. Some think he is the 'scapegoat' of ancient times who carries away from the community all evil influences. Whatever the explanation, the ceremony of the Burry Man is well entrenched at Queensferry. So well entrenched, in fact, that it is unlikely to be discontinued and it would, indeed, be a pity if it was. Such time-honoured customs, in addition to the simple pleasure they provide for the onlooker, serve as a kind of chain of continuity through the years. The Burry Man links, possibly, the early settlers here on the shore of the Forth with the boatmen who brought Margaret across the water from Fife, with medieval men and women thronging the Ferry Fair, with seventeenth-century shipmasters, eighteenth-century fishermen, the men who manned the first steam ferry boats 150 years ago, and with the motorists who speed across the Forth Road Bridge. All of them, except perhaps the last, who are in too great a hurry, have seen the Burry Man. All of them have wondered what he signifies – except the first because, presumably, they knew.

Another story running right through the history of Queensferry is that of the crossing of the Forth. Though one tends to date everything connected with the Queensferry Passage from Queen Margaret who made it fashionable, it must have been a recognized route long before her day. However, the first regular ferry service seems to have been started in 1130 when David I made a grant to the Abbot and Convent of Dunfermline authorizing them to provide a ferry on condition that all travellers to and from the Court would have free passage. Later, the right of providing passage was leased to 'substantial seamen'; and, in 1474, the fares were fixed by Act of Parliament at one penny Scots for a man and twopence for his horse.

The landing place on the south was generally at the Binks or later at the 'Garnock and Gray Shippings' near the harbour. But at some states of wind and tide, the beach at Newhalls, about half a mile east of the town, was used. There, opposite the landing place an inn was built – the Hawes Inn, to which at the beginning of R. L. Stevenson's *Kidnapped*, David Balfour was brought by his scheming uncle and handed over to Captain Hoseason of the brig *Covenant*. The modern Hawes Inn incorporates remnants of a seventeenth-century building which may have been the very inn that Stevenson had in mind.

At any rate, somewhat to the displeasure of Queensferry Town Council who would have preferred their harbour to be used, the Newhalls landing place came more and more into use and, there, Hawes Pier was built. It remained the regular ferry-point until the ferries were discontinued in 1964, but many years passed before a satisfactory pier was provided. As late as 1802, Alexander Campbell, a tourist who made a *Journey through parts of North Britain* wrote in his journal: 'At Spring tides, when the sea has retired, the landing-place is inconvenient in the extreme. Passengers are obliged to scramble over huge rocks and vast stones covered with seaweed so slippery that they are in danger of falling every instant.' Of the crossing itself he said: 'The passage is pretty safe and is usually performed in 20 minutes'; but he recommended that boats loaded with black cattle should be avoided 'in case they are upset'. As for the twenty minutes' crossing time, that was when the wind was set fair for the opposite shore. With contrary winds and difficult tides the crossing could easily take two hours or more, clearly not a pleasant voyage in a small boat carrying horses, cattle or sheep as well as passengers. Given the landing facilities, or lack of them, described by Campbell, how horses and cattle, let alone carriages, were got aboard is a mystery. Nevertheless they were.

There were other problems too. A report on the state of the ferry service about the time of Campbell's journey, stated that boats were stationed at the village of North Queensferry only, where all the boatmen lived and that they were not always willing to cross over to South Queensferry to pick up passengers. When the boatmen were at hand, 'insubordination was often a cause of just complaint' and there was no superintendent to take charge of them. So in 1809 the ferries were placed under the control of a trust, the landing-places were improved and a competent superintendent with naval experience was appointed.

Things improved. But soon the introduction of steam-boats crossing the Forth from Leith and Newhaven to Burntisland, Kinghorn and other Fife ports, and others sailing up the Forth to Alloa and Stirling, diminished the use of the Queensferry boats. So, in an effort to regain custom, the ferry trustees had a steamboat built to a design prepared by their own superintendent to meet the special needs of the crossing. Inevitably, it was named the *Queen Margaret*. It was put into service on 1 October 1821. Besides carrying her own passengers, her task was to tow the sailing boats, so that they became independent of wind and tide. It was reported that 'in calm weather, she could tow three boats carrying cattle and sheep while she carried carriages, horses, and carts'.

The next great development was the opening of the Forth Railway Bridge, with its intricate pattern of tubes and girders towering above Hawes Pier and the ferry boats. It was opened by HRH the Prince of Wales (later Edward VII) on 4 March 1890. Seventy-four years later, on 4 September 1964, Queen Elizabeth opened the Forth Road Bridge. Suspended on seemingly fragile cords, the bridge soars between its 500-foot-high towers above the roof tops of Queensferry. Except that both perform the same task of carrying traffic across water, no two structures could be less alike. They represent the heights of engineering achievement of two ages, separated by seventy years. Each in its own way is entirely functional, with nothing added that does not have a purpose; and because of that, each in its own way is a work of art.

The ceremonial opening of the new bridge was almost spoiled by the weather, for the day began with the bridge lost in a thick grey mist. But, as the time for the ceremony approached, the mist gradually cleared and the bridge slowly and dramatically came into view. It could not have been stage-managed better. Then, with the bridge declared open, the Queen drove across it and down to the village of North Queensferry. From there, almost exactly 900 years after Queen Margaret had first crossed the Forth, Queen Elizabeth made the crossing in the last ferry boat of all.

With the opening of the road bridge, Queensferry's long era as the town at the ferry had ended. But the town has continued to thrive and grow steadily since. Eleven years later, on 16 May 1975, the ancient Royal Burgh became a part of the City of Edinburgh District, not thereby losing its identity as a community, but adding its own chapter to the city's rich chronicle of history and tradition. At the same time, for the city which grew from a cluster of houses on the Castle ridge and now covers a hundred square miles of town, country, coast and hill, yet another new chapter had begun.

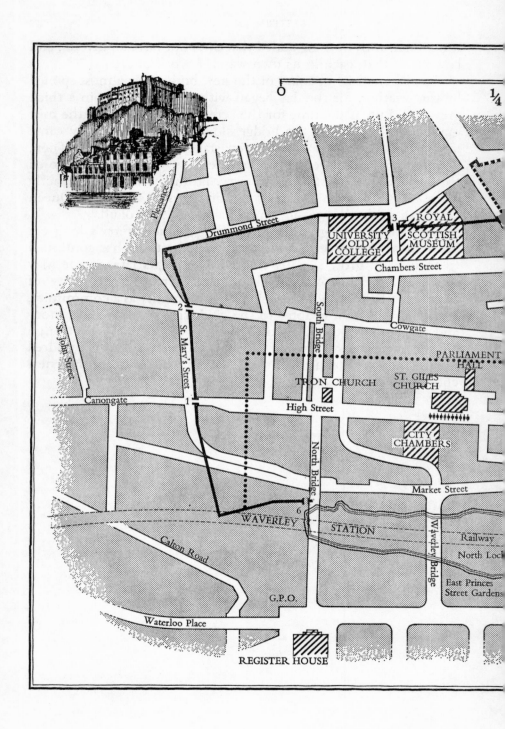

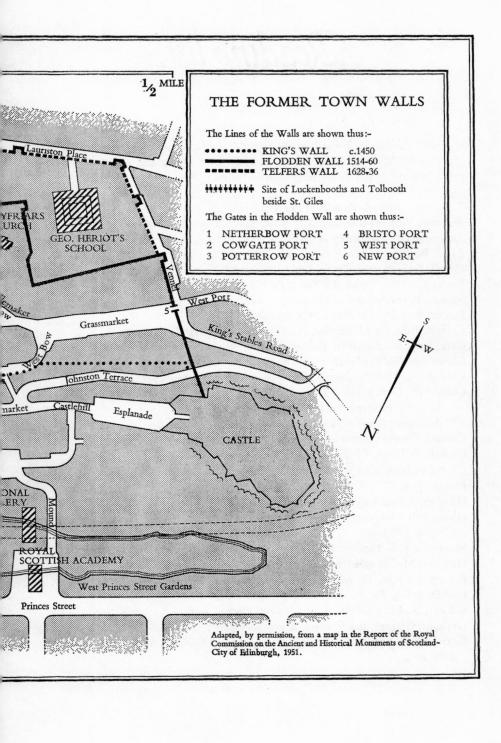

THE FORMER TOWN WALLS

The Lines of the Walls are shown thus:-

•••••••• KING'S WALL   c.1450

▬▬▬▬▬ FLODDEN WALL 1514-60

▬ ▬ ▬ ▬ TELFERS WALL 1628-36

┼┼┼┼┼┼┼┼ Site of Luckenbooths and Tolbooth
beside St. Giles

The Gates in the Flodden Wall are shown thus:-

1 NETHERBOW PORT   4 BRISTO PORT
2 COWGATE PORT   5 WEST PORT
3 POTTERROW PORT   6 NEW PORT

½ MILE

Lauriston Place

GEO. HERIOT'S
SCHOOL

YFRIARS
URCH

Vennel

West Port

5

Grassmarket

King's Stables Road

West Bow

Johnston Terrace

Castlehill

Esplanade

CASTLE

market

ONAL
ERY

Mound

ROYAL
SCOTTISH ACADEMY

West Princes Street Gardens

Princes Street

S
E W
N

Adapted, by permission, from a map in the Report of the Royal
Commission on the Ancient and Historical Monuments of Scotland-
City of Edinburgh, 1951.

Reading list

Some of the books consulted during the preparation of *Edinburgh – the Story of a City* are shown below. Many of the older books are, of course, out of print but are available in reference libraries.

Anderson, William P., *Silences that Speak*, 1931.

Andrew, William Raeburn, *Life of Sir Henry Raeburn* R.A., 1886.

Arnot, Hugo, *The History of Edinburgh*, 1779.

Baird, William, *Annals of Duddingston and Portobello*, 1898.

Birrell, Robert, *Diary* (completed 1605), 1798.

Boswell, James, *Journal of a Tour to the Hebrides*, 1785.

Brown, P. Hume, *Early Travellers in Scotland*, 1891.

Butler, Rev. D., *The Tron Kirk of Edinburgh*, 1906.

Carlyle, Rev. Dr Alexander, *Autobiography* (completed 1805), 1860.

Carr, Sir John, *Caledonian Sketches, or a Tour through Scotland*, 1809.

Chambers, Robert, *Traditions of Edinburgh; and Walks in Edinburgh*, 1825.

Chambers, William, *Memoir of William and Robert Chambers*, 1872.

Cockburn, Henry, *Life of Lord Jeffrey*, 1852.
   Memorials (completed 1830), 1856.
   An Examination of the Trials for Sedition in Scotland, 1868.

Cowan, Charles, *Reminiscences*, 1878.

Creech, William, *Edinburgh: Fugitive Pieces*, 1791.

Crombie, Benjamin W., *Modern Athenians 1837–1847*, 1882.

Dibdin, James C., *Annals of the Edinburgh Stage*, 1888.

Dunlop, Alison Hay, *Anent Old Edinburgh*, 1890.

Edinburgh Architectural Association and The Civic Trust, *The Conservation of Georgian Edinburgh*, 1972.

Ferguson, J. de Lancey, *The Letters of Robert Burns*, 1931.

Fletcher, Mrs, *Autobiography*, 1876.

Forrest, George, *The History and Antiquities of St Leonard's, Edinburgh*, 1865.

Geddie, John, *The Water of Leith from Source to Sea*, 1896.

Gilbert, W. M., *Edinburgh in the Nineteenth Century*, 1901.

Graham, Clementina Stirling, *Mystifications*, 1865.

Grant, Sir Alexander, *The Story of the University of Edinburgh during its first 300 years*, 1884.

Grant, James, *Old and New Edinburgh*, 1883.

Hill, Rev. Cumberland, *Historic Memorials of Stockbridge, the Dean and the Water of Leith*, 1887.

Irons, J. Campbell, *Leith and its Antiquities*, 1897.

Japp, Alexander H., *Thomas de Quincey: His Life and Writings*, 1890.

Kay, John, *Original Portraits and Caricature Etchings (1784–1826)*, 1838.

Lauder, Sir John, of Fountainhall, *Decisions of the Lords of Council and Session* (completed 1712), 1761.

Lindsay, Ian G., *Georgian Edinburgh*, 1948.

Littlejohn, Henry D., *Report on the Sanitary Condition of the City of Edinburgh*, 1865.

Lockhart, J. G., *Life of Sir Walter Scott*, 1848.

Macdonald, Sir J. H. A., *Life-jottings of an Old Edinburgh Citizen*, 1915.

Mackay, John, *History of the Burgh of Canongate*, 1879.

Mackenzie, Henry, *Anecdotes and Egotisms* (completed 1825), 1927.

Maitland, William, *History of Edinburgh from its Foundation*, 1753.

Meikle, Dr Henry W., *Scotland and the French Revolution*, 1912.

Miller, Hugh, *My Schools and Schoolmasters*, 1875.

Miller, Robert, *The Municipal Buildings of Edinburgh*, 1895.

Mossner, Ernest C., *Life of David Hume*, 1954.

Mudie, R., *A Historical Account of His Majesty's Visit to Scotland*, 1822.

New Statistical Account of Scotland, *Edinburghshire (Midlothian) and Linlithgowshire (West Lothian)*, 1845.

Nicoll, John, *A Diary of Public Transactions* (completed 1667), 1836.

Petrie, Mrs John, *The History of the Abbey, Palace and Chapel-Royal of Holyroodhouse, including an account of the Sanctuary*, 1819.

Pope-Hennessey, Una, *Charles Dickens 1812–1876*, 1936.

Priestley, Lady Eliza, *The Story of a Life-time*, 1908.

Reid, John, *New Lights on Old Edinburgh*, 1894.

Robertson, David, *The Bailies of Leith*, 1915.

 The Princes Street Proprietors, 1935.

Robertson, David and Wood, Dr M., *Castle and Town*, 1928.

Roughead, William, *The Trial of Deacon Brodie*, 1906.

 The Trial of Captain Porteous, 1909.

Royal Commission on the Ancient Monuments of Scotland, *City of Edinburgh*, 1951.

Shepherd, Thomas H., *Modern Athens, Displayed in a Series of Views*, 1829.

Simpson, David C., *Edinburgh Displayed*, 1962.

Sinclair, Sir John, *Statistical Account of Scotland (Edinburgh and adjoining Parishes)*, 1793.

Skinner, Robert T., *The Royal Mile*, 1928.

Snyder, Franklyn Bliss, *Life of Robert Burns*, 1968.

Somerville, Rev. Thomas, *My Own Life and Times*, 1861.

Stevenson, Robert Louis, *Edinburgh: Picturesque Notes*, 1879.

Stewart, A. Francis, *The Exiled Bourbons in Scotland*, 1908.

Stoddart, John, *Remarks on Local Scenery and Manners in Scotland*, 1801.

Story, Mrs, *Early Reminiscences*, 1911.

Terry, Charles S., *The Scottish Parliament: Its Constitution and Procedure, 1603–1707*, 1905.

Third Statistical Account of Scotland, *City of Edinburgh*, 1966.

Willis, R. L., *Journal of a Tour from London to Elgin* (written 1793), 1897.

Wilson, Sir Daniel, *Memorials of Edinburgh in the Olden Time*, 1848.

Wood, John Philp, *The Antient and Modern State of the Parish of Cramond*, 1794.

Wood, Dr Marguerite, *Book of Records of the Ancient Privileges of Canongate*, 1956.

Wood, Dr Marguerite and others, *Edinburgh, 1329–1929*, 1929.

Youngson, Professor A. J., *The Making of Classical Edinburgh*, 1966.

Other sources include:

Minutes and other records of the Town Council of Edinburgh, the Police Commissioners of Edinburgh, the Bailies of Canongate, the Town Council of Queensferry.

Mason, Dr John, 'The History of Queensferry' (manuscript volume).

Court of Session papers in the Signet Library, Edinburgh.

Register of Protections of the Sanctuary of Holyroodhouse.

Early Minute Books of the Edinburgh Chamber of Commerce.

Volumes of Proceedings of the Society of Antiquaries of Scotland (1792–1972).

Books of the Old Edinburgh Club (1908–1972).

Index

Abbey Strand, 24, 96, 108
Abercorn, 8th Earl, 249, 250
Abercromby Place, 145, 242
Abercromby, Sir Ralph, 69
Academy, Edinburgh, 151–3
Acheson House, 91
Adam, Dr Alexander, 69, 72
Adam, John, 63,
Adam, Robert, 63, 79, 120, 121
Adam Square, 127
Adamson, John, 50
Ainslie Place, 148
Alison, Dr William P., 187, 188
Almond, River, 230, 256, 260
Ann Street, 150
Anne of Denmark, 30, 53
Antiquaries of Scotland Society, 27, 208
Appleton, Sir Edward, 80
Art Centre, Edinburgh, 154
Arthur's Seat, 12, 13, 99, 136, 247
Assembly Rooms, 105, 123–5, 128–30, 173, 175
'Athens, the Modern', 151, 153, 154–6
Austin, Dominie, 57
Aytoun, Professor, 167

Balerno, 259
Balfour, The Rev. Lewis, 227
Balmuto, Lord, 72
Barnbougle Castle, 260
Baxters, Incorporation, 224, 225
Beard, Tom, 181
Begg, the Rev. James, 189, 190, 192
Belford Bridge, 226
Bell, Dr Joseph, 203
Bell-house, 43
Bell's Brae, 224
Bernard Street, 214
'Bickers', 73–5, 77, 257
Birrell, Robert, 52, 53
Blackford Hill, 21, 245
Blackfriars Street, 197
Blair, Dr Hugh, 56

Bonnington, 21, 215, 216
Borrow, George, 74
Boswell, James, 25, 56, 71
Boyd, George, 117, 136
Braid Hills, 21
Braxfield, Lord (Robert McQueen), 70, 72, 178
Brereton, William, 24
Bristo Place, 19
Bristo Port, 19
Brodie, William (Deacon), 85–7, 132
Brougham, Lord, 232
Broun, Bailie Adam, 37
Brown, James, 67, 68, 72
Brown Square, 67
Brown, Dr Thomas, 165
Bruce, Robert the, 15, 16, 214, 237
Bruntsfield Links, 178
Burgh Muir, 21, 48
'Burgh Reformers – Committee of', 135
Burleigh, Master of – escape, 37
Burn, Robert, 137
Burn, William, 27, 152, 153, 246, 266
Burnett, Elizabeth, 89
Burns Monument, 138, 155
Burns, Robert
  First visit, 126–39
    Arrival, 126
    Assemblies, 128–31
    Creech, William, 132, 133
    Fergusson, Robert – memorial stone, 137, 138
    Kay, John, caricatures, 134–36
    Lawnmarket Lodgings, 126
    Mackenzie, Henry, 127, 133, 134
    Monboddo, Lord, 89, 135
    Nasmyth, Alexander – portraits, 136
    Scott, meeting, 138
    South Bridge, 126, 127
  Second visit, 139–42
    'Clarinda' – Mrs McLehose, 138, 141, 142
    Cruickshank, William and Janet, 150

Burns, Robert—*cont.*
St Andrew's Church, 140–1

Cadies (messengers), 25
Caledonian Hunt, 130, 173
Calton Gaol, 146, 203
Calton Hill, 12, 136, 155, 172
Calton Hill building development, 147
Camperdown, Earl (Adam Duncan), 69
Canal – proposed for New Town, 111
Canal Street, 111
Canal, Union, 227, 260
Candlemaker Row, 19
Canongate, 17, 81–95
  Acheson House, 91
  Bailies, 82
  Bible Land, 87
  Building Restoration, 26
  Burgh Records, 90
  Chessel's Court, 85–7
  Cordiners (Shoemakers), 87, 88
  Crosses, 82, 83, 96
  Foundation, 17, 81
  Golfer's Land, 93, 94, 236
  Hammermen, 91
  Huntly House, 90, 91
  Kirkyard, 64, 82, 137, 138
  Moray House, 88
  Morocco Land, 83–5
  Panmure House, 92–3
  Playhouse, 157, 159
  Queensberry House, 94, 95
  St John Street, 88–9
  Shoemakers' Land, 87
  Tolbooth, 89
  Water Gate, 83, 90
  White Horse Close, 95
Canonmills, 21, 217, 223
Carfrae, Mrs, 126
Carlyle, Alex., the Rev., 93
Carlyle, Thomas, 145, 171, 228
Caroline, Queen, 39, 42
Carr, Sir John, 144
Carse, Alexander, 171, 215
Castlehill, 17, 24
Castle Wynd, 17
Chalmers, the Rev. Thomas, 187, 188
Chambers, Robert, 64, 144, 155, 166, 190
Chambers Street, 19, 189, 197
Chambers, William (Lord Provost), 36, 102,
  196–9

Chambers, William (Sir), 114, 249
Chantrelle, Eugene, 202–3
Charity Workhouse, 187
Charles I, 19, 30, 48–50, 98, 265
Charles II, 32, 97
Charles X of France, 103–7, 228 (*see also*
  Sanctuary of Holyrood)
'Charlie, Bonnie Prince', 60, 249
Charlotte, Queen, 245, 249
Charlotte Square, 22, 111, 120, 121, 122, 164
Chessel's Court, 85–7
Cholera epidemic, 185, 186
Chopin, Frederick, 217
City Chambers (Royal Exchange), 15, 62–3
City of Edinburgh District, 63, 195, 213, 230,
  259–73
Coach-drivers' tombstone, 138
Coaches for London, 95
Cockburn, Mrs Alison, 128
Cockburn, Henry (Lord Cockburn)
  Academy, Founder of, 152, 153
  Adam, Dr, Praise of, 69
  Counsel for Henry Raeburn, 223
  Mound, dislike of, 118
  Parliamentary reform, supporter of,
    178
  Portobello Sands case, 232
  Recollections, 31, 44–5, 148, 152
Colinton, 66, 213, 227
College Street, 19
Comely Bank, 211, 228
Commerce, Chamber of, 132, 133, 198
Comte d'Artois – *see* Sanctuary of
  Holyrood
Cooperative Building Societies, 190
Corstorphine Hill, 12, 23, 247, 258
  Village, 246–7
Cowgate, 17, 18
Craig, James, 110, 111, 122, 140, 155
Craig, Sir Thomas, of Riccarton, 263
Craigcrook Castle, 218
Craiglockhart Dell, 227
Cramond 253–8
  Almond Estuary, 230, 243, 247, 253
  Iron Mills, 256, 257
  'Lammas Feast', 257, 258
  Mansionhouse, 255
  Oyster-fishing, 256
  Roman Fort, 253, 254, 255
  Tower, 255
  Village houses, 255

Creech, William, 46, 75, 132–3, 139, 228
Cromwell, 20, 32, 88, 237
Cruickshank, William and Janet, 140, 141
Currie, 259

Dalmahoy Hill, 262–3
Dalmeny – Church, 261
    Estate, 106, 174, 260–1
    Village, 261, 262
Darnley, Lord, 97
David I, 15, 17, 81, 96
Dean Bridge, 151, 221, 222, 224
    Development beyond, 222
Dean Valley, 219
    Village, 16, 222–6
Defoe, Daniel, 24
De Quincey, Thomas, 102
Dick, Sir Alexander, 248
Dickens, Charles, 181, 182, 183, 191
Donaldson's School for Deaf, 226
Douglas – a Tragedy, 159, 161, 166
Doune Terrace, 166
Dowie, Johnnie, 126
Drummond, George
    Diary, 65
    House, 144
    Infirmary, founder, 61
    Life, 59, 60, 64, 65
    Lord Provost, terms as, 59, 60
    New Town, founder, 63, 64, 110
    Royal Exchange, founder, 62
    University, services to, 60, 79
Drummond, James, R.S.A., 38
Drummond of Hawthornden, 49
Drummond Place, 66, 144
Drummond Street, 18, 19, 62
Duddingston House, 249, 250
Duddingston Loch, 99, 248, 251, 252
Duddingston Village, 99, 108, 247–53
    Church, 247, 250
    Cultivation Terraces, 247, 248
    Dalkeith (Innocent) Railway, 252, 253
    Dunsapie Loch and Rock, 248
    Prince Charlie's House, 249
    Thomson, John, 250, 251
    Turner, J. M. W. – visits, 250, 251
    Weaving, 248
Duff, Jamie ('Bailie Duff'), 136
Duncan Adam (Earl of Camperdown), 69
Dundas, Henry (Viscount Melville), 69, 71,
    73, 127

Dundas, Sir Laurence, 114
Dundas, Robert, 127

Eagle Rock, 260
Edinburgh
    Approaches to, 11–13
    Capital City, 210–12, 213
    Castle, 11, 13–14, 16, 19, 20
    Charters, 15, 16
    Descriptions, 17th and 18th centuries, 24
    Growth
        18th century, 109–24
        19th century, 143–56, 194, 234
        20th century, 229, 230, 239–40, 247, 259
        Summary, 14–23
    Improvement Scheme, 1867, 196–9
    Local Government Changes, 63, 146, 194,
        195
    Origin, 14
    Police Commissioners, 194
    Population, 20, 170
    Southern Districts, 73
Eglinton, Countess, 130
Elizabeth, H.M. Queen, 272, 273
Erskine, Hon. Henry, 71–2, 75–6, 98, 128, 228

Falconer, Sir John, 212
Ferguson, Adam, 79, 138
Fergusson, Robert, 137, 187
Festival, Edinburgh International, 131, 212
Festival Musical (1815), 31
Fettes College, 211
Fettes Row, 145
Fettes, Sir William, 211, 216
Figgate Whins, 230–1
Findlay, John R., 225, 226
Fletcher, Miles, 176
Fletcher, Mr and Mrs, 164–6, 176–8
Flodden, Battle, 18, 240
Flodden Wall, 18, 19, 20, 49
Forrester, Sir Adam, 246
Forth, Firth of, 21, 144, 264, 271–2
Forth Railway Bridge, 23, 264, 272–3
Forth Road Bridge, 12, 23, 264, 272–3
Fountainhall, Lord, 32
'Friends of the People', 70, 164, 178

Gaol Calton, 146, 203
Gaol, Tolbooth, 35–41
Gardenstone, Lord, 219
Gay, John, 94

Geddes, Jenny, 50–1
Geddes, Patrick, 54, 226
Gentle Shepherd, The, 158, 228
'Geordie Boyd's Mud Brig' – see Mound
George IV visit, 1822, 120, 169–75, 214–15
    Arrival, 169, 172, 214–15
    Artists' Records, 171, 239
    Dalkeith House, residence at, 172
    Departure, 171, 175
    Events, 155, 172, 173, 175
    Grant, Jane and Mary, letters, 172–4
    Highlanders, 169, 170, 171
    Illuminations, 174
    Organisation, 169–70, 172, 175
George IV Bridge, 19, 196
George Square, 67–80
    Assembly Rooms, 129
    'Bickers', 73, 77
    Building, 67–8
    Early residents, 69–70
    Lunardi visits, 75–7
    University development, 77–80
George Street, 21, 22, 110–12, 119, 164
    Assembly Rooms, 105, 123, 124-5, 130, 173 175
Gillespie, James, 228
Gilpin, William, 12
Gladstone's Land, 47, 48, 49
Glencairn, Lord, 128
Goldsmith, Oliver, 129
Golfers of Edinburgh, Hon. Company of, 236
Gordon, Duke and Duchess of, 58, 128
Gordon of Rothiemay – drawing of Edinburgh, 31, 83
Graham, James Gillespie, 148, 149
Graham, Miss Stirling, 167, 168
Grant, Elizabeth, 163, 164, 172
Grant, Dr Gregory, 57, 58
Grant, Jane and Mary, 172–4
Granton, 22, 243
Grassmarket, 17, 18, 19, 20, 38–40
Gray, Andrew, 84, 85
Great King Street, 144
'Great Michael', the, 22, 240
'Green-breeks', 74
Greenshields, Gavin, joiner, 192, 193
Grey, Earl – celebrations, 177, 179–182
    Pavilion, 180
Greyfriars Kirk and Kirkyard, 19, 40
Grieve, Bailie John, 116, 117, 136
Guthrie, the Rev. Thomas, 189, 190, 192

Hamilton, George, 231
Hamilton, Thomas, 153, 155, 180
Health, Cholera Board of, 186
'Heave awa' Hoose', 191
Heriot, George, 45
    Row, 143, 187
    Trust, 46, 144
Heriot's Garden, 75, 76
    Hospital (school), 19, 20, 45, 46, 75
High School, Royal
    High School Yards, 52, 72, 152
    Regent Road (Calton Hill), 151, 153, 154, 180
    Transfer to Barnton, 154
High Street, 17, 24–34, 35, 40, 43–4
High Street, collapse of house, 191, 192
Hill, Peter, 132, 137, 139
Hillside Crescent, 147
Holyrood Abbey, 15, 17, 48, 81, 96, 97
    Bailie, 98, 99, 108
    High Constables, 108, 249
    Sanctuary – see Sanctuary of Holyrood
Holyroodhouse, Palace of, 13, 29, 97, 172
Holyrood Park, 90, 96, 99, 247
Holy Rood School, 251
Home, the Rev. John, 159
Hopetoun House, 175
Howard Place, 217
Hume, David, 55–6, 79, 93, 109, 159, 207
Hunter Square, 33

Improvement Scheme, 197–9
Industrial (Ragged) Schools, 190
Infectious disease – measures, 185–6, 199–201
Infirmary, Royal – first, 61, 62
    present, 20, 62
'Innocent Railway', 252, 253

Jamaica Street, 145
James IV, 22, 97, 240
James VI and I, 15, 28, 29, 53
James VII and II, 17, 64, 94, 236
James Court, Lawnmarket, 25, 55, 56, 57
Jameson, William, 231
Jeffrey, Francis (Lord), 165, 167–8, 174, 178, 223
Johnson, Dr Samuel, 12, 25, 56, 57, 71
Johnston Terrace, 17, 20, 196, 211
Jordan Burn, 244, 245
Juniper Green, 213, 228, 259
Jury Court, 223

Kaimes Hill, 262-3
Kay, John, 58, 134, 136
Keys of the City, 49, 172
King's Wall, 17, 18
Kirkliston, Village and Church, 261
Knox, John, 27, 28, 29, 236
Krames, 44, 45

Lamash, Mrs, 76
Lamb's House, Leith, 215
Lauder, Sir Thomas Dick, 245
Lauriston Place, 19
Lavengro, 74
Lawnmarket, 17, 24, 26, 47-58, 117, 125-6, 135
Learmonth, John, 106, 221
Leith
    Amalgamation, 22, 239-40
    Bailies, 238
    Burgh, 238-9
    Citadel, 237
    Civic Trust, 214
    Comte d'Artois (Charles X) arrival at,
        103, 105
    Docks, 236, 238
    George IV landing, 170, 172, 214, 215, 239
    History, 236-9
    Lamb's House, 215
    Links, 94, 236, 237
    Mary, Queen, Landing, 28, 215
    Magistrates and Masters, 238-9
    Miller, Hugh, arrival at, 13
    Races, 234-6
    Siege of, 236, 237
    Superiorities, 237
    Water of - *see* Water of Leith
Liberton, 66, 244
Littlejohn, Henry D. (Sir), first MOH
    Appointed, 192, 193
    Career, 193, 194-203, 204
    Character, 201
    Expert Witness, 193, 202
    Forensic Medicine, professor, 193, 201
    Improvement Scheme 1867, 197
    Infectious Disease Measures, 199-200
    Police Surgeon, 194
    Sanitary Report, 119, 195, 196
    'Sherlock Holmes' prototype, 203
    Smoking, Views on, 201
    Tuberculosis Scheme, 200-1
Local Government changes
    1833, 146, 238

1856, 194, 195
1896, 233, 234
1920, 239, 240, 247
1975, 23, 63, 259, 273
Loch - Burgh (South), 21, 68
    Corstorphine, 246
    Duddingston, 99, 247, 248, 251
    Dunsapie, 248
    North (Nor'), 17, 18, 20, 63
Lockhart, J. G., 169, 171, 176, 232
Luckenbooths, 35, 43-6
Lunardi, Vincent, 75, 76, 77, 135

Macdonald, Sir J. H. A., 242
Mackay, Charles, actor, 174, 176
Mackenzie, Henry, 104, 133-4, 159, 165, 166
McLaren, Duncan, 186
McLehose, Mrs Agnes ('Clarinda'), 125, 138,
    141-2
McMorran, Bailie John, 51, 52, 53
McMorran, Ninian, 53
McQueen, Robert (Lord Braxfield), 70,
    72, 178
Maitland, William, 210
Malcolm III (Canmore), 15, 264
Margaret, Queen, 15, 23, 264-5
Market (Mercat), Cross, 25, 29, 30, 69
Marlin's Wynd, 34
Mary King's Close, 62
Mary of Guise, 237
Mary, Queen of Scots, 28, 29, 97, 215
Meadowbank, Lord, 175
Meadows, The, 20, 68
Medical Officer of Health, first, 192, 193,
    194-204
    last, 195
Melville Street, 151, 211
Memoirs of a Highland Lady, 163, 164, 172
Merchiston Castle, 244, 245
Miller, Hugh, 13
Mills, 16, 213, 215-17, 222-5
Milne, James, 150
Minibus, 204, 205
Minto House Hospital, 189
Mitchell, Sydney, Architect, 225
Monboddo, Lord (James Burnett), 89, 135
Moray Place Development, 148-50
Moray's Grounds, Lord, 148, 149, 208
Morning Chronicle, 181-3
Morocco Land, 84, 85
Mound, the, 21, 117, 118, 135, 136

Moyle, General, 41
Multrie's Hill, 21
Murray, Hon. Mrs, 28
Murray, William, 175
Museums – Antiquities, Scottish National, 50
   Huntly House (City Museum), 90, 91
   Lady Stair's House, 208
   Royal Scottish, 19, 197
Mylne, Robert (17th cent.), 97
Mylne, Robert (18th cent.), 113
Mystifications – Miss Stirling Graham's, 167–8

Nasmyth, Alexander, 68, 136, 219, 250
Nasmyth, James, 68
Nasmyth, Michael, 68
National Gallery, Scottish, 11, 38, 154
National Monument, Calton Hill, 155
National Trust for Scotland, 48, 266
Nelson Monument, 12, 137
Nelson, William, 220
Nether Bow, 24, 27
Netherbow Art Centre, 18
   Port, 18, 42, 49
New Town Conservation Area, 143, 218
New Town Dispensary, 187
New Town, first phase
   Building Regulations, 116
   Canals, proposed, 111
   Charlotte Square – design and building, 120, 121, 122
   Competition for Plan, 64, 110
   Craig, James, winning design, 110, 111, 112, 122
      Freedom of City, 111
   Houses, original, 119
   Mound – formation, 117–18
   North Bridge – building, 112–14
   Princes Street – first houses, 112, 118–19
      Future buildings, 119
      Naming, 112
      South side preserved, 114–16, 207, 210
   St Andrew Square, 114
   St Andrew's Church, 114, 140
   St George's Church, 121–2
   Sedan chairs in, 122–4
New Town, second phase
   Abercromby Place, 145
   Drummond Place, 144
   Great King Street, 144
   Heriot Row, 143–44

Playfair, William, 145
Reid, Robert, 143, 144
Royal Circus, 145
Sibbald, William, 143, 144
New Town, later phases
   Ann Street, 150
   Calton developments, 146, 147
   Graham, James Gillespie, 148
   Grecian phase, 151–6
   Hamilton, Thomas, 153
   Moray Estate, 148–50
   Outlying extensions, 151
   Playfair, William, 154–5
   Raeburn Estate, 150–1
   Regent Road, Terrace, 146–8
   Royal Terrace, 147, 148
   St Bernard's Crescent, 150, 151
New Town–Old Town, Division, 191
New Town, Social Life in, 163–8, 184
Newhaven
   Chain Pier, 107, 243
   Fishwives, 103, 216, 242
   James IV Charter, 240
   Oysters, 92, 230, 241, 242
Nicoll, John, diarist, 223
Nicolson, Lady, 68
Nicolson Square, 67, 141
   Street, 67
Nimmo, Christian, 246
Noddy, 204–5
Norrie, James, 54
North Bridge, 21, 64, 112–14, 157

Observatory, City (Calton Hill), 155
   Royal, 21
Officers of State v. Smith, 232
Old Town – crowding and neglect, 185, 191
Orde, Chief Baron, 109, 119
   Nancy, 109
Oysters, 92, 230, 241, 242, 256

Parliament Hall, 30, 31, 71, 173
   Square, 32, 41, 45
Patersone, John, 94, 236
Paxton, Sir Joseph, 147
Pentland Hills, 12, 21, 136, 213, 228–9, 259
Philip, Dr R. W., 200
Physicians, Royal College of, 119, 198, 201
Pitcairne, Dr Archibald, 94
Pitscottie, Lindsay of, 240
Plague, 48, 84, 237

Playfair, Professor John, 155, 165
Playfair, Dr Lyon, 167
Playfair, William (W. H.), 79, 145, 147, 155, 226
Playhouse, Canongate, 157, 159
Pleasance, 18
Police Court, first, 53
Political Martyrs – Trials, 70, 178
Poor Relief, 186–9
Port Edgar, 175
Porteous, John, 38, 39
Porteous Riot, 38–43
Portobello, 230–4
    Amalgamation, 234
    Bathing machines, 231, 233
    Burgh, 12, 233
    Holiday Resort, 231, 232, 233, 234
    Industries, 231, 234
    Jameson, William, 231
    Origin, 230–1
    Sands, 173, 232, 233
Portrait Gallery, Scottish National, 136
Portsburgh, Easter and Wester, 67
Potterrow, 19, 141
Powderhall, 217, 223
Prestonpans, 60, 241
Priestley, Lady Eliza, 166
Princes Street
    Houses, first, 118–19
    Modern buildings, 119
    Naming, 112
    South side preserved, 115–16, 207, 210
    Tramcars in, 206
Princes Street Gardens, 17
    Building prevented, 115–16, 207, 210
Princes Street Gardens, West
    Layout, 207–9
    Opened to public, 207, 209
    Regulations, 209
    Trains, 209

Queen Street, 50, 110, 119, 144, 164
Queensferry, 23, 259, 264–73
    Bridges, railway and road, 23, 272, 273
    'Burry Man', 269, 271
    Carmelite Friars, 266
    Charter, 265
    Edinburgh District, within, 23, 273
    Elizabeth, H.M. Queen, 272, 273
    Ferry Fair, 269
    Hawes Pier and Inn, 271

    Herring Fishing, 267
    Margaret, Queen (St), 264, 265, 273
    Plewlands House, 266,
    Shipping and Trade, 267, 268
    Town Council records, 268, 269
Queensferry Passage, 271–3

Rae, Sir William, 232
Raeburn, Sir Henry, 150, 174, 208, 218, 223
Ramsay, Allan (artist), 160
Ramsay, Allan (poet), 46, 94, 132, 158, 228
Ramsay, Kirsty, 105
Randolph Crescent, 148
Reform Act, Burgh, 146, 177, 178, 238
Reform Act, Parliamentary, 177, 179
Reform Act Processions, 106, 178, 179
Regent Road, 90, 146, 211
Regent Terrace, 147, 148
Register House, 121
Register House, West, 122
Reid, Robert, 31, 121, 143, 215
Riccarton, 78, 263
Riccio, David, 97
Richmond, John, 126, 140
Riddle's Close and Court, 51–5
    Adult Education Centre, 54
    Banquet to James VI, 53
    Geddes Patrick, 54
    Hume, David, 55
    McMorran, Bailie, 51–2
    Mechanics Library, 54
    Shawfield's Lodging, 53, 57
    Student residence, 54
Roberts, David, 180, 218, 219
Robertson, William, 79, 250
Romilly, Sir Samuel, 176
Rose Street, 112
Rosebery, 5th Lord, 260
Roseburn, 60, 226, 246
Roslin, 136
Ross House, 68
Royal Circus, 145, 146, 201
Royal Crescent, 145
Royal Exchange – see City Chambers
Royal High School – see High School
Royal Mile, 13, 24–34, 35–46, 47–58, 81–95
Royal Scottish Academy, 11, 154
Royal Terrace, 147, 148
'Royalty', Ancient, 20, 72
'Royalty', Extended, 22

St Andrew Square, 21, 109, 110, 111, 114
St Andrew's Church, 114, 121, 140–1
St Bernard's Bridge, 223
    Cresent, 150
    House, 150, 223
    Well, 71, 219, 223
St Cecilia's Concert Hall, 123
St David Street, 109
St George's Church, 22, 121
St Giles Church, 17, 27, 50, 173
St James Square, 21, 125, 140
St John Street, 82, 135
St Margaret's Chapel, 15, 21
St Mary's Cathedral, 211
St Mary's Street, 17, 18, 197
St Stephen's Church, 153
Saltire Society, 48
Sanctuary of Holyrood, 96–108
    Bailie's duties, 98
    'Bread for Monsieur', 104
    Chambers, William, visits, 102
    Court Books, 101
    Debtors in Sanctuary,
        Accommodation, 99
        Comte d'Artois, 103–7, 228
        De Quincey, Thomas, 102
        Dilks, Mrs, 101
        Haliburton, Patrick, 100
        Privileges, 99
        Procedures, 99–100
    Extent of Sanctuary, 96
Saughton Park, 227
Sciennes House, 138, 139
Scott Monument, 11
Scott, Sir Gilbert, 212
Scott, Sir Walter
    Academy, a founder of, 152, 153
    Boyhood, 72, 74, 75, 152
    Burns, meeting, 138
    Castle Street home, 123
    Character, 177
    Duddingston, connection with,
        250–1
    George IV visit, 120, 169, 170, 173, 175
    Heart of Midlothian, The, 38
    Mound, opinion of, 118
    Portobello, visits to, 232
    Princes Street Gardens, Key, 208
    Theatre – sponsors H. Siddons, 162
    Theatrical Fund Dinner, 175, 176
Scott, Walter, W.S., 72

Scottish Wildlife Trust, 251
Seafield, 234
Sedan chairs, 122–4
Shakespeare Square, 157
Shale oil industry, 261
Sharpe, Charles Kirkpatrick, 208
Shore, Leith, 214
Sibbald, William, 140, 143
Siddons, Henry, 162
Siddons, Mrs Henry, 163, 168, 172, 173
Siddons, Mrs Sarah, 58, 160–3
Silvermills Village, 21, 218, 223
Simpson, Sir J. Y., 166, 167, 189, 195
Skene, James 57, 171, 208, 209
Skinners Hill, 158
Slateford Village, 227
Smith, Adam, 93
Smollett, Tobias, 89
Smuggling, 39, 216
South Bridge, 33, 126–7, 152
Southern Districts, Commissioners, 73, 75
Soutra Hill, 11
Spittal, James, 179
Spylaw House, 228
Stark, William, 147
Stevenson Robert, 146
Stevenson, Robert Louis, 13, 21, 70, 217, 227,
    271
Stewart, Archibald, 60
Stewart, Dugald, 155
Stewart's College, Daniel, 211
Stockbridge, 21, 145, 150, 190, 219, 223
Stockbridge Bus, 205
Stoddart, John, 243, 253
Story, Mrs, Reminiscences, 242
Stow, John, 15
Stuart, James ('Athenian'), 156
Syme, James, 189

Tailors' Hall, Cowgate, 159
Taylor, Dr J., 220
Taylor, Joseph, 24
Telfer, Mrs, 89
Telfer's Wall, 20
Telford, Thomas, 221, 222
Theatre Royal, 157, 160–3, 173, 180, 218
    'New', 162
Theatrical Fund Dinner, 175
Theatricals, Home, 166–7
Thistle Street, 112
Thomson, John, 250, 251

Tipperlinn, 244–5
Tolbooth, Canongate, 89–90, 98
   New, 36
   Old, 35–43
Town Guard, 38, 39, 40, 41, 42
Trained Bands, 41
Tramcars, 205–7
Tron Church, 30, 32, 33, 34
Turner, J. M. W., 171, 250, 251
Tweeddale Court, 17

Union Canal, 227, 260
University, Heriot–Watt, 78, 263–4
University of Edinburgh
   George Square Development, 77–80
   Improvement Scheme, 1867 – comments,
      198
   Old College, 19, 52, 79
   Scottish Studies, School of, 71

Vennel, the, 19
Victoria, Queen, 219, 226

Walker, Misses, 211
Walks in Edinburgh (R. Chambers), 144,
   155

Wallace, Sir William, 16
Warriston Close, 28
Warriston Cresent, 217
Water of Leith, 16, 21, 213–29, 259
Water of Leith Village – see Dean Village
Waterloo Place, 146, 179, 196, 207
Watson's George – Ladies College, 77
Waverley Station, 11, 18
Well Court, 225
Wells o' Wearie, 248, 252
West Bow, 40, 48, 49, 51
West Port, 19, 49
Whyte, the Rev. Thomas, 159
Williams, Hugh W. (Grecian), 156
Williamson, Peter, 44, 141
Wilson, Alexander, 40, 41, 42
Wilson, Andrew, 38, 39
Wood, Dr Alexander ('Lang Sandy Wood'),
   135
Wood, John Philp, 256, 257, 260
Woodhouselee, Lord, 69
Wood's Farm, 21

Yetts, Willie, 136
York, H. R. H. Duke of, 16
Young, John ('Paraffin Young'), 261